A STUDY OF FREGE

A STUDY OF

FREGE

By JEREMY D. B. WALKER

Assistant Lecturer in the University of Leicester

CORNELL UNIVERSITY PRESS
ITHACA   NEW YORK
1965

Printed in Great Britain

ACKNOWLEDGEMENTS

I am indebted to Professor Ryle for reading this book in manuscript and making many valuable criticisms and suggestions; the responsibility for any errors of fact or presentation that remain is my own. I must also record my gratitude to him for many hours' discussion of these topics, during which I have learnt more than I can say. I also owe much to Mr. E. J. Lemmon, who first aroused my interest in Frege and has since encouraged it. Professor L. W. Forster gave me essential advice on the translation of certain German terms. I would like also to take this opportunity of thanking him and Mrs. Forster for their kindness in giving me hospitality while the book was being drafted. Professor Nowell-Smith was good enough to suspend for one term my obligation to lecture at Leicester University. Without this help I could not have found time to complete the work. I am grateful to the editors of *Mind* and *Philosophical Review* for permission to quote from articles printed in these journals. Miss Irene Brennan was of great service in helping to correct proofs.

Mawgan Porth, 1963.

CONTENTS

In this book I give an account of Frege's philosophical views. Frege was not primarily a philosopher; it would even be wrong to think of him as a logician. He was rather a mathematician, and since mathematics in the late nineteenth century was in a critical state, he spent most of his life working towards the solution of these crises. It was this that compelled him into his logical inquiries. The existing apparatus of logical systems, methods and theories was quite inadequate to deal with much of the reasoning typical of mathematics. So Frege was forced to construct a set of logical tools for his professional needs. This in turn entailed consideration of the philosophical foundations of traditional logic, and justification of his own. It was in this way that he reached his characteristic philosophical theories.

It follows that his philosophy is not presented in a typically philosophical manner. Valuable remarks are often squeezed into footnotes or between passages of symbolism. His two principal works deal with the foundations of a logically valid mathematics, and most of his articles serve to explain terms and distinctions used in these works. Although it is possible to grasp his philosophical views without attending to their contexts, such an attempt would be of little value. Nobody who is ignorant of the basic problems and techniques of logical and mathematical reasoning can fully understand the subjects comprised in philosophical logic. Perhaps appreciation of modern philosophy as a whole demands the same technical awareness. Therefore what is said in this book is not meant to stand on its own, though it does not presuppose a detailed knowledge of formal logic or mathematics.

I shall not discuss Frege's technical achievements. Despite what has been said, an attempt to present both the more general and the more technical together would risk dissatisfying all parties. The only exception to this limitation is Chapter 12, which is meant in part to introduce Frege's philosophy of mathematics. I have also omitted to compare Frege's views with Russell's. Such comparison would have doubled the length of this book; and while there are many excellent accounts of Russell, there are few of Frege. I must at this point acknowledge a general debt to the existing accounts of Frege. I have listed some of these in the Further Reading.

Frege's life as a thinker falls into three parts. The first extends from the publication of the *Begriffsschrift* in 1879 to the publication of the *Grundlagen der Arithmetik* in 1884. In the *Begriffsschrift* Frege elaborated a logical script which was to be the basis of his formal presentation of arithmetic, though as yet it lacked certain refinements. But in the *Grundlagen* he presented his theories about arithmetic quite informally; this work is also the best introduction to the range of his thought. In the second period he began to concentrate on language. This period is characterised by the publication of the two volumes of the *Grundgesetze der Arithmetik* in 1893 and 1903. It ends abruptly with the Appendix to the second volume, in which Frege discussed the paradox in his axioms discovered by Russell. This great work is the crown of Frege's achievement and should be read by all who are seriously interested. Unfortunately the complexity of his symbolism made reprinting expensive, and copies of the original edition are not common.

There are a number of important articles during these middle years. They deal for the most part with philosophical points raised by or presupposed in the logical techniques of the *Grundgesetze*. Some of their content is reproduced in the early pages of the *Grundgesetze*, but for full understanding it is still necessary to consult the articles. Besides his investigations into the philosophy of language Frege discusses in the *Grundgesetze* various philosophical theories about mathematics; philosophical theories about logic; and the particular subject of definition.

The third period of Frege's working life is sad. It began with his acknowledgement of the contradiction contained in the axioms of his system. It seems that he was never able to regain his former faith in the possibility of giving arithmetic a purely logical basis. It is interesting that a parallel fate overtook Russell himself some years later at the hands of Wittgenstein, whose work issued largely from Frege's. He too answered by abandoning his logical researches. For many years Frege published very little except a series of articles on the foundations of geometry, with special reference to Hilbert's formalist theory, and a few other articles on formalism. Then in 1918 he began a series of four articles called 'Logical Investigations', in which he discusses the nature of propositions, truth, negation and connected subjects. The fourth of these has not yet been published. It is here that we find his mature views about the relations between facts, thoughts and linguistic expressions. We can therefore see Frege as moving from symbolic logic, through a concern with ordinary language, to a more general interest in thought and its expression.

The plan of my book is very roughly based on this development. It starts with Frege's notion of a function, which is central to his whole thought and perhaps his most important contribution to philosophy. This is followed by a discussion of its analogue in language, namely the concept. This goes over into consideration of Frege's views on the significance of facts of grammar and syntax. Next, I turn to the notion of 'incompleteness', which is given as a criterion for distinguishing functions and concepts from objects. It now becomes clear that for fuller understanding we must examine Frege's general theories of meaning and truth; these occupy most of the remaining chapters. In the last chapters I deal briefly with some general aspects of his position, namely his theory of definition, his view of the nature of science, and his notion of mathematics. Chapter 12 takes up again the notion of a concept regarded as a function, and shows how this notion is central in Frege's definition of number.

I would like to have discussed Wittgenstein's relation to Frege. A great deal of what is most important in the *Notebooks* and the *Tractatus* cannot be understood until their reader is acquainted with Frege's doctrines. More speculatively, the Kantian elements in Wittgenstein's philosophy seem to me to be traceable through Frege. But reasons of space made both examinations impossible.

I have quoted from and referred to the following editions and articles of Frege:

1. *The Foundations of Arithmetic* (*Die Grundlagen der Arithmetik*, 1884), translated by J. L. Austin (Blackwell, 1953). At some points I have altered Austin's translation slightly.

2. *Translations from The Philosophical Writings of Gottlob Frege*, edited by Peter Geach and Max Black (Blackwell, 1960). This contains partial translations of the *Begriffsschrift* (1879) and the *Grundgesetze der Arithmetik* (1893 and 1903); also complete or partial translations of the following articles:
   'Function and Concept' ('Funktion und Begriff', 1891)
   'On Concept and Object' ('Ueber Begriff und Gegenstand', 1892)
   'On Sense and Reference' ('Ueber Sinn und Bedeutung', 1892)
   'What is a Function?' ('Was ist eine Funktion?' 1904)
   'Negation' ('Die Verneinung', 1918)
   'Review of Husserl's *Philosophie der Arithmetik*' (1894)
   'Critical Elucidation of some points in E. Schroeder's *Vorlesungen ueber die Algebra der Logik*' (1895)

3. 'The Foundations of Geometry' ('Ueber die Grundlagen der Geometrie', 1903) translated by M. Szabo, *Philosophical Review*, 1960

4. 'The Thought' ('Der Gedanke', 1919), translated by A. M. and Marcelle Quinton, *Mind*, 1956

5. 'Compound Thoughts' ('Gedankengefuege', 1923–26) translated by R. Stoothoff, *Mind*, 1963

6. *Grundgesetze der Arithmetik* (Jena, 1893 and 1903) and *Vol.* 1 reissued in 1962 (Darmstadt u. Hildesheim)

Methods of reference are as follows. Passages from the *Grundlagen* are identified by the page on which they occur in the above edition. Passages from the *Grundgesetze* are identified by the volume and the *section* in which they occur, rather than by page number, except when explicitly indicated. In this case reference is made to the page on which they occur in the German edition. Passages from the other writings are identified by the page on which they occur in the Blackwell's volume of translations, or by the page on which they occur in the periodicals named. In general I have tried to be sparing of references. Instead, an indication of general sources is given at the end of each chapter.

CHAPTER ONE

FUNCTION AND CONCEPT

IT will help to see the immediate point of Frege's theory of functions, if we cast our minds back to the sort of thing often said about them in schools. Those who are beginning mathematical analysis are often told two quite different things about equations such as '$y=x^2$', and both are confused. They are told either that in this equation y is a function of x, or that x^2 is a function of x. But since x, they are told, can take any value we please, it seems to follow that y will be different for each different value of the variable x. It then becomes puzzling to see what kind of entity y can be, if it can appear at different times as different numbers and still be 'the' function x^2 or 'the' value of this function. And it is puzzling to see how x can 'take' any value we like. Surely we have no power to make unequal things equal at will, and if this is so, how are we justified in letting x equal now 3 and now 4? And, for the other case, if we let x equal 3 and calculate that x^2 is then 9, are we to say that 9 is a function of 3? Why should we not say with as much right that 8 is a function of 3?

Frege's clarification of the related notions of function, value and argument sprang from his dissatisfaction with the kinds of confusion exhibited in the above passage, kinds of confusion which were common among mathematical analysts of the highest calibre in the middle of the nineteenth century. The first confusion is comparatively easy to see, once it has been pointed out; perhaps it is so obvious that we normally overlook it. It consists in saying things which are true of the number signified by the x-expression of the x-expression itself. It is in general to confuse the sign with the object it signifies. The second is not quite so obvious. It is the confusion committed most strikingly in this definition of a function, which I have seen in some dictionary of the period. A function is 'a quantity so connected with another that any change in the one correspondingly affects the other'. The best way to elucidate the notion is to make clear exactly what state of affairs is described by the equation '$y=x^2$'. As a first attempt, we say that the equation states that whatever number x may be, a different number x^2 corresponds to it in some way. But this does not make sufficiently clear the distinction between the number, say 3 or 4, and the letter 'x' which signifies the number. So as a second approximation we may say that whatever number we let the letter 'x' signify, the expression 'x^2' signifies some corresponding number. Now it is easy to see the point of introducing a different letter, namely 'y', if we remember that the problem arose originally in the context of mathematical analysis. For one technique of analysis is the construction of the curves of given equations on graphs. These graphs conventionally begin with a horizontal line called the 'x-axis' and a vertical line intersecting it at the point of origin called the 'y-axis'. To describe a function by means of the equation '$y=x^2$' is to say that whatever number we select on the x-axis, we must select the number which is its square on the y-axis in constructing the curve of this equation. The 'value' of the function x^2 is always the square of whatever number is selected as x. We can therefore make a third attempt to state precisely what situation is described by the equation '$y=x^2$', leaving out reference to the graphical context. We begin with the expression 'x^2'. Taking some definite number, say 3, we construct an expression of the same form by writing the numeral '3' where the letter 'x' occurred, and obtain the expression '3^2'. By convention, we interpret this numerical expression as signifying the number 9. We can therefore say that the number 9 is the value of the function x^2 for the argument 3. Similarly, the number 16 is its value for the argument 4.

Much of Frege's theory of the function consists in elucidating these related notions, and trying to explain precisely the meanings of the terms 'function', 'value', 'argument' and 'variable'. Although these are mathematical notions, and Frege's efforts towards a set of definitions were an essential part of his general attempt to put mathematics upon a firm foundation of logic, they have also a general importance in view of his assimilation of concepts to functions, and of objects to the possible arguments of functions. It is with this more general context that I am concerned in the first half of this book.

(ii)

When trying to define the notion of a function, it is best to start with a numerical expression. Let us take once more the expression '3^2' as our example. We can say of this expression that the numeral '3' stands for the *argument* of the function, and that the expression '3^2' itself stands for the value of the function which corresponds to this argument. The argument is the number 3, not the numeral '3', and the value is the number 9 or 3^2, not the numerical expression '3^2'. If we analyse the expression '3^2' in this way, then the *function* we are dealing with is that signified by the functional expression '$(\ )^2$'. We could equally well analyse the same expression '3^2' in a different way. We could say that the numeral '2' in this expression stood for the argument. In this case the function in question would be that signified by the functional expression '$3^{(\ )}$'.

It is clear that the function is closely related to the *form* of the expression. But from the two examples I gave it seems that we can interpret any given expression containing more than one distinguishable element as exemplifying more than one such form. The expression '3^2' exemplifies the form '$3^{(\ )}$' just as much as it exemplifies the form '$(\ )^2$'. Indeed it also exemplifies the quite indeterminate form '$(\ )^{(\ )}$'. It is therefore important when talking of the *forms* of expressions to consider not just one expression on its own but several expressions together. We cannot talk of *the* form of an expression by itself, but we can talk of *the* form common to several different expressions. If the two expressions in question are '3^2' and '4^2', we can say that '$(\ )^2$' is *the* form common to each expression. Again it is important not to confuse the expression '$(\ )^2$' with the entity, whatever it may be, signified by this expression, which I have just called a form. The importance of all this will be brought out later in considering Frege's application of this terminology to sentences and linguistic expressions. For part of the work of the logician is to investigate those relations which hold between sentences solely in virtue of their logical forms. Analysing sentences in the functional mode is one means of giving concrete sense to talk about their forms ('Function and Concept', p. 24).

I have been using expressions of the form '$(\ )^2$' rather than of the more commonly used form '$(x)^2$' or 'x^2'. Frege is careful to distinguish the use of the letter 'x' in such expressions from the use of the gap indicated by empty brackets. The expression for a function should not contain the letter 'x', and should contain a gap. However in practice it would be clumsy and misleading to use brackets or gaps in this way. One use of the letter is to show clearly the place in the expression where the expressions for definite arguments, for example definite numerals, are to be substituted. Frege himself prefers to use the Greek equivalent 'ξ' rather than the Roman 'x' for the purpose of indicating argument places. In referring to functions it is best to write their expressions in the form '$\varphi(\xi)$' rather than the form '$f(x)$'. The reason Frege had for using the Greek letter rather than the Roman was that there are two distinct functions performed by the letters in a functional expression, for one of which he reserves the Roman figure. I shall use an example to show this. In order to express our symbolism for the various powers of numbers we may say that for any number x the expression 'x^2' stands for the second power of that number, and in general that the expression 'x^n' stands for the nth power, where n is some definite number. Similarly we may say that for any number x the expression '$x^2 - 1$' and the expression '$(x-1)(x+1)$' stand for the same number. In each case our use of one and the same letter 'x' throughout the proposition in question is intended to signify the generality of the proposition. Ordinarily this generality is implicitly understood in the case of mathematical expressions and equations. In logic, on the other hand, where everything must be made explicit, the device of quantification is used to make it explicit. Frege therefore distinguishes the use of letters to indicate argument places from their use to indicate generality, and he reserves the latter use to the Roman letters. It may appear now that it is essential that some letter should occur as part of a functional expression. This is not so, as I said above. In an expression of the form '$\varphi(\xi)$' or '$f(x)$' what actually signifies the function is the part '$f(\ )$'. The argument sign is not part of the sign which signifies the function itself.

The letter 'x' has yet another use which is distinct from either of these though related to both. If an equation is written out explicitly with the universal quantifier before it, we are to understand that if we substitute a particular numeral in the expression we must substitute the same numeral in each argument place filled by the same letter. This is obviously so when only one such letter occurs, but becomes important where more than one argument is called for. In the equation '$(x)\ (y)\ x^2 + 2xy + y^2 = (x+y)^2$' the point of using the letter 'y' as well as the letter 'x' is to indicate the respective places in the expression where the substitutions of definite numerals are independent of each other. We need not substitute the same numeral in every place filled by an 'x' or a 'y', though there is nothing to prevent us doing so, but we must substitute the same numeral in any one place filled by an 'x' as in any other, and the same in any one place filled by a 'y' as in another. Understanding these multiple points of the notation by letters therefore comes to understanding the necessary rules of substitution in such expressions, which is itself part of understanding the meaning of such expressions.

Another way of representing the nature of the function is by drawing its curve on a conventional graph. In such a case it is easy to see that the function correlates pairs of numbers in a particular way. We may be tempted for this reason to think that a function is simply a relation between pairs of numbers. This is not correct. For the relation between the numbers 3 and 9, although in one way it can be regarded as identical with the relation between the numbers 4 and 16, in another way must be regarded as different. On the one hand we can regard both 9 and 16 as numbers of the form 'x times x' and therefore we might say that the common relation in question was 'multiplied by itself'. On the other hand, it is obvious that while 9 is 3 multiplied by 3, 16 is 4 multiplied by 4. The term 'itself' in the expression 'multiplied by itself' depends for its meaning on the number we take as argument. We may prefer to say that the function is a kind of *law* for correlating pairs of numbers ('What is a Function?', p. 112). But once again it is not correct to say that 'x^2' or 'ξ^2' or '$(\ )^2$' stands for this law. Rather, the law is what is expressed in the equation '$y=x^2$'.

So far it has been assumed that only numbers can be the arguments to functions. Indeed if we understand the symbols of algebra in the usual way, it only makes sense to substitute numbers. Expressions like 'The Moon$+3$' appear to be nonsensical. But it seems that if we are not to rely on intuitions of nonsense, we must find some way of saying what kinds of object can be the arguments to given functions. Since nothing prevents our constructing expressions out of functional expressions by writing proper names and definite descriptions in the argument places, the real problem clearly concerns the value of such expressions. Ordinarily we should simply say that only numbers were to be possible arguments, only numerals were to be substitutable in argument places in such functions, since only numbers can be the values of the kind of expression we get after substituting definite argument signs into functional expressions. This is the notion which underlies the type theory adopted by Russell in face of such problems.

Frege however, did not think this kind of solution adequate. For it would involve, he thought, setting up a complete set of rules describing the kinds of argument to each given kind of function. He believed that the full definition of a function must enable us to decide the value got by taking every object in turn as its argument. Only objects indeed can be arguments of ordinary functions, but this fact about the proper use of the notation is yet another thing implicit in the use of the letters 'ξ' or 'x'. As we might say, the terms 'object' and 'what can be substituted for 'ξ' or 'x'' are equivalent. Frege's solution to this problem of apparently nonsensical expressions is quite different. We are to allow the substitution of every object as possible argument into any function, subject only to the rules of the notation. There are to be no rules restricting the range of objects which are possible arguments to any given function. We are instead to stipulate that the values of expressions which do not appear to stand for anything, such as 'The Moon+3', shall be some arbitrary object or objects. Frege chooses to say that all apparently nonsensical expressions like the one above are to be taken as signifying that object he calls 'The False'. (I describe this object in section (v) below and also in Chapter 10). Thus we are to say by stipulation that the value of the function x^2 for the argument 3 is the number 9, and for the argument The Moon it is The False. If this seems strange we may recall that it was originally just as much a matter of stipulation that expressions of the form 'x^2' were to be regarded as standing for the second power of whatever number x was.

Frege's method therefore comes to this. If an expression can be formed in accordance with the rules for the notation, the rules for the use of the symbols, it must be given some reference. What cannot be allowed is the possibility that the rules for forming complex expressions in accordance with the principles of the notation should permit the formation of nonsensical expressions or expressions which fail to signify anything. In Frege's view the most important rule governing the formation of functional expressions is the rule that only meaningful functional expressions shall be admitted into the symbolic system, that is only functional expressions which signify or refer to something. Such an expression is only meaningful if we can substitute the name of any object into its argument place or places, and always get some expression with a definite reference.

(iii)

We are taught to say that certain functions are equal to one another. For instance we say that the functions $x^2 - 1$ and $(x - 1)(x + 1)$ are equal. This way of talking is imprecise, but it contains a notion of great importance which Frege clearly brought out into the open. If we draw the two curves for the functions I mentioned above they will be seen to coincide. For any argument the value of the one function is identical with the value of the other. The numerical expression got by substituting any numeral in the argument places in the expression for the one will stand for the same number as the expression got by substituting the same numeral in the argument places in the expression for the other. We may add that if we substitute signs which are not numerals but, for example, proper names, the values of the two functions will still be identical. They will be The False.

If the values of two functions are identical for every argument then Frege says that the *value-ranges* of the two functions may be said to be identical ('Function and Concept', p. 26). This notion is fundamental to his whole theory of numbers. I shall say a little about it in this chapter, but more in Chapter 12, which is designed partly to show the application of the theory of functions to the definition of number. The sentence at the head of this paragraph refers to two distinct equivalences. The first may be put in this way. For any argument x, $x^2 - 1 = (x-1)(x+1)$. Here we are saying that an equality holds quite generally ('Function and Concept', p. 27). We are saying, for instance, that $3^2 - 1$ is equal to $(3-1)(3+1)$. In this way the function of the letter in allowing the expression of generality comes out very clearly. The second equivalence is Frege's. The *value-range* of the function $x^2 - 1$ is identical with the value-range of the function $(x-1)(x+1)$. Here we are speaking of a quite definite and particular equivalence, namely the equivalence of two definite objects or their identity.

In view of the importance of this notion in Frege's thought about the foundations of mathematics, one should be clear what a value-range is. But it seems extraordinarily hard to state this precisely. For Frege's introduction of the notion only seems to apply to contexts where we are comparing the value-ranges of two different functions, namely where we are saying either that two value-ranges are identical or that they are different. We do not seem to have any clear way of talking about a particular value-range on its own, or about the value-range of just one given function. However it is possible to mention a number of different things that must be distinguished from a value-range. Obviously the value-range of a function is not just the set of all its possible arguments, nor the set of all possible values of the function. It is not just the set of all possible arguments and all possible values. What such sets lack is the element of correlation between particular arguments and particular values which is essential to the notion of a function. It is therefore more to the point to wonder whether the value-range of a function is the set of correlated pairs of arguments and values, or even the common relation between pairs of arguments and values. The latter can be dismissed at once, since Frege tells us that the value-range of a function must be regarded as a kind of object, and he sharply distinguished relations from objects. Since he elsewhere describes the value-range as something we recognise to be common to given functions we may wonder whether to construe it as the peculiar law of correlation which is said to contain the essence of the function. But laws are dangerously like relations. Later we shall see how Frege took the notion of a concept's *extension* as a particular case of the *value-range* of functions. This assimilation may throw more light on the notion of the value-range.

Frege says that if we have already seen something generally common to two functions we are justified in assuming that there is something particular which is common to them (*Grundgesetze*, ii, 146). This is a 'fundamental law of logic', and we have just seen the kind of intuitive support it has. The importance of the notion of the value-range is that it gives us a way of moving from general truths to particular truths. It is not of course the only way. We can move from the general truth 'The value of the functions $f(x)$ and $g(x)$ for the same argument is the same' to any particular truth like 'The value of the functions $f(x)$ and $g(x)$ for the argument 3 is the same'. Frege introduces a notation for value-ranges which shows clearly the relation between general and particular. To construct the expression which signifies the value-range of a given function, we take the expression for the function, write a Greek epsilon 'ε' in each empty argument place, enclose the whole in brackets, and then write the 'ε' again in front of the brackets with a smooth breathing above it. The sign for the value-range of the function $x^2 - 1$ is '$\acute{\varepsilon}(\varepsilon^2 - 1)$'. Russell's notation for classes is similar in form to this.

(iv)

Frege says of himself that although he began with the simple notion of a function as it occurs in mathematics, he came to extend the notion in two distinct ways ('Function and Concept', pp. 21 and 28). We must examine the extended notion, since it is here that philosophical interest is aroused most strongly. The first extension consists in allowing objects of any kind and not just objects of the particular kind called 'numbers' as possible arguments of functions. The second consists in extending the reference of the term 'function' itself. It is with the latter that I am concerned now.

Earlier we regarded algebraic equations as stating the equality of different functions. Now we are to construe them as themselves expressions for particular functions, so that '$x^2 - 1 = (x-1)(x+1)$' will be the expression for a particular function and '$x^2 = 4$' the expression for another. (Strictly we should replace the letter 'x' which occurs in these algebraic equations by the letter 'ξ' which is appropriate to be used in signifying argument places in functional expressions). As before the arguments we are at first concerned with are numbers, though we must bear in mind that it is permissible to substitute the name for an object of any kind into the argument places. It is over the question of the value of such functions that difficulty arises. If we take a particular number, say 2, as the argument of the two functions signified above, we shall get two numerical, arithmetical equations after substitution. It is these arithmetical equations which stand for the values of the respective functions for the argument 2. So the equation '$2^2 = 4$' stands for the value of the second function for this argument, and the equation '$3^2 = 4$' stands for its value for the argument 3.

The most obvious difference between these two equations last signified is that the former is true and the latter is false. It is this that underlies Frege's idea. For he construes the values of those functions which are equations as truth and falsity. We do indeed say that for any argument an algebraic equation will turn out either true or false. Those arguments which yield after substitution true arithmetical equations are called the *solutions* of the given algebraic equation, so that for instance the numbers 2 and -2 are solutions of the equation $x^2 = 4$. This may explain why there is at first a temptation to think that only the numbers 2 and -2 can be taken as proper arguments to the function $x^2 = 4$. This is not so. We have to admit that there is something common to the equations $3^2 = 4$ and $4^2 = 4$, and this is what Frege calls the function $x^2 = 4$. Truth and Falsity are taken to be two objects of a peculiar kind, namely logical objects or rational objects. Because they are so peculiar, Frege allows us in speaking of equations as a kind of function to refer to Truth and Falsity as *truth-values* rather than simply as values. Truth, or The True, as Frege also calls it, is therefore the truth-value of the equation '$x^2 = 4$' for the arguments 2 and -2, and Falsity or The False is its truth-value for every other argument. It will be explained in Chapter 2 what Frege means by an object. And in Chapter 9 I shall try to present his reasons for taking the truth and falsity of sentences as objects.

The first extension of the notion of a function, then, consists in treating algebraic equations as a kind of function, or treating arith- metical equations as functional expressions, one part of which is regarded as invariant, while the other parts are seen as substitutions into argument places. The second extension consists in treating expressions in ordinary words as functional. This is done in the same way as before. We can either construe a descriptive expression like 'The capital of Germany' as functional by imagining that the name 'Germany' is filling an argument place, or we can treat the expression as standing for a particular value of the function *The capital of*——. The only real difference between such descriptive functions and the kind we began with is that in the latter case there is an agreed mathematical symbolism which corresponds to expressions of ordinary language. We could treat of the function *Square of x* just as well as the function x^2. We could treat of the function *Something which when squared is 4* just as well as the algebraic form $x^2 = 4$.

The essential extension at this stage then consists in allowing objects of all kinds, and not just numbers, as possible arguments to such functions. In the case mentioned above, Germany was the argument of the function *The capital of x*. We must be careful to understand that it is the actual country of Germany which is the argument, and not the name 'Germany'. Objects of other kinds than numbers must be admitted as the possible values of such functions. The value of the function *The capital of x* for the argument Germany is the city of Berlin. However this intuitive way of describing the difference between descriptive or linguistic functions and mathematical functions would not seem useful or valuable to Frege, since he makes no essential distinction between numbers and objects of other kinds. In theory any object whatever can be taken as argument to any function whatever. Nevertheless it is helpful to distinguish functions by the types of objects that can be their values.

(v)

Descriptive expressions are not the only kind of linguistic expression that can be construed as functional. Any expression can be seen as functional if we construe it as part invariant and part variable in the way described. In particular this kind of analysis can be performed upon complete sentences. If we take the sentence 'The cat is on the mat', we can replace the particular term 'The cat' by the indefinite indicator 'x', and by doing this we shall obtain the functional expression 'x is on the mat'. Similarly we could replace the definite term 'The mat' by the indefinite indicator and obtain a different functional expression. This extension of the original notion brings together the two different extensions discussed above. Like equations, sentences are statements of fact, that are capable of truth and falsehood; like descriptions they are composed of words of ordinary language. They may therefore be construed as a kind of functional expression, having objects of all kinds as their possible arguments. As in the case of equations we are to take the values of the resulting expressions, namely sentences, as truth-values. Such expressions will be quite definite and complete sentences.

Frege calls the kind of function involved here a *concept* ('Function and Concept', p. 30). This seems surprising at first, since there is no obvious relation between sentences construed as particular values of functional expressions of a certain type and those entities we call concepts. But the relation can in fact be brought out in the following way. If we want to express the fact that something is red, a horse, or on the mat, we have several distinct ways of doing it. We can, for instance, say that the thing in question falls under the concept of redness, of equinity or of being-on-the-mat; we can say that the concept of redness, etc., applies to the thing; or that the thing instantiates the concept, is an instance of the concept. With ways of talking such as these goes much of the traditional problem of universals, for one goes on, perhaps, to wonder how concepts can apply to particular objects, how they can apply to different objects simultaneously, and so forth. Another way of expressing the same fact is to say that redness or equinity or being on the mat is *true of* the object in question, or that it is true that the thing is red or a horse or on the mat. Now if we consider the functional expressions 'x is a horse', 'x is red', 'x is on the mat', we see that what we mean when we say that Pegasus is a horse or that the pillarbox is red can be expressed in terms appropriate to the language of function and value. For we can say that Pegasus is an argument of the function x *is a horse* that the pillarbox is an argument of the function x *is red* for which the values are in each case The True. Similarly we can say that the number 2 is an argument of the function $x^2 = 4$ for which the corresponding value is The True.

By describing concepts as a kind of function Frege performed with great simplicity two philosophical tasks of the highest difficulty and importance. He showed that when we speak of concepts applying to objects, or of individuals partaking of universals, we are in fact talking about predicates being true or false of particular objects, or about the truth or falsity of sets of sentences sharing a common predicate, e.g.

'is red' or 'is a horse'. And by relating these notions to the symbolism for functional expressions he shows us one way of symbolising the generality of concepts, and in so doing shows us part of what it means to say that concepts are called 'universals'.

Since concepts are functions they too must be allowed to admit any object whatever as a possible argument. It must not be the case that expressions of no definite value can be formed by substituting the names of definite objects into the argument places of such functional expressions. Therefore every sentence which expresses an object's falling under a concept must be regarded as possessing a definite truth-value. And once more we are to construe sentences we should ordinarily regard as meaningless or lacking truth-value as false, as standing for the logical object named 'The False'. The condition that all concepts must be definite, so that every sentence obtained from the corresponding functional expression is either true or false, is imposed by the nature of logic. For Frege thought that the laws of logic treated of and applied to concepts and objects. They expressed quite general truths about the relations between concepts and objects, irrespective of the particular contents of either. Frege says that this rule is a version of the Law of the Excluded Middle, namely that for any object and any concept either the object definitely falls under the concept or it definitely does not (*Grundgesetze*, ii, 56). His argument, which will be examined in detail later, is that if this were not the case sentences constructed from the expression for the concept would not have a complete sense. Granted his identification of the truth or falsity of a given sentence with what the sentence as a whole stands for or signifies, we can see that the requirement of definiteness for concepts is simply part of the general requirement for functions that there should be some definite value corresponding to every possible argument.

Frege identifies the *extension* of a concept with its value-range ('Function and Concept', p. 30). This at once tells us that he understands by 'extension' something different from the term's ordinary meaning. For when we speak of a concept's extension, we are usually referring to the set of objects that fall under it. Now this set would be in Frege's terms the set of arguments that yield the value The True for the concept in question. But whatever a *value*-range is, it is not simply a set of *arguments*, not even a restricted set of arguments of this kind. It is true, on the other hand, that most of what Frege says about the extensions of concepts is appropriate only if we interpret them as sets of arguments. Most of his review of Schrœder's *Algebra der Logik* is concerned with distinguishing extensions from mere collections of objects falling under a concept, which would be pointless unless there was grave risk of confusion. I shall say more about this apparent paradox in Chapter 12, where I discuss Frege's definition of numbers as the extensions of certain concepts.

Corresponding to the general version of the fundamental law of logic there is a particular version which applies to the extensions of concepts. If two concepts always have the same truth-value for each particular argument, then we may say that the extension of the first concept is identical with, or equal to, the extension of the second. Now there are two ways of putting this equivalence. First, we can say that if and only if the extensions of two concepts are identical, then any object which falls under either concept falls under both. For without worrying what an extension is precisely we can see from the general conditions for value-ranges that all objects which as arguments yield the value The True for either concept will also yield the value The True for the other. And to say that an object yields the value The True as argument to a concept is to say that it falls under the concept. It does not, I think, follow from this that we must identify the extension of a concept with the class of objects that fall under it.

The second equivalence which is related to the particular version of the fundamental law I quoted is this. If the extensions of two concepts are identical then, Frege says, we are justified in saying that the two concepts are themselves equivalent. He does not mean that we can identify the concepts. He means rather that the number of objects falling under the one is identical with the number of objects falling under the other. There are two considerations, however, which may suggest that the equivalence of concepts is construable as identity. In the kind of case under discussion the extensions of the two concepts are supposed to be identical, since exactly the same set of objects falls under both. And there is a certain attractive gain in simplicity in saying that if this is so, then we may regard the concepts as identical. Another consideration is that for the purposes of logic it is irrelevant what the 'meaning' of a concept is. Logic is concerned only with the truth of sentences containing the concept.

Frege's views about concepts and their extensions as I have just described them were radically altered later in his life. After he had received the letter from Russell in which Russell pointed out a contradiction latent in Frege's set of axioms for the *Grundgesetze* system, Frege decided to abandon the fundamental law of logic as quoted. He still allows us to move from the general equality of two functions having identical values for corresponding arguments to the particular identity of their value-ranges, but he will no longer allow the converse move (*Grundgesetze*, ii, Appendix, p. 239). We may not conclude because two concepts have the same extension that any object falling under either also falls under the other. I shall say more about this in Chapter 12.

(vi)

We have so far been talking in terms of *the* argument of a function and *the* value corresponding to it. But there is no need to restrict ourselves to functions that take only one argument. For every kind of function of one argument there is a general kind of function of two arguments, or of several. Instead of discussing the function $x^2 - 1$, we might discuss the function $x^2 + 2y + 1$, for example, which is a function of two arguments. Now the conventions of notation must be carefully observed in the case of functions of more than one argument. It would be quite wrong to symbolise the function last mentioned by the expression '$x^2 + 2x + 1$'. For by the conventions of notation we should always have to substitute the same argument-sign in each of the argument places, and therefore the function would simply be of one argument. By using different letters in the argument places of expressions for functions of many arguments, it is shown that substitution in certain places is quite independent of substitution in certain other places.

If we take the functional expression for a function of two arguments, we see that by substituting a definite argument-sign in one argument place we obtain an expression which still contains one argument place unfilled. If we substitute the numeral '3' into the argument place marked by the letter 'y' in the expression '$x^2 + 2y + 1$', we obtain the expression '$x^2 + 2.3 + 1$' or '$x^2 + 7$'. This is of course the expression for a function of one argument. Therefore in order to obtain a definite value from the original function of two arguments, we must make a second substitution in the remaining argument place. The two arguments we need in order to obtain some definite value may now be taken as a 'composite' argument. The importance of this comes out when we turn to the particular case of concepts of two arguments. Such a concept is the one signified by the expression '— is larger than —', and we call such concepts *relations*. From the expression for a relation we can obtain the expression for a concept by substituting some particular argument sign in just one argument place. From the one mentioned, '— is larger than —', we can obtain for instance the concept expression '— is larger than London' or the concept expression '— is larger than the Moon', or the concept expression 'London is larger than —' or 'The Moon is larger than —'. Just as a concept can be regarded as something common to different objects, a relation can be regarded as something common to different concepts. We can derive the expression for a relation in the opposite way from that described, namely by replacing some definite name in the concept expression by a gap-sign or a letter indicating indefinitely. From the concept expression '— is larger than London' we can derive the relation expression '— is larger than —'. The *values* of relations too will be truth-values, since the expressions obtained by filling both argument places will be complete sentences, e.g. 'New York is larger than London'. For most relations the order of the pair of arguments is highly relevant to the value obtained by substituting them. With the same two arguments New York and London, and the same relation *x is larger than y*, we can obtain the quite different sentence 'London is larger than New York'. The reader will be able to work out easily similarities and differences between relations and other functions of many variables, and concepts and functions of one variable in general.

Since Frege regards truth and falsity as objects, and since every object must be a possible argument to every function, it follows that in his view truth and falsity themselves must be capable of appearing as the arguments of functions and concepts. Frege introduces two special functions in the *Grundgesetze* for which this condition is important. The first of these special functions is symbolised by writing a horizontal line in front of the given expression, e.g. '—ξ', and the second by adding a vertical line to this horizontal line, e.g. '$\top\xi$'. The rule governing our interpretation of these two functions is this. When The True is argument to the first, and only when, then the value of the resulting expression is The True; when The True is argument to the second, and only when, then the value of the resulting expression will be The False. We may express these functions as 'is identical with The True' and 'is not identical with The True'. In the *Begriffsschrift* Frege called the horizontal line the *content-stroke*, meaning the stroke that signified that the expression following was to be taken as the content of a judgment (section 2). A sign of the form '—p' is there to be read as 'the fact that p' or 'the proposition that p'. Now in view of Frege's theory that truth and falsity are objects, and his interpretation of the 'is' which precedes proper names of objects as the identificatory rather than the predicative, I think we may take the two functions mentioned above, namely the function *Is identical with The True* and the function *Is not identical with the True* in a more intuitive fashion. We may interpret them as the functions *Is a fact* and *Is not a fact* (see 'Function and Concept, p. 35). Therefore the later interpretation of signs of the form '—p' is to be 'p is a fact'. There is an obvious difference between this and the earlier interpretation. Now, since 'is a fact' is a concept, we obtain actual statements of fact under substitution, for the resulting expressions are no longer what Frege called proper names of a certain kind, but complete sentences.

There are other functions which, like the two discussed, take propositions as their appropriate arguments. These are the functions often described as *intensional*. The expressions 'I judge that p' and 'I fancy that p' are expressions for intensional functions. The peculiarity of such functions is that, unlike other functions, the value of the complete expression appears to be independent of the value of the sentence which is one of its components. The truth or falsity of 'I judge that p' is independent of the truth or falsity of the sentence 'p' itself. A more general way of putting the matter is that we have here a set of cases where the reference of a complete expression is not wholly dependent on the references of its components. Frege does not say much about such functions, and seems to have thought that his theory of sense and reference could give a satisfactory account of them.

So far we have been discussing only such functions as take objects as their possible arguments. Indeed it has been implied that it is essential to the very notion of a function that only objects could be possible arguments to them. For even propositions, or *thoughts*, as Frege terms them, are taken by him as objects of a certain kind, and so are truth and falsity, and numbers. But Frege extends the notion of function even wider than this. For he gives us a type of function which can take ordinary functions themselves, and not objects, as their possible arguments. These functions are called *functions of the second level* or *second order*; functions of the type discussed earlier in this chapter are *functions of the first level*. I shall not say much about second level functions, with one particular exception, since their place in Frege's thought lies outside the intended scope of this book. But there are three particular functions which are of rather general interest and importance. These are the two functions known as the *existential* and *universal quantifiers*, and the function known as the *class abstractor*, namely the value-range function described in section (iii) above. In terms of ordinary language, the expressions for the first two functions are 'It is not the case that for every $a f(a)$ is not The True' and 'For every $a f(a)$ is The True'. In simpler terms, 'For some argument the value of the function $f(\ )$ is the True', and 'For all arguments the value of the function $f(\ )$ is The True', or ' 'ξ is f' is true of something' and ' 'ξ is f' is true of everything'. An ordinary language expression for the value-range function is the expression 'The value-range of the function $f(\ )$'.

The existential quantifier is the particular function I said I should deal with as an exception. There are two related contexts in which it is important in Frege's theory, his theory of definite descriptions, and his analysis of the notion of existence and the notion of number. For the first, Frege insists as strongly as Russell that we are only justified in using expressions which have the form of singular definite descriptions, e.g. 'The so-and-so', if we know that at least one thing is so-and-so, namely if we know the truth of some existentially quantified statement (see for example *Grundlagen*, p. 87, note 1).

The existential quantifier takes functions of the first level as its arguments. The values yielded by particular substitutions will be truth-values. The corresponding expressions are complete sentences of the form 'There is a so-and-so' or 'Something is so-and-so'. The significance of Frege's analysis will be brought out in Chapter 2, in discussing his distinction between existence and objectivity. It is enough to remark here that we are partly provided with a form of answer to the old question whether existence is a predicate or not. Frege's immediate answer is that it is a predicate of predicates, in the old terms, and not a predicate of objects.

There is, of course, something odd in the whole way of talking which calls such functions of the second level 'functions'. If it is essential to the ordinary notion of a function that only objects can be their possible arguments, then what is the justification for also using the term 'function' to refer to entities that can take functions as possible arguments? For there is, as Frege himself points out, just as great a difference between functions of the second level and functions of the first as there is between functions of the first level and objects. But the possible justification is not hard to see. There is something common to all functions of whatever level which distinguishes them from objects, namely the property of all functional expressions of containing empty places or argument places. Of course argument places in expressions for functions of the second level are clearly designed to be filled only by the expressions for functions of the first level. But it is here irrelevant what kind of expression has to be inserted; what is relevant is only that some expression has to be. In Frege's view this common property of the symbolism for all functions of whatever level reflects a common property of all functions in themselves, namely what he calls their *incompleteness* or *unsaturatedness*. It is because the distinction between complete entities and incomplete ones is of absolutely fundamental importance to a correct philosophy of logic that we are justified in using a common term to cover all entities on the latter side of the distinction.

SOURCES FOR CHAPTER ONE

'Function and Concept'; 'What is a Function?'; *Grundgesetze*, i, 1 ff; *Begriffsschrift*, section 9 ff.

CHAPTER TWO

CONCEPT AND OBJECT

Throughout his entire work Frege insists upon the radical distinction between the nature of concepts and the nature of objects. He regarded the clarifying of this distinction as one of his most powerful tools of philosophical criticism and construction (see, e.g., *Grundgesetze*, i, Preface). One aspect of the distinction was briefly discussed in Chapter 1, namely the need for the rules for correct formation of functional expressions in logical notation to show clearly a distinction between signs for possible arguments and signs for functions. But Frege speaks as if there were more to the distinction than this; he seems to have thought that it was not just a necessity of perspicuous symbolism, but a distinction grounded in the nature of things. It is this belief that I shall discuss in Chapters 2 and 3.

At the end of the Introduction to the *Grundlagen* Frege states three fundamental principles which, he says, underlie his methods of thought (p. x). The first is always to 'separate sharply the psychological from the logical, the subjective from the objective'; the second is 'never to ask for the meaning of a word in isolation, but only in the context of a proposition'; and the third is always to bear in mind the distinction between concept and object. These principles are clearly related to one another. For according to the first we must distinguish concepts from ideas, *Vorstellungen*. Ideas are mental entities, belonging to the realm of the psychological, and therefore subjective; concepts are not mental entities, and the science that investigates their nature and properties is not psychology but logic. According to the second principle we understand that concepts are in some way essentially propositional. Instead of talking, for example, about the concept *Red* or the concept *Horse* we should be careful to make explicit the connection with the form of a proposition by talking rather of the concept *Is a horse* or the concept *Is red*. It is not clear yet whether we should go further still, and say that concepts only occur in propositions. Frege's answer to this will be explored in Chapter 5 below, and further in Chapters 6 and 7 (section (iv)).

Frege has criteria of two distinct types for distinguishing concepts

19

from objects. Some are properties of the expressions for concepts and
the expressions for objects, and some are properties of concepts and
objects themselves. I shall deal with the first group in Chapter 3 below;
in this chapter I concentrate on the second group, and in so doing
hope to throw some light on what Frege means by calling concepts
objective as opposed to ideas, and why this yields a connection with
logic rather than psychology.

The first distinguishing property is that objects fall under concepts,
but that concepts cannot be said to fall under objects nor under other
concepts of the first level. The German term used by Frege, *fallen
unter*, is idiomatic, and therefore not to be pressed for any special
content. It is quite easy to see two things implied by Frege's use of this
common idiom. The first is that to say that a particular object falls
under a concept, say the concept *Horse*, is no different from saying
that the object is a horse. So saying that an object falls under some
particular concept is at least partly saying that the corresponding concept expression can be truly applied to the name of the object. The
second is that there are at least two distinct types of thing in the world,
namely objects and properties; again, nothing of philosophical significance need yet be extracted from this common way of thinking. Saying an object falls under the concept *Redness* is therefore at least
partly saying that it possesses the property of redness. And obviously
these two points are closely related; for in the common terms a predicate can be truly applied to the name of some object only if the object
possesses the property signified by the predicate in question.

This criterion for the concept-object distinction does not therefore
help us very much, except that it reminds us that Frege's notion of a
concept is at least related quite closely to the ordinary notion of a
property. A second deficiency is that it does not serve to distinguish the
concept-object distinction from the quite different relation between
second level concepts and first level concepts. Frege does indeed introduce a special term for this latter relation, namely that first level concepts 'fall within' second level ones. But apart from telling us that the
relation of falling within must not be confused with the relation of
species to genus he gives little help as to his meaning. A third deficiency
is some unclarity in Frege's presentation of the notion of *falling under*.
Most of the time he calls it a relation, but it is distinct from the relation
between the given object and the property in question and from the
relation between the name of the object and the relevant predicate.
But at other times he says that it signifies a distinction of 'logical

places'. One part of his meaning is that the peculiar relation in question can only hold between entities of different natures; but this would only help us to distinguish concepts and objects if we already knew what the relation was. Another part of his meaning is that the grammatical position of subject expression and predicate expression are not differentiated just by particular forms of grammar, e.g., by the difference between nouns and adjectives; these positions are somehow imposed by logic.

The rest of the non-grammatical criteria for the concept-object distinction can be detailed briefly. One concerns our means of apprehending entities of the two types. Frege shows no great interest in this criterion, to which Locke, Hume, Kant and Russell devoted much of their thought. But it becomes important at one point, namely in discussing the nature of classes and the extensions of concepts. Frege denies that we can reach concepts only by abstraction, though he does not deny that this is one valid way of reaching them. We also reach them, he says, by constructing them from simpler concepts, and by analysing propositions whose complete sense is known into sets of complementary concepts. And none of this can be applied to objects, even to such objects as numbers which Frege calls objects of reason.

A second distinction is contained in the description of concepts as incomplete or unsaturated as opposed to objects, which are described as complete, self-sufficient and standing by themselves. Now Frege often expresses a similar principle by saying that a criterion for the distinction is given by the necessary forms of expressions for concepts and objects; the expressions for concepts must themselves be incomplete, while the expressions for objects are complete. It is not clear yet what the former version is supposed to mean if it is not simply another way of putting the latter. For the latter can at least be put in a definite and fairly clear form; expressions for concepts must always contain some empty place, a place filled in logical notation by an indefinitely indicating letter.

(ii)

We are not yet much further in understanding the distinction between concepts and objects. Now the idea of an *object* seems at first sight to be less problematic and closer to ordinary modes of thought than the idea of a concept. So let us turn to the notion of a concept first, to see whether it can throw any light on the distinction in question.

In the *Grundlagen* Frege distinguishes concepts from ideas and mental images; these are subjective entities while concepts are objective (p. 37, note 1). I shall go into this later in the chapter. But at least part of what Frege means is that while a man's ideas are private in the sense that only he has access to them, concepts are essentially public. They are not possessed by you or by me, and if I happen to possess one it is because I have got in touch with something that already existed independently of my mental processes or of yours. There is no doubt that Frege was an extreme realist in one sense. He believed not only that concepts and propositions are independent of all mental processes, but also that they actually subsist before our minds come into contact with them, and presumably afterwards as well. This is the point of his repeated comparison of mathematics with exploration; the mathematician and the logician too can only discover what is already there waiting to be discovered (see *Grundlagen*, p. 108; *Grundgesetze*, i, Preface, p. 145).

Concepts can be handled by us in several ways. They can be discovered or recognised, they can be known, they can be defined and they can be communicated. In these respects they resemble objects, for we are used to thinking that objects are essentially discoverable and recognisable, as Frege did. Moreover concepts like objects have properties (*Grundlagen*, p. 65); but here a distinction must be drawn. If we say that a concept has a certain property, we are saying that it falls within a concept of the second level. But there is another quite different relation between concepts. There are complex concepts, which are composed of sets of simpler concepts; and in this case the component concepts must be on the same level as the complex one. They are not in fact properties of the complex concept but rather *marks* of it, and in the old terminology the relation of a concept to its marks is that of a species to its differences.

Concepts resemble very much what people sometimes call the *meanings* of words of a certain kind, namely general words. It makes good sense to speak as if meanings were objective entities, parts of our public world as opposed to our private worlds of thought. And we often speak as if the meanings of words can be discovered, recognised, known or not known, defined and communicated. In view of the similarity between Frege's notion and this one we should be on our guard against unrestricted borrowings from our intuition in the interpretation of Frege's remarks about concepts.

Concepts, like the meanings of words, form the *content* of sentences. To each sentence of our language, Frege says, there corresponds a definite thought (see 'The Thought'). But this thought does not consist only of one particular set of concepts, for we can analyse it, or rather the sentence that expresses it, in different ways, and to each mode of analysis there will correspond a different set of component concepts. Although, we might say, the meaning of the sentence remains the same and although it consists of the meanings of the various expressions which compose it, still we can analyse it into different sets of complementary expressions, and these of course will have different meanings. Like the meanings of words too, concepts are something we use in our thinking; they occur in our *conceptual thinking* as opposed to our intuitive thinking. When we think intuitively, we use only our intuitions, we might say, and according to Frege intuitions are subjective entities like ideas or mental images. To say that concepts are not used in intuitive thinking is partly to say that they cannot be intuited. And whatever Frege thought intuition was, it is clear that he did not consider it to be a mental act of the kind that presupposed the objectivity of its object, such as recognition or communication. (*Grundlagen*, p. 20 on 'conceptual thinking').

Some of the things Frege says about concepts do not fit the ordinary notion of a general word's meaning so well. He attributes to concepts a power of grouping or collecting objects together (ibid., p. 61), and says that some concepts but not all isolate in a definite way the objects that fall under them (ibid., p. 66). These remarks are similar to some of the things traditionally said about ideas or mental images by empiricist philosophers. It would be quite wrong to think Frege had any such thing in mind, at least when he had emancipated himself from the crude doctrines of the *Grundlagen*. It is nearer his meaning to say that he is referring implicitly to certain properties of general words or predicative expressions. Isolating concepts are concepts like *Cat* and *Horse* that contain as part of their conditions of application a condition of distinguishing particular objects that fall under them; non-isolating concepts are concepts like *Red*, *Snow* and *Is running*, which contain no such condition. And when Frege speaks of concepts' grouping force, he is referring to the fact that the possession of concept expressions in our language enables us to deal in our thinking with whole sets of objects simultaneously; we can speak of horses, of red things and so forth. A further respect in which Frege's concept seems to resemble mental images more than meanings is that concepts can be obtained by taking a set of objects and abstracting from their distinguishing properties until the common property is reached. It is in places like these that one should look for the remnants of typical empiricist confusions between logic and psychology in Frege's thought.

(iii)

It is now time to turn to consider Frege's notion of an *object*, which he calls in quite ordinary German a *Gegenstand*. However, as seen above, that a philosopher uses a word thought to be absolutely transparent is no guarantee of the transparency of his use of that word; and this goes for Frege's use of the term 'object' or '*Gegenstand*'. Now in the *Grundlagen* he takes this as his basic and undefined notion, defining the notion of concept with respect to it; here he treats the words 'object' and 'thing' ('*Ding*') as interchangeable. It was only later that he came to give the term a peculiar philosophical content. And at the same time he took to defining objects in terms of functions, which thus took over the role of basic entity.

Objects are described in the *Grundlagen* as definite and particular. Frege calls the expression 'indefinite object' a self-contradictory one (p. 61). It was against this sort of sloppy thinking that much of his theory of the functional *variable* was directed. People sometimes think that the letter 'x' in a functional expression stands for a variable number. But though the properties of an object can alter with time, how can an object itself alter with time and yet remain the same object? And Frege's objection to the notion of a variable number is that if a number's properties vary, then the number itself must vary. He certainly believed the ancient doctrine that where there is change there must be something that does not vary throughout the change; and this was partly the function of his objects.

No two objects are identical; no object, as he puts it, 'is repeated' or 'makes a second appearance'. We shall have to qualify this when we come to his theory of meaning. For one of the uses of this theory is that it can explain how one and the same object can, as it were, make more than one different appearance in language. It explains how there can be different signs for one and the same thing, which are nevertheless all recognisably signs for the same thing. Frege believed too that all objects were necessarily identical with themselves. We can gloss these two conditions by saying that in his view identity was essentially a relation of any object to itself. This will be discussed in Chapter 4 below.

Objects are also described in various places in the *Grundlagen* by the terms 'bounded off', 'self-sufficient', 'undivided', 'standing by them-selves' and 'unity' (e.g. p. 42). Now these too are all notions we might use intuitively without a clear understanding of their bearings and relations, or without an ability to state criteria for their application. Much of Frege's general theory of language deals with this. For we can put his meaning, at least in part, in these words: the typical expres-sions of language which stand for objects are proper names, and there are two properties of proper names that distinguish them quite clearly from expressions typical of functions or concepts. One is that in some sense proper names are *complete* expressions, whereas concept expres-sions and functional expressions in general must contain an empty place or a letter that indefinitely indicates without definitely designat-ing. The other follows on. Names can sensibly stand on their own, whereas expressions containing gaps or free variables cannot.

There is one important property of objects in themselves which does not need to be clarified in terms of grammar and syntax. This is their essential *recognisability*. Frege believed that it was a necessary condition for our construing some entity as an object that there should be some way of recognising it as it appeared at different times and places or in different guises (*Grundlagen*, p. 116). For certain kinds of objects, for example numbers, this presents a difficulty of interpretation. Here Frege says that our 'recognition' is expressed in the putting of two signs for the same object as identities. We express our recognition of the number 4 when it appears under the guise of the sign '2^2' by saying that 2^2 is equal to 4. In the same way the recognition of the object described as the capital of England could be expressed by saying that the capital of England is London (ibid., p. 116). But usually when we speak of recognising an object we are implicitly referring to our apprehension of its properties. Frege was not interested in epistemo-logical problems about properties. In general he seems to have accepted the common view that objects have properties, that an object's pro-perties can in some cases change without the object itself becoming a different object, and that different objects can share one and the same common property.

No object can possess properties which are mutually contradictory (*Grundgesetze*, ii, 143; *Grundlagen*, p. 87). Now in calling properties 'contradictory', we are using of them a term usually applied to proposi-tions or to predicative expressions. So Frege's point is that if 'A' is the name of some object, and 'F' the expression for some concept, the sentence 'A is both F and not F' is a logical contradiction. This is one version of the Law of Contradiction. Now it seems that it is only when the two expressions in question are explicitly of the forms '*F*' and 'not *F*' that we are justified in taking the corresponding properties to be mutually contradictory. In general, Frege says, there is no criterion for the inconsistency of properties, and the only criterion for the consistency of properties is the occurrence of some object actually possessing the properties in question. It follows that we cannot say in advance of experience what objects can exist; we can only say that certain objects cannot exist. This point is of the highest importance in mathematics. For one common method that is used in many different branches of the subject is the method of constructing entities that are to be used in the course of a proof. Frege insists that we have no right to construct entities. They either already exist or they do not exist, in which case we cannot make them exist. And in any case we must be sure before we are justified in using them in systems of reasoning that they do not contain any latent contradictions, and the only way of knowing this is by discovering them before putting them to use.

People often think that we can call each distinct object 'one', as if Oneness was a property that every object necessarily possessed. Another candidate for similar treatment is the notion of existence. Even if people refuse to call Existence a predicate, they will still often be found to say that objects exist. Many of the terms Frege applies in general to objects seem to imply that he held the former view. But Frege did not believe that number words like 'one' and 'three' were genuine predicates. He did not believe that it made sense to call an object 'one'. For he took expressions like 'one' and 'the number one' as names for certain objects. Now sometimes we seem to predicate numbers. In 'There are nine planets', we seem to predicate the number nine either of the set of planets or of the concept *Planet*. It would then be a concept of the first level or of the second. Frege analysed such sentences quite differently. 'There are nine planets' can be rewritten as 'The number of planets is nine', and he construed such sentences as expressing identities of the form 'The number of planets = The number nine'. This proposition can also be expressed in the form 'The concept *Planet* falls within the concept *Has nine instances*', which states that a certain concept falls within a certain second-level concept. There is a second-level concept *Has N instances* corresponding to each natural number N. This analysis explains why the natural numbers seem to be predicable of sets or concepts. For it shows that number-words are components of a certain type of expression predicable of concepts, i.e. of expressions for a certain type of second-level concept.

Frege's analysis is not immediately appealing. There is still a strong desire to say that numbers are the properties of sets of objects. There are however two points that can be made on Frege's side at once. The first is that someone who takes the line mentioned is committed to saying that Oneness is not a property of objects in themselves, but rather a property of all those sets of objects that contain just one member. Now there does correspond to each particular object a set that contains just that object as its only member. Oneness will be a property of each of these sets, not of the objects themselves. But this immediately makes the proposed line less plausible, and further from the ordinary mode of thinking from which it sprang. It is only because it is easy to confuse the notion of a set that contains just one object as its only member with the notion of an object that it seems near to common sense. Frege attacked this line of thought in another way too. He thought that it involved a mistaken notion of class. For in his view what is important about a class is not simply that it is composed of a number of different objects, but that what objects it contains is determined by their falling under one and the same concept. So even if, in this way, we allowed numbers to be the properties of classes, they would still have to be treated as the properties of extensions of concepts.

Frege also brings out a connection between the notions of existence and of number. 'Affirmation of existence is nothing but denial of the number nought' (*Grundlagen*, p. 65). This does not mean that affirmation of existence is affirmation of the number one. Since existence is not a possible predicate of objects, to say of an object that it exists can only be construed as saying that it falls under some concept, or perhaps that it falls under some concept which has at least one instance. Affirmation of existence is denial that some concept has no instances. It is affirmation that it has at least one instance. It is through this connection that people treat the existential quantifier both as if it asserted existence and as if it asserted some number. We can now see that it is safer to deal with it as Frege does, namely by dropping the notion of existence and treating it simply as the negative form of the universal quantifier. To say that there is a so-and-so is simply to say that it is not the case that for every object whatever that object is not a so-and-so; it is simply 'denial of the number nought'. Perspicuity would then best be achieved by calling this quantifier 'particular' or 'numerical' rather than 'existential'.

(iv)

I described Frege in an earlier section as a Realist. In this section I shall try to justify my remark by describing Frege's notion of *objectivity*, and in the next by discussing his notion of *existence*. He drew a sharp distinction between objectivity and existence, and he firmly believed in the objectivity of concepts, thoughts and senses. I shall argue later, however, that he defended the objectivity of these entities only in upholding the objectivity of truth and falsehood. The point of this was to uphold the objectivity of statements about the natural numbers, and therefore to support his derivation of mathematics from logic.

What is objective must be distinguished from what is *subjective*. When Frege calls something subjective, he means that it is part of some psychological event or mental act (see *Grundlagen*, p. x). Such events and acts are themselves subjective in a slightly different sense. They are essentially private and accessible only to the particular person in whose mind they take place. We can therefore distinguish two threads of thought. Mental acts have both contents and objects. The mental act itself is the act of some particular agent and so far as this is private to him. I cannot make the judgments you make. The content of a mental act is generically part of the content of some particular person's consciousness, and therefore private in a different way. For Frege takes it that one man cannot have direct access to another man's mind. I cannot know what you are feeling, perceiving or thinking. We can express the distinction between the objective and the subjective, then, by saying that Frege distinguishes the content of a mental act from its object. If I think of a horse, the horse itself which is the object of my thinking is not a part of my thinking. It is not even, as some have thought, a kind of quality of or property possessed by my mind at the time in question. Frege never denies that there are things going on in our minds all the time we are thinking about objects or thinking thoughts. He allows that to certain words and sentences there may very well correspond mental images, vague feelings, associated thoughts and ideas, and so forth ('On Sense and Reference', p. 59). Only he insists that these associated psychological phenomena are neither the only entities in the situation nor the ones with which the logician is concerned.

He makes this distinction in what seems a curious way. In the *Grundlagen* he defines what is objective as 'what is independent of our sensing, intuiting and imagining, and of the constructing of inner pictures out of the memories of earlier sensations, but not what is independent of reason (*Vernunft*); for to answer the question what things are when they are independent of reason would be like judging without judging or washing the fur without wetting it' (*Grundlagen*, p. 36). And immediately above he says, referring to space, that 'what is objective in it is what is subject to law, what can be conceived (*Begriffliche*), what can be judged, what can be expressed in words' (ibid., p. 35). And a third passage which expresses the same idea occurs in Section 105 of the *Grundlagen*. 'In arithmetic we are not concerned with objects which we come to know as something alien from without through the medium of our senses, but with objects given directly to our reason and as its own, utterly transparent to it . . . For that very reason, these objects are not subjective fantasies. There is nothing more objective than the laws of arithmetic.' From these passages we gather two things; that the property of objectivity is closely related in some way to the faculty of reason, and that reason itself is related to the power of expressing facts and necessary truths. Now Frege elsewhere describes logic as the science which studies not minds but mind, and says that its subject matter is the laws of thought, or the laws of truth, rather than the laws of thinking ('The Thought', p. 289). Logical laws do not describe in wholly general terms our actual processes of thought and inference. Rather, they prescribe the conditions under which our thought-processes may achieve logical validity or correctness. And one such condition is that from true premisses only true conclusions can be correctly inferred.

It looks as if Frege was still under a confusion when he wrote the *Grundlagen*, under the same confusion as his opponents, who failed to see that no mere description of actual thought-processes could take take the place of a prescription for the correct use of thought. For otherwise, why does he talk in terms of *reason*? The fact that something is an object of reason does not distinguish it from objects of sensation, perception or imagination. It is just as much the object of a mental act, we might say, as they are. It does not seem to constitute a sufficient reason for calling it objective. Reasoning, judging and inferring are after all just as much psychological events as perceiving and imagining. Another explanation of Frege's curious mode of making his point is that at the time when he was writing the *Grundlagen* he was very much under Kant's influence. One way in which Kant marks the objective-subjective distinction is by referring it to the distinction between reason and 'sensibility'.

But beneath any superficial confusion of terminology Frege has got hold of two important truths. The first is that logic is not a descriptive science, but that its laws are normative, as Ramsey said. They impose norms or conditions to which our rational operations must conform if they are to achieve validity. They lay down the necessary conditions for *validity* of reasoning. It is here that we see why it is a profound description to call them 'laws of truth', as Frege does. For truth and falsity are notions which operate in definite ways; the ordinary truth-tables of propositional logic contain the ways in which they operate. So if our remarks, written or spoken, are to be true or false, they must be subject to the mode of operation symbolised in the truth-tables. In particular, when we are concerned with validity of proof and correctness of inference, we must see that both premisses and conclusions conform to the laws of truth, namely the conditions implicit in the truth-tables. The second important truth in Frege's view that objectivity is related to the faculty of reason is that what is fundamental in the problem of objectivity is the objective truth and falsehood of propositions. Logic, we may say, is in Frege's view the science which studies the conditions for the objective truth and falsehood of propositions.

It follows directly from this second point that talking about the objectivity of entities is secondary to talking about the objectivity of the truth-value of propositions concerning those entities. This involves their having objective senses or meanings. It involves the objectivity of the meanings of the words and component expressions in such propositions. We may provisionally put the relation between Frege's theories of truth and meaning like this. A proposition can be objectively true or false, which is to say that it can be true or false, only if each separate term in it has an objective meaning. So when we speak of the objectivity of concepts we are actually talking about the objective truth-values of propositions containing concept expressions or predicative expressions, and saying that the concept expressions they contain have objective meanings. And when Frege distinguishes concepts as objective from ideas or mental images, part of his meaning is that the objective meaning of a concept expression, such as 'red' or 'a horse' or 'likes John', is not any mental image the expression calls up in our minds. Similarly, when we say truth is objective part of our meaning is that merely thinking a proposition to be true is neither sufficient nor necessary for its being true. The question whether it is true or false can be settled without reference to our mental attitudes, e.g. of belief or disbelief, towards it. And when we say that number is objective, part of our meaning is that it is a fact that there are nine planets and four sides to a square, and not something that could be altered if we adopted a different set of numerals or a different method of counting or different multiplication tables.

We can now see something of what is implied in calling Frege a Realist. He believed quite simply that certain things were facts about the world and certain others were not. We can definitely say that some things are true and others false, and moreover we can definitely say that it is true that the former are true and the latter false, and false that the former are false. Among the things that are definitely either true or false are propositions attributing determinate predicates to objects or qualities to things, and propositions about the numbers of sets of objects. This seems innocuous, but it becomes less innocuous when related to Frege's theories of meaning and truth.

(v)

Finally Frege's notion of *existence* needs further examination. Existence was sharply distinguished by him from objectivity. So if all that he means by describing concepts as objective is that predicative propositions are either true or false, he does not yet seem to be committed to a Platonic view that universals are in some sense *real* just as individuals are. Frege does indeed point out that objectivity is not to be confused with reality or actuality, *Wirklichkeit* (*Grundlagen*, p. 35).

Existence is a concept of the second order in Frege's view. In effect this is to deny that it is an ordinary predicate. And even though it allows us to say that it is a second order predicate predicable of first order predicates but not of objects, we must be clear what such predication amounts to. In discussing sentences of the form 'There is . . .', Frege remarks that we cannot fill the gap with a proper name, but only with a concept expression, a predicative expression. 'There is Julius Caesar', if construed in the way in which we construe 'There is no unicorn' or 'There is virtue in the world', is nonsensical, although it can be given sense by different interpretations. Sentences where a predicative expression fills the gap are construed as predicating existence of the concept signified by the predicative expression. 'There is a horse' predicates existence of the concept *Horse*. It can be rewritten in the form 'The concept *Horse* has instances', and this is equivalent to the more explicit forms 'The concept *Horse* falls within the concept

Existence' or 'The concept *Horse* falls within the concept *Concept having instances'*.

Put crudely, what Frege is saying is this. We cannot just say that Julius Caesar exists. This is not just an empty remark but a senseless one ('On Concept and Object', p. 50). We can on the other hand sensibly say, for instance, that he was an emperor of Rome. Now to predicate the concept *Emperor of Rome* truly of Julius Caesar entails saying that the concept *Emperor of Rome* has at least one instance. Predicating a definite concept of some object is therefore implicitly predicating what we confusedly call 'existence' of it. The truth of the predication entails that the object is a proper instance of the concept in question, and so a possible instance of other concepts as well. Frege treats existential propositions as if they were incomplete predicative propositions, so that '*x* exists' should be written rather in the form '*x* is . . .'. It is clear that this can be completed by a predicative expression.

Frege re-expressed in a similar way statements attributing numbers to sets of objects (*Grundlagen*, p. 63). 'There are nine planets' is re-written in the form 'The concept *Planet* falls within the concept *Concept having nine instances'*. It is clear from this why attributions of a definite number to sets of objects are simply particular cases of the general attribution of 'existence'. For attributing existence is predicating instantiation of the concept in question in not less than one object.

Frege's analysis of existence does not allow us any longer to say that objects exist. But it does not allow us either to go on saying that concepts exist. All that we may say is that concepts have instances or do not have any, just as all we may say of objects is that they either fall under some concept or do not. To say explicitly of some concept that it existed would appear to be involving oneself in contradiction, since 'There is the concept *Horse*' has, on Frege's analysis, exactly the same logical form as 'There is Julius Caesar', and 'There is a concept *Horse*' does not have any clear sense. We can, however, provide a context. If we consider the form 'There is a concept such that it . . .', we see that the gap can perfectly well be filled by the expression for a second order concept, for example by the expression 'is a concept having nine instances' or the expression 'has instances'. The resulting sentences can then be rewritten in the forms 'The concept *Concept having nine instances* has instances' and 'The concept *Concept having instances* has instances'. Another perfectly good context is that exhibited in the expression 'There is a concept such that everything falls under it' or the expression 'There is a concept such that whatever is a man falls under this concept', namely the concept *Male*. The former contexts are all reducible to the notion of *instantiation* of concepts. And even the latter context can be reduced to the same notion, since it can be rewritten in the form 'The concept *Concept such that whatever is a man falls under this concept* has at least one instance'. At least one instance of this second order concept is the concept *Male*.

This reduction of the notion of existence as applied to concepts to the notion of instantiation may serve to distinguish Frege from the Platonists, to whom the existence of universals is a problem to be discussed together with the problem of the existence of particulars. But concepts, although we may not say in a simple way that they exist, can still be objective (*Grundlagen*, p. 37, note 1). And there is a logical connection between the existence of objects and the objectivity of a concept. To say that a concept is objective we may for the time being construe as saying that sentences containing the corresponding concept expression are either objective truths or objective falsehoods. Then the sentence 'The concept *Horse* is objective' may be taken as meaning much the same as the sentence 'Sentences predicating the expression "is a horse" of the names of objects are either true or false'. And Frege believed as we shall see that the latter sentence entailed that the expression 'is a horse' possessed an objective meaning. Now in line with his theory of definition this means that it must be either true or false of every object whatever that it is a horse. He frequently puts the same point in a simpler and more forceful way. Concepts must be 'sharp' or 'definite' or have sharp 'boundaries' (see, e.g., *Grundgesetze*, ii, 56).

It is a condition for the objectivity of any concept that it be decided for every object whether or not it falls under the given concept. But this condition does not of course entail that any object actually falls under the concept. So long as it is objectively false of every object that it falls under some concept, say the concept *Centaur*, then the condition for the objectivity of this concept is fulfilled. Frege goes further. There are some concepts, he says, under which no object can possibly fall. To say of any object that it fell under such a concept would not merely be to say something false but to say something self-contradictory. But if it is impossible for any object to fall under such a concept, it must be false that any object does in fact fall under it. So the objectivity of such a concept is guaranteed *apriori*. Frege cites the concept *Not identical with itself* as one such concept (*Grundlagen*, p. 87). It is logically impossible, he says, that any object should not be identical with itself. Since we know this *apriori*, we know *apriori* that no object does fall under this concept, and therefore that it is objective. Indeed it is perhaps easier to see *apriori* that such a concept is objective than it is to see that the concept *Horse*, for example, is objective. For it is by no means clear that every object either definitely is a horse or definitely is not.

In making this distinction Frege ironed out yet another problem that was still confusing people many years after he had solved it. People sometimes think that because a concept is self-inconsistent, like the one cited, it cannot 'exist', just as self-inconsistent objects cannot exist. It has even been thought that because a concept happens to have no instances it does not exist, that because there are no ancient Greeks left on earth, the concept *Ancient Greek* too has ceased to exist. Frege's answer to this particular form of the confusion would still be valid even if we also held the false theory that concept expressions actually stood for the objects they applied to; even if 'Ancient Greek' actually stood for all and only the ancient Greeks.

SOURCES FOR CHAPTER TWO

'On Concept and Object'; *Grundlagen*, sections 26–27, 46–54, 57–61, 70–74.

CHAPTER THREE

SUBJECT AND PREDICATE

I N this chapter I examine the second group of criteria Frege gives for the concept-object distinction. These are the criteria provided by grammatical and syntactical forms of expression. Frege assumes throughout that facts about the forms and uses of words and sentences are capable of standing as signs of or criteria for facts about reality; I shall go into this in Chapter 10. Here, if we like, we can treat these questions of grammar and the use of language on their own merits, forgetting the ontological background they are supposed to spring from and point to. We may, that is, think for the time being of the terminology of objects and concepts as simply one mode of expressing the given facts about language. Of course Frege himself did not think this was all that was in the case. He thought it possible to say things in this terminology which were neither solely about the use of language and expressions, nor expressible solely in the terms 'subject', 'predicate' and so forth (e.g., 'On Concept and Object', p. 45 and *passim*).

The basic distinction we are here dealing with is a distinction between two types of expression; between what Frege calls *proper names*, *Eigenname*, and what he calls *concept-words*, *Begriffsworte*. These categories do not apply only to single words like 'Socrates' and 'horse'; complex expressions too can be proper names or concept words. Frege regards definite descriptions as a kind of proper name, for example, so that the expression 'The tallest man on earth' is just as much a proper name as 'Socrates'. Similarly, expressions like 'is a horse', 'ran from John o'Groats to Land's End' are concept-words. Frege neither claims nor intends that these two types of expression exhaust what language contains. But not every expression that occurs in a significant proposition is logically an expression; the expression 'every man', which occurs for instance in the sentence 'Every man is mortal', is not a logically complete or self-subsistent expression. This sentence falls rather into the separate expressions 'Every . . .', '. . . is mortal', and '. . . man'.

In discussing the distinctions between proper names and concept-words we are discussing signs of, or criteria for, a distinction between objects and concepts. For Frege thought that if a language or symbolic notation answered in its properties to the logical properties of the subject-matter it was to express, then it would be a logically adequate language; if not, not. And he clearly thought that ordinary language was up to a point logically correct; so that up to this point the properties of ordinary language and its expressions, i.e. facts of grammar and syntax, could be taken to correspond to or mirror real logical properties of whatever can be expressed in language.

Sometimes he defines proper names as 'whatever expressions stand for objects' (e.g., 'On Sense and Reference', p. 57); and sometimes he defines objects as 'whatever proper names stand for' (e.g., 'Function and Concept', p. 32). And a similar ambiguity attends his definitions of concept and concept-word. Now if we take the latter to represent his intention, then as I said we may ignore his terminology of object and concepts, and simply interpret his work as philosophy of language. But I do not think this is correct. For since his category of proper names is considerably wider than ours, he must presumably have some way of specifying a proper name; and it seem that he does this precisely in the former way, namely by saying that any expression which stands for or signifies an object is to be considered in logic as a proper name. His thought can here be put in another form. The kind of standing for that ordinary proper names do, i.e. naming objects, is only one kind of a general relation between certain expressions and things; and it is this general relation of *standing for* or *signifying* or *referring to* objects which is of logical importance. But the case is different for concept-words. Here it seems that we must start with the notion of the concept-word, and define concepts as the entities such expressions stand for. For Frege only defines concepts in terms of functions, at least in writings later than the *Grundlagen*, and the terminology of functions makes sense only when we are considering the logical analysis of propositions. So it appears that his definitions are asymmetrical; proper names are defined in terms of objects, but contrariwise concepts are defined in terms of concept-words. We can put the whole thing in another way. We start with a singular predicative sentence such as 'Socrates is wise'. Corresponding to the predicative part of the sentence there is a concept, namely the concept *Wisdom*. Now we already know that any sentence of this form states that some object falls under some concept; this fact is given in the mode of analysis. It follows that what is left of the subject matter of the whole sentence when the concept *Wisdom* is subtracted is the object. And this will be what is signified by the expression which remains when the concept word that signifies the concept *Wisdom* is removed from the sentence, namely the proper name 'Socrates'. So that this expression must be taken as a logically proper name.

This analysis rests upon three assumptions of completeness; that every complete singular proposition can be analysed without remainder into a subject part and a predicate part; that every sentence which expresses a singular proposition, namely every singular sentence, can be analysed without remainder into a proper name and a concept-word or predicative expression; and that every complete singular proposition predicates, without remainder, some concept of some object falling under it. In this account the exceptional cases of particular and universal sentences, existential sentences and complex sentences are ignored for the time being. Now the third of these assumptions need not be questioned, since it may be seen as simply expressing a mode of analysis of propositions, namely the analysis in terms of function, argument and value. And perhaps the second and first can be conflated; for Frege certainly identifies concept-words and *predicative expressions*, and I think he also less explicitly identifies proper names and possible subject expressions of singular sentences. The main problem that is to be solved is therefore why Frege believed that every singular proposition could be completely analysed into a *subject* and a *predicate*, and what he meant by these terms.

(ii)

At this point it is worth detailing the explicitly grammatical criteria for distinguishing proper names in Frege's sense from concept-words. There are not many, and only two seem to play a great part in his thinking.

Only concept-words can have grammatically plural forms (*Grundlagen*, pp. 50, 64); occurrence in the plural is sufficient to show that an expression is a concept-word, since proper names cannot have plural forms. This follows from the fact that concept-words can in principle be applicable to more than one object simultaneously, while each proper name is essentially the proper name of one distinct and definite particular object. Even if there are several men called 'John Smith', still the proper name of the first John Smith is not the proper name of the second; what differentiates the two names is just that each is the name of a different man. An apparent exception to the rule of grammatical singularity for proper names concerns definite descriptions, which Frege classes as proper names; are there not plural descriptions, like 'The white horses'? Frege does not discuss these forms, though he alludes to them in 'On Concept and Object' only to say that they are specifically excluded from the scope of his remarks in that essay.

This criterion is related to a second criterion. Only concept-words can be preceded by the words 'all', 'every', 'some', 'no' and 'any' ('On Concept and Object', p. 48). These words correspond to the universal and existential quantifiers of logical notation. It is sensible to prefix these terms to an expression only if the expression can in principle be applicable to more than one object. 'Any John Smith' and 'all John Smiths', unless they are interpreted to mean the same as 'any man named "John Smith"' and 'all men named "John Smith"', are senseless. Concept-words, rather, are preceded in grammar by these analogues of the quantifiers. It would however be a bad mistake to construe legitimate expressions like 'all men' or 'some whales' as logically complete and coherent expressions. To do this would be to make the mistake of construing universal and particular sentences as if they were species of singular sentences. 'All men' is not the logical subject of the proposition expressed by the sentence 'All men are mortal', nor 'Some whales' of the proposition expressed by the sentence 'Some whales are blue'. I discuss this in section (iii) below.

Related to these criteria is a third, which applies only to some expressions, namely to descriptive phrases formed by prefixing some general term with the definite or indefinite article. Expressions prefixed by the definite article 'the' are proper names, expressions prefixed by the indefinite article 'a' are concept-words; of course here too we are only speaking of cases where the general word in question is grammatically singular. Expressions of the kind dealt with by these last two criteria were assimilated by Russell into what he called the class of *denoting phrases*. It is obvious that Frege makes a special case of definite descriptions; Russell on the other hand does not, but treats them in exactly the same way as he treats denoting phrases of other types, a way almost identical with Frege's treatment of them. The justification for Frege's making an exception of definite descriptions will be dealt with in Chapter 4.

One further criterion should be mentioned. Concept-words are said to be capable of appearing in the adjectival form, the attributive construction and the predicative position (*Grundlagen*, p. 27, p. 72; 'On Concept and Object', p. 43). Proper names, on the other hand, are characteristically substantive, and are incapable of appearing by themselves in the predicative position. I shall discuss this point later.

These explicitly grammatical or linguistic criteria for the concept-object distinction are not meant by Frege as anything more than guides or first steps towards the logical analysis of expressions. He pays little attention to them, and if taken at face value they appear to conflict with one another and with Frege's own views. The rest of this chapter therefore ignores them and discusses instead the notions of subject and predicate. But in Chapter 4 I shall come back indirectly to these problems, when dealing with Frege's interpretation of definite descriptions as proper names.

(iii)

Frege does not define his use of the terms 'subject' and 'predicate'; he took it that we should naturally understand his meaning, and it is not hard to do so. For we can simply say that the subject is what a given proposition is about, and the predicate is what is said about the subject. In terms of sentences, the subject is the expression that stands for what the sentence is about, and the predicate the expression that completes the sentence into an assertion about this thing. The subjects and predicates of sentences are words or expressions and are investigated by the study of grammar and syntax; the subjects and predicates of propositions are not words or expressions. Frege equates the subject and predicate of singular propositions with an object and the concept it falls under.

So there is a distinction between the grammatical and the real subject and predicate. But there is also a further and more difficult distinction to be made; the distinction between the apparent and the *logical* subject and predicate of a proposition (*Grundlagen*, p. 68; 'On Concept and Object', pp. 44, 48). If we consider the proposition expressed by the sentence 'All men are mortal', it seems at first that the subject of this proposition is the entity termed 'all men', and its predicate the concept *Mortality* or *Is mortal*. But this analysis is logically incoherent. The correct analysis of such a proposition shows that the logical predicate of the proposition is what is expressed by the words 'All . . . are mortal'. The proposition is not to be construed as predicating mortality of

Socrates, Plato, Aristotle, etc., but as saying that for every object whatever, if that object is a man, it is mortal. In Frege's view it states a relation between the two concepts *Man* and *Mortality;* therefore the logical subject of the proposition may be said to be the concept *Man.* We could give as an explicit equivalent to the original proposition, the proposition 'The concept *Man* is contained in the concept *Mortality*'. The distinction between apparent and logical subject and predicate does not have to be drawn only with propositions of this kind. Russell came to apply it even to the case of singular propositions, first to those expressed in sentences whose subjects were singular definite descriptions and later even to those expressed in sentences whose subjects were proper names in the usual sense.

Frege believed that the logical predicate of every proposition could be expressed by the grammatical predicate of some possible sentence (*Grundlagen*, p. 77, note 2). For this is simply how he analyses certain puzzling kinds of sentence. It is assumed that, although the sentence stated does not express the proposition it appears to but a different proposition, nevertheless we can state a different sentence which expresses the same proposition as the first sentence expresses. And he certainly thought that every proposition can be expressed in some sentence, although this will later be subject to qualification. It is here that the grammatical points described in the last section are relevant; for it now follows that an expression which cannot stand in a grammatical predicate position in virtue of the rules of grammar and syntax cannot be the expression signifying any concept. We might express Frege's point in this way; a concept is the possible predicate of some proposition.

Not all propositions bring objects under concepts. There are propositions where a second level concept is predicated of a first level concept, for instance existential propositions and statements of number. In these propositions the subject position is occupied by a concept. Now we might express a proposition of this kind by, for example, the sentence 'The concept *Horse* has instances'. It seems from the form of the expression 'The concept *Horse*' and from the fact that it occupies the subject position in this sentence that contrary to hypothesis it stands for some object. This apparent anomaly was exploited by opponents of Frege, and caused him some trouble to explain; I shall go further into it in Chapter 5. But the lines of Frege's answer can be indicated easily; the same proposition can be expressed by the quite different sentence 'Something is a horse'. Here the term 'horse' reoccupies its proper predicative position in the sentence, and the subject position is taken over by the indefinite indicator 'something', which Frege says 'indicates an object indefinitely' but fails to designate any object ('What is a Function?', p. 110). There are other kinds of proposition which do not predicate a concept of an object, notably universal propositions and hypothetical and disjunctive propositions. But Frege remarks in the *Begriffsschrift* that the distinction between categorical propositions and hypothetical and disjunctive ones seems to be merely a grammatical distinction; his only significant discussion of hypothetical ones occurs in 'On Sense and Reference'. And it is in that analysis made plain that the logical analysis of hypothetical propositions would show that their component concept expressions still occupied logically predicative positions within the various component propositions into which Frege analyses a hypothetical.

There are on the face of it two ways of defining the predicates of propositions. One is to say that they are what the predicates of sentences stand for or express, where it is taken as possible to specify the criteria for a grammatically predicative expression. The other is to say that they are what are predicated in predicative propositions; here the activity of predication is taken as fundamental. Frege speaks in one or two places as if he had something like this in mind. He mentions the case of expressions which cannot be used predicatively ('On Concept and Object', p. 43), and he speaks of the 'predicative occurrence' of expressions. But it is safer to say that he did not really take this line seriously, and thought instead about facts of grammar and syntax. However one qualification must be made; early on he had confused predication with assertion, and this confusion occupied him for some years. Later he became quite clear that assertion was an act performed by the speaker, and distinguished it sharply from the fact of predication within the asserted proposition. And earlier part of his confusion had consisted in locating the proposition's being asserted within its own predicate; so even here it looks as if predication did not mean to Frege any kind of act, but rather a grammatical function within language.

(iv)

There are two characteristics of the simple subject-predicate sentence which play important roles in helping to determine the correct logical state of affairs. These are the ordinary *copula*, the verb 'to be' and its appropriate forms, and the *negative*, especially the word 'not'. For the syntactical functions of these two terms are indices to the facts about logical predicativity which Frege has brought out.

He makes a sharp distinction between the 'is' which is the ordinary copula involved in predication and the 'is' which is involved in statements of identity ('On Concept and Object', p. 44). I think any predicative proposition could in his view be re-expressed in a sentence containing the copula; for any predicative expression must contain a verb in the indicative mood, and such a verb can always be expressed by the copula together with a participle. 'Runs' can be replaced for logical purposes by 'is running', and 'walked' by 'is having-walked'; this kind of thing is familiar to students of highly inflected languages like Greek. The sentence 'Socrates is wise' contains the predicative copula; on the other hand the 'is' in 'Socrates is Xanthippe's husband' is identificatory according to Frege. We could rewrite this sentence in the form 'Socrates=Xanthippe's husband', except that the symbol '=' is normally used only in mathematical contexts; Frege did not believe that this gave it a different meaning in any way. 'Socrates is Xanthippe's husband' is therefore of the same form as '$2^2=4$'. But even statements of identity are predicative, though what is predicated is not what is said to be identical with the subject, i.e., in our case Xanthippe's husband; this is an object, and no object can be predicated. Rather it is 'is identical with Xanthippe's husband' which is predicated in the sentence quoted. Identity is a relation in general, and therefore 'identical with Xanthippe's husband', since one argument place has been filled by the proper name 'Xanthippe's husband', stands for a concept. Statements of identity predicate identity with the object signified by the second name of the object signified by the first, and vice versa. On the other hand predicative propositions are in general not identificatory. Frege is here taking a stand against people who said that since 'Socrates is wise', for instance, states the identity of Socrates and Wisdom, it is necessarily false, a conclusion extended to cover all ordinary predicative propositions.

The copula must also be distinguished from the use of the same verb 'to be' in asserting existence; a rare use, which has however led some philosophers to construe all predicative propositions as asserting the existence of their subjects. Finally two distinct varieties of copula must be distinguished within the simple predicative use of 'to be', namely the timeless 'is' and the present-tense 'is'. Ordinary predications are said by Frege to be dependent for their truth-values on the times of their utterances (*Grundlagen*, p. 59; 'The Thought', p. 309). The sen-

tence 'Socrates is wise' is true at certain times but false at others. Here
we may regard the 'is' as implicitly containing a reference to the time
of utterance. If the sentence did not somehow refer to the time at
which the fact it states is asserted to obtain, its truth-value would not
be definite; and the verb is the only plausible candidate for containing
such a time-reference, though this is a peculiarity of certain languages
and not all. Time-references might be marked in the grammatical
form of the predicative term, e.g., 'wise', just as well. In other cases
there is no reference to time, since the truth-value of the proposition
stated is quite independent of the time of utterance. If the sentence
'Socrates is wise' expresses a true proposition, then we may say 'It is
true that Socrates is wise'; and here the truth of 'Socrates is wise' is
timeless. If it is now true that this particular proposition is true, then
it is always true. Perhaps the truth-values of sentences stating conceptual
relations are similarly timeless; the truth of 'All men are mortal' may
not depend on its time of utterance. Frege does not seem to determine
this one way or the other.

We can distinguish the copula from the 'is' of identification with
help from another Fregean source. For if an expression follows directly
after the copula in accordance with ordinary rules of syntax, then it
must be a concept-word; while if it follows directly after the identificatory 'is' it must be a proper name. And conversely in each case. Therefore we can tell immediately by inspecting the sentences 'Socrates is
wise' and 'Xanthippe's husband is Socrates' that the first contains the
copula, and the second contains the identificatory 'is'. This criterion
works in most cases, since we can generally distinguish concept-words
from proper names without prior recourse to the distinction between
predication and identification. But it does not work in the crucial case
of singular definite descriptions. For it seems just as plausible to construe the 'is' in the sentence 'Socrates is Xanthippe's husband' as
predicative as it is to construe it with Frege as identificatory. I shall
discuss the relation between definite descriptions and statements of
identity in Chapter 4.

The second point to examine is Frege's doctrine of the function of
the word 'not' and of negation or negativity in general. Like the words
which do the same in ordinary language as the symbols of quantification, the word 'not' can be used as a criterion for distinguishing logical
and apparent predicates. What can be negated? Frege answers that
negation applies to propositions. Even in the *Begriffsschrift* he said that
'negation attaches to the content (of judgement), no matter whether

this occurs in the form of a judgement or not . . . I therefore regard negation as a mark of a possible content of judgement' (p. 4). The point of this is in part to warn us that we must not think that we can negate just terms or even just predicates. The attachment of a sign of negation to a predicative expression, as in the sentence 'Socrates is not wise', is understood to negate the whole proposition expressed by the sentence 'Socrates is wise', and not to negate just the predicate, namely the concept *Wisdom*. This is not to say that we cannot construct forms in which it is explicitly the predicate that is negated; 'Socrates is not-wise' is an artificial way of doing this, and perhaps 'Socrates is unwise' is a happier way of expressing the same proposition. But this proposition is quite different from the negation of the proposition 'Socrates is wise'. Frege's point is that we should construe the word 'not' in general as if it meant the same as the expression 'It is not the case that . . .', where only the expressions for complete propositions, i.e. complete sentences, can fill the argument place indicated.

The sign of negation is attached to the predicate; but once again it is the logical and not the apparent grammatical predicate. For the negation of 'All men are mortal' is not 'All men are not mortal' but rather 'Not all men are mortal', and here the 'not' is attached to the grammatical subject expression. We have already seen how in this case the logical predicate captures part of the subject expression, and in fact the sign of negation attaches precisely to this captured part, namely the term 'all'. Frege says that 'this makes it clear that so far as their sense goes these words (i.e. 'all' and 'some') must be counted in with the predicative part of the sentence' ('On Concept and Object', p. 48). So the fact that the word 'not' attaches to these quantifying expressions is used to show that they are logically predicative. Why does Frege assume, as he appears to, that the only way of negating a proposition is by attaching a sign of negation to the corresponding predicative expression? The answer seems to be that all singular propositions can be construed as examples of the form 'The object A falls under the concept F', and their negations as of the form 'It is not the case that object A falls under the concept F'. Now this can be expressed in the form 'The object A does not fall under the concept F'. And just as the Fregean form 'A falls under the concept F' corresponds to a normal form of sentences 'A is F' (e.g. 'Socrates is wise'), so the Fregean form 'A does not fall under the concept F' corresponds to a normal form 'A is not F'. This account is only designed to be persuasive and probable. A second consideration is that if we attached the sign of negation to the subject expression, e.g. in the sentence 'Not-Socrates is wise', we should get a senseless sentence. For 'Not-Socrates' is certainly not the name of any object, and the sentence obtained is certainly not the negation of 'Socrates is wise'. If it means anything, it means 'Every object with the exception of Socrates is wise'.

Towards the end of his life Frege became sceptical about negation; he came to doubt that we could give any general definition of a 'negative term' in language further than the mere detailing of particular instances. He also came to doubt that we could give any general method for distinguishing negative and positive propositions. We know that one of the pair of sentences 'Socrates is wise' and 'Socrates is not wise' must be construed as the negative version of the other; and in this particular type of case, because 'not' is our paradigm of a negative term, we ordinarily take the latter as the negative and the former as the positive. But of course the positive can be regarded as the negative of the negative. And when we consider the sentence 'Not all men are mortal', we see how the two doubts are related; for it expresses the same proposition as the sentence 'Some men are immortal', and is this a negative proposition or not? If we could say definitely whether 'immortal' was a negative term or not, we should perhaps be able to say definitely whether 'Some men are immortal', and for example 'Socrates is unwise', were positive or negative. I say more about Frege's theory of negation in Chapter 8 below.

(v)

Frege was not concerned with subject-predicate analysis for its own sake. What he was concerned with was the possibility of the object-concept analysis of propositions, i.e. the application of the theory of functions to propositions. Everything he says about subject and predicate must be taken in this way. In the *Begriffsschrift* he said 'A distinction of subject and predicate finds no place in my way of representing a judgement' (p. 2), and he kept to this all his life. If this seems to contradict what has gone before, we should reflect that facts of language were of importance to him only insofar as they threw light on facts of logic. What does find a place in his notation is the logical distinction between object and concept. The fact that this distinction quite often coincides with the distinction between what the subject of a sentence signifies and what its predicate signifies is of no more interest than that. Frege took the grammatical distinctions to be merely results of the accident, as he thought it, that language is used to communicate a speaker's thoughts to a hearer (*Begriffsschrift*, p. 3).

A second related point is that Frege thought even the grammatical analysis into subject and predicate was arbitrary, as Ramsey did later (*Begriffsschrift*, section 3; 'On Concept and Object', p. 49). We could construe the sentence 'Socrates is wise' as being about Wisdom, not about Socrates. But such scepticism would not throw any doubt upon his logical views. For if we construe the sentence quoted as being about Wisdom, then the proposition expressed will be 'Wisdom is a property of Socrates'; and the subject of this proposition will be the first order concept *Wisdom*, while its predicate will be the second order concept *Property of Socrates* or *Concept truly predicable of Socrates*. And this analysis fits Frege's views perfectly well.

SOURCES FOR CHAPTER THREE

'On Concept and Object'; *Begriffsschrift*, section 3; 'On Sense and Reference'; 'Negation'.

CHAPTER FOUR

NAME AND DESCRIPTION

In the last chapter it was seen how at one point Frege's theory of logical predication relies on construing singular definite descriptions as proper names that signify definite objects, rather than as concept words signifying predicable entities. In this chapter I examine Frege's theory of descriptions, and try to show how his view may be justified; I also discuss his method of analysing sentences containing singular definitely descriptive expressions. Finally I say a little about his analysis of identity and statements of identity, to which the problem of definite descriptions is fundamental.

Frege uses the term *name* of any *sign* which stands for, signifies or refers to a definite object. So not only persons and places can have proper names, but so can points of space and instants of time, since these too are logically objects ('On Sense and Reference', p. 71). He speaks in the *Grundgesetze* of 'function-names' also; the expression 'ξ^2' is a function-name, since it may be said to stand for the function ξ^2. It is therefore clear that Frege's use of the term is considerably wider than the first definition allows. It seems to mean something like 'expression signifying something', where the type of entity signified and the type of signification involved are not determined. However I shall ignore the use of the term 'name' to cover the expressions that signify functions and concepts, and use it only of signs that signify objects.

The crucial terms in this account are 'signify' and 'stand for' (*bezeichnen* and *bedeuten*). Frege's analysis of the notion of standing for, or *reference* to, will be explored in detail in Chapters 6 and 7; however something must be said here. The first distinction to get clear is that between standing for and *indicating* (*bedeuten* and *andeuten*). Indication is a function of certain signs, notably functional signs; the sign 'x^2' is said not to stand for the numbers 1, 4, 9 etc., but to indicate them indefinitely. The letter 'x' which occurs in such a functional sign, or on its own, is called an indefinite indicator, since it does not itself stand for the various numbers which are possible arguments of the function in question, but rather only indicates them indefinitely. It is important to put the matter in Frege's way; we must not say that 'x^2' indicates an indefinite number, or that the '*x*' in '*x* is a horse' indicates an indefinite object. For Frege says that no object can be indefinite; if it is an object at all, it must be a definite object. The converse of his principle of completeness in defining concepts is a principle of completeness in defining objects. It must be determined one way or the other for each concept whether or not each object falls under it; it follows that it must be determined for each object whether or not it falls under each particular concept.

Signs are objects. The question then arises how we are to tell that a given instance is the same sign as another instance; how we tell, for example, that the signs '1' and '1' are the same sign in some sense. This is often called the problem of tokens and types. Frege gives two criteria. The first is simply that particular instances, or tokens, of a sign must be similar to each other; not exactly similar, since we neither need nor could get exact similarity between the instances of '1' that we produce. The second criterion is that the object must be produced with the intention that it be a sign for the object normally signified; e.g. that in writing a token '1' the writer should intend the sign to signify the number 1. If two tokens of the same type are similar enough for us to recognise that they are both intended to signify the same thing, both criteria are simultaneously fulfilled. Now in extreme cases these criteria may conflict; my writing may be so bad that you fail to recognise what I intend as a token '1' as an instance of the sign '1' at all; you fail to see the thing written as signifying the number 1. This is a failure of communication; for there is no reason why I should not use the badly written '1' as an instance of the numeral '1' myself. The criterion of similarity of appearance seems to be necessary simply in order to guarantee recognition and communication. And as we shall see in Chapter 10, Frege thought communication was essentially posterior to self-communication.

It is not a condition for the logically correct use of signs that to each object there should correspond only one sign. One and the same object can be given in many different ways, under many different aspects, through many different senses. Corresponding to a different mode of presentation we demand a different sign. The use of identity statements rests according to Frege upon this fact. For if there could only be one sign that signified any given object, the only possible identities would be of the form '*a*=*a*', which is useless for the purposes of real knowledge. Now a difficulty arises at this point. For how are we to tell in general whether two slightly different signs are to be taken as the same sign with irrelevant differences of production or as instances of two different signs, i.e. types? This difficulty is not peculiar to Frege's account of signification; and it does not seem to arise except in odd cases. Nobody will quarrel over the question whether 'Aristotle' and 'Aristoteles' are the same name or not.

(ii)

Names, i.e. proper names in Frege's sense, are signs of a certain kind. As such they must conform to the logical conditions of signification; a proper name must stand for or signify some one definite object, and signify it in some definite way. To each proper name possessed by an object there must correspond some definite way in which the object named is presented to us, some definite mode in which it is introduced to us ('On Sense and Reference', p. 57). Frege gives two examples of his meaning. In the *Begriffsschrift* he says that if we take a point 'A' on the circumference of a circle and draw a line through 'A' so as to cut the circumference at another point, we may call the second point 'B'. But the limiting case of a line's cutting the circumference of a circle twice occurs when it is a tangent to the circle; in this case we may call one and the same point, namely the point at which the tangent touches the circumference of the circle, either 'A' or 'B'. 'It is clear from this that different names for the same content are not always just a trivial matter of formulation; if they go along with different ways of determining the content, they are relevant to the essential nature of the case' (p. 12). Similarly, since one and the same object, namely the planet Venus, can be correctly described as the evening star and as the morning star, we may say that these two descriptions embody different ways in which the planet Venus is presented to us.

It follows from Frege's doctrine of the sense and reference of expressions that ordinary proper names such as 'Aristotle' and 'Berlin' must not only have a reference, i.e. signify some object, but also have a sense; the name 'Aristotle' must present the individual Aristotle to us in a certain definite characteristic manner. 'In the case of an actual proper name such as 'Aristotle', opinions as to the sense may differ. It might, for instance, be taken to be the following; the pupil of Plato and teacher of Alexander the Great. Anybody who does this will attach another sense to the sentence 'Aristotle was born in Stagira' than will a man who takes as the sense of the name: the teacher of Alexander the Great who was born in Stagira ('On Sense and Reference', p. 58, note). Frege goes on to say that such possible variations of sense ought not to occur in a 'perfect language'. The name 'Aristotle' should have a perfectly definite and unambiguous sense. Now one thing is quite clear from this account; that the sense of a genuine proper name can be expressed by a definite description. This is immediately reminiscent of Russell's treatment of proper names; only Russell held that no 'logically proper name' should have any sense at all, in Frege's terms. He therefore held that all ordinary proper names such as 'Aristotle' were not logically proper names; he restricted the class of logically proper names to signs which simply signified without describing the object signified in any way, whereas Frege extended the class to cover all signs which signified. They agree that the use of ordinary proper names does in some way entail possession of definite descriptions.

A more important condition for the logically valid use of proper names in Frege's view is that there should be something they signify. This does not of course mean that we are to abandon the use of signs which indefinitely indicate without signifying and functional signs; rather it applies to cases where the form of the sign leads us to believe that something is signified by it when this is not in fact the case. There are two important kinds of case for which this condition is often unfulfilled in everday uses of language. The first is of proper names of fictional and mythical entities; 'Pegasus' and 'Ulysses' both appear to name definite objects, but there are in fact no such objects named by them. The second is of singular definite descriptions; the expression 'the largest integer' appears to signify some definite number, but in fact there is no such integer. In this case the reasons for failure to comply with the conditions of signhood are more complex. A second condition is that there should be not more than one entity signified by a name. 'Aristotle' was and is the name of several different persons; 'the square root of 4', given our system of numerals, refers to two distinct numbers. According to Frege's second condition neither expression can be admitted into a logically perfect language.

The reasons why these last two conditions must be fulfilled by a perfect language or a notation adequate to express logical truths are related. They are related in the fact that proper names are used as the subjects of sentences. Now if we say something about Pegasus or Ulysses, supposing that what we say has a definite meaning, how can what is said be either true or false? For Pegasus and Ulysses, since they are not objects at all, cannot fall under any concepts; nothing can be either true or false of them, since there is nothing for anything to be true or false of. Now if we are not concerned with truth, as when we are making poetry or writing stories, Frege is quite willing to allow us to continue to use such apparent proper names. For as we shall see he did not believe that the fact that 'Pegasus' fails to signify anything entailed that sentences about Pegasus were meaningless. But when truth and knowledge are in question, i.e. as Frege says in 'science', such words must be avoided.

For ordinary definite descriptions a second reason is forthcoming. This is already contained implicitly in Frege's demand that concepts should be definite, *bestimmt*. For if a definite description applies to more than one object, it will not be clear which object any particular sentence containing the corresponding expression is about. And it is not simply that this is not clear; it cannot possibly be clear, since the description applies to several different objects. Again, it is in the nature of the case that no sentence about the white-haired man can have a definite truth-value; if individual *A* is meant it may be true, if *B* is meant it may be false. And again it is not just that we do not know whether the sentence is meant to be about *A* or *B*; the sentence, we might say, is as it stands just as much about the one as it is about the other. In this respect it resembles a functional expression; the subject-term 'the white-haired man' is analogous to a functional sign, in that it does not signify any individual, but rather serves to indicate indefinitely among a possible range.

Therefore two conditions which must be fulfilled if the use of a proper name is to be logically justifiable are that its object of reference should exist and be uniquely determined. And this amounts to the conditions under which a proper name has sense; for both requirements seem to entail that each object shall fall under a unique set of concepts. And this is simply a way of expressing Leibniz' axiom of the Identity of Indiscernibles.

(iii)

Frege's theory of definite descriptions resembles Russell's theory in some ways, although it differs in that Frege construes them as expressions that signify or refer to particular objects. Both make quite explicit the fact that correct use of such expressions involves as a condition the existence of some one object to which they apply. But there are two immediate differences. The first concerns the logical relation between a sentence whose subject is such an expression and the sentence that states the existence of a corresponding object. Russell takes the former to contain and imply the latter, while Frege takes it to *presuppose* the latter. The second difference is over the truth-value of propositions of the former kind in cases where the condition of existence is not fulfilled. Russell takes such propositions to be false, since they imply a false proposition, while Frege takes them to be nether true nor false, since their having any truth-value depends on the fulfilment of the condition of existence.

Definite descriptions occur in two principal positions. The first is the subject position, as in the sentence 'The King of France is bald'; the second is the apparent predicate position, as in the sentence 'Scott is the author of *Waverley*'. Frege's analysis of the former kind of occurrence is as follows. According to the conditions for correct use as a proper name, it is presupposed that (a) there is a King of France and that (b) there is not more than one King of France. These two presuppositions merely serve to state the unique existence of some object falling under the concept *King of France*; they do not specify which object does nor do they name it. Now if there actually is a King of France whose name is Louis, then the expressions 'Louis' and 'The King of France' refer to the same object but do so in different ways; they have different senses in Frege's terminology. So the sentence 'The King of France is bald' will have as a whole the same 'reference' as the sentence 'Louis is bald'; for the time being, we can gloss this Fregean expression as saying that 'The King of France is bald' will be true or false precisely according to whether 'Louis is bald' is true or false. The two sentences have the same truth-value. But they do not have the same sense.

Analysis of occurrences of the former kind seem to demand a prior understanding of occurrences of the latter kind; I shall therefore discuss Frege's analysis of sentences of the form 'Scott is the author of *Waverley*' in section (iv) below. Meanwhile his notion of *presupposition* must be clarified; for it is with this notion that his analysis of sentences containing definite descriptions diverges most from Russell's. Now Russell analyses the sentence 'The King of France is bald' into the set of propositions that (a) there is at least one King of France, that (b) there is at most one King of France, and that (c) whoever is King of France is bald. In Frege's analysis propositions (a) and (b) are not part of the meaning, i.e. sense, of the sentence, since he allows the sentence to continue to have the same sense when there is no King of France as when there is. Rather, their joint truth is a necessary condition for the truth or falsity of the sentence. Frege allows that there are sentences which are neither true nor false, yet still have perfectly definite senses, and when there is no King of France, 'The King of France is bald' will be such a sentence.

The notion of presupposition relates to the normal use of material implication and truth-values as follows. (See 'On Sense and Reference', pp. 61ff, pp. 69ff, especially p. 71, note 2). If a proposition P presupposes a proposition Q, then if Q is false, P is neither true nor false; and if Q is neither true nor false, P is neither true nor false. If Q is true, then P is either true or false, and may be either. The difference between presupposition and material implication on this account is that falsity of an implied proposition implies non-truth of the implying proposition, but falsity of a presupposed proposition implies both non-truth and non-falsehood of the presupposing proposition. This raises the question whether a proposition can be neither true nor false. Now Frege construes sentences as essentially true-or-false. This is part of his general method of attributing definite references to properly constructed expressions; therefore just as we are to count 'The Moon+3' as standing for The False, if it does not have a prior use for us, we are to count sentences which are neither true nor false as false sentences. (As I shall show later, he took the relation of a sentence to its truth-value as an instance of the general relation of a sign to the object signified.) This treatment is only needed for the purposes of logic and in general what Frege calls science; it is not required for ordinary everyday purposes.

I think we can see how Russell and Frege came to diverge from identical assumptions. They agree that (i) a namelike expression 'A' only designates an object if (ii) there actually is some object designated by 'A' and (iii) there is just one such object. As Frege puts it, whether a proper name has reference 'depends on the truth of a thought'. They would further agree to reformulate all this as follows: proposition (i) is true if and only if propositions (ii) and (iii) are true, and proposition (i) is false if and only if the complex proposition (ii)-plus-(iii) is false. They would also, I think, agree that therefore proposition (i) was equivalent to proposition (ii)-plus-(iii). It is in their interpretations of this that they differ. Russell interprets it to mean that (i) and (ii)-plus-(iii) have the same meaning; Frege does not. For as in general he distinguishes the sense and reference of a sign, he distinguishes in particular the sense of a sentence, i.e. the proposition it expresses, from its reference, i.e. truth-value. It follows that two propositions can have the same truth-value but still be different propositions, and that two sentences can have the same truth-value but express different propositions. This is the case in point. Frege would say that (i) and (ii)-plus-(iii) have different senses although identical truth-values. The proposition expressed by 'The expression "The King of France" has a reference' does not mean the same as the proposition expressed by 'There is just one King of France'; and surely Frege was right in this.

His chief reason for opposing a Russellian treatment seems to have been something like this. ('On Sense and Reference', pp. 68–71). If we say that a proposition of the form 'Louis is bald' contains or implies the proposition 'The name "Louis" has reference', we shall have to say that the negation of 'Louis is bald' is not 'Louis is not bald' but rather 'Either Louis is not bald, or the name "Louis" does not refer to anyone'. The argument can be applied to definite descriptions. If we say that the proposition 'The King of France is bald' implies the proposition 'Just one thing is King of France', we shall have to say that the negation of 'The King of France is bald' is not 'The King of France is not bald' but rather 'Either the King of France is not bald, or there is no King of France or there is more than one King of France'.

Perhaps the greatest difference between Frege's treatment and Russell's is that Russell does not allow that definite descriptions are of the logical form they appear to be; in his analysis there is left no entity which is referred to or meant by the phrase 'The King of France'. As I said earlier, in this he is more consistent than Frege, since he merely extends the Fregean analysis of 'denoting phrases', phrases beginning 'All . . .', 'Some . . .' and so on, to this case. In a fully analysed version of 'The King of France is bald', there occurs no sign which designates or signifies or stands for a particular object; there occurs rather only the letter 'x' which indicates indefinitely. In terms of ordinary language, we are left with the indicating term 'something' and various pronouns bound by this term. One reason why Russell denied that propositions of the form 'The so-and-so . . .' were logically singular propositions was because of the connection between his theory of meaning and his theory of knowledge by acquaintance. 'Every proposition which we can understand must be composed wholly of constituents with which we are acquainted'. In other words, to know what a sentence means is to know what each of its constituent expressions means, and this is to be acquainted with each of these meanings. Now in Russell's terminology 'mean' comes to much the same as 'stand for' or 'name'; so understanding what a sentence means is being acquainted with the objects, i.e. particulars and universals, which its constituent expressions stand for. And in a case such as that of the sentence 'The King of France is bald', which Russell takes without argument to be false, we understand the proposition although apparently not being acquainted with the King of France. He therefore denies that 'The King of France' has any meaning, unlike 'Louis' or 'Scott', which mean Louis and Scott respectively; this is to say that he denies that 'The King of France' is a genuine constituent expression of the sentence 'The King of France is bald'.

Frege was not under pressure from his theory of meaning in the way that Russell was; in distinguishing the sense of an expression from its reference, i.e. from Russell's *meaning*, he showed how we can understand sentences without *ipso facto* having anything to do with the entities referred to (*meant*) by its constituent expressions. In Frege's theory an expression's having sense does not depend on its having reference (*meaning*). Therefore he was not forced to show that the logical form of 'The King of France is bald' differed from the logical form of 'Louis is bald'.

In section (v) I shall come back to the question whether Russell's theory is finally more convincing than Frege's or not. Meanwhile it is time to turn to the second principal context of definite descriptions, namely their occurrence in apparently predicative positions.

(iv)

The two problems we are here concerned with are first, why Frege thought definite descriptions were not of a logically predicative form and why they could not be predicated, but only used to refer to and identify objects; second, how in general he treats statements of identity.

One might think that definite descriptions are logically predicative because they contain predicative expressions, e.g. 'King of France' or 'winged horse'. The proposition that Scott is an author of Waverley certainly seems to follow from the proposition that Scott is the author of Waverley; 'The King of France is bald' certainly seems to imply 'A King of France is bald'. Now the temptation to analyse definite descriptions as predicative does not readily arise for the latter kind of context, but rather for the former. Can we not say that in the former proposition 'is an author of Waverley' or even 'is the author of Waverley' is being *predicated* of Scott? This is not all. We might also say, for instance, that the logical form of the proposition is more complex. We might say that its expression conceals the fact that 'is an author of Waverley' is being predicated of Scott, and that 'is a concept having one instance' is being predicated of the concept *Author of Waverley* simultaneously. This would be in accord with Frege's principles of predication.

It might also be the case that definite descriptions are both proper names of some kind and nevertheless also predicable of objects. But if we put this suggestion into Fregean terms we see why it is absurd. For it amounts to the suggestion that an object might be predicable of another object, or that some other object might fall under this object. This is incoherent. Frege is careful to distinguish the 'is' of identity and the 'is' of predication, and it is worth repeating his method. He says that sentences like 'The morning star is Venus' can indeed be understood as predicative ('On Concept and Object', p. 44); only what they predicate of the morning star is not Venus but rather the concept *Identical with Venus*. We have here a general method for reinterpreting statements of identity as predicative statements. Instead of the form '$A=B$', where 'A' and 'B' are Fregean proper names, we can write the form 'A is identical with B', where the 'is' is the ordinary copula and 'identical with B' stands for the concept predicated of A. Identity is therefore on Frege's view a relation between objects (see *Grundlagen*, sections 63–5; p. 87; 'On Sense and Reference', p. 56; *Grundgesetze*, ii, Appendix p. 235).

There are trivial cases in ordinary use where we really do seem to be predicating a proper name, and Frege noticed some cases of this kind. If a man says 'Trieste is no Vienna', it seems that 'Vienna' is being predicated; in other terms, it seems as if the city of Vienna is being predicated of the city of Trieste. But this is only apparent; in fact the speaker is implicitly predicating a proper concept such as *City as large and cultured as Vienna*.

If a further explanation is wanted why proper names cannot occur as grammatical predicates on their own, although they can quite well occur as components of grammatical predicates, perhaps the reason is simply that predication is saying something about the subject of predication. And it is in the nature of a genuine proper name such as 'Aristotle' that to say someone is called Aristotle is not to give any information about him; it is not even to say that he is a man, since owls too can be called Aristotle. It is however precisely at this point that definite descriptions differ from genuine proper names. For even if sentences of the form '*A* is the *F*' are not allowed to be predicative, still it seems that saying *A* may be described as the *F* really is saying something about *A*; it gives genuine information about *A*. And Frege realised this. Only he accounted for the fact in another part of his theory, namely in his theory of sense and reference. One intended point of this theory is to explain how sentences of the form '*A* is the *F*' can impart genuine knowledge while nevertheless being statements of identity. And once we realise that the intuitive demand that they should give us information is satisfied in Frege's theory, much of our objection to his theory of definite descriptions may vanish. But of course we must first satisfy ourselves that his theory can do what he promises and we demand.

The problem we are concerned with now is how to analyse sentences of the form 'Scott is the author of Waverley'. Exactly which two entities are being identified in such a sentence, and how can their identification, if correct, be anything but analytic? Frege's answer to the first question is simple; the object named 'Scott' is identified with the object named 'The author of Waverley'. If there is discomfort in the notion that two distinct objects can be identified and also in the notion that one object can be identified with itself, we can put his answer in terms of predication. We can say that in this sentence the concept *Identical with the author of Waverley* is predicated of Scott, and vice versa. But there is still some unclarity. If this sentence is not to be analytic like the sentence 'Scott is Scott', then presumably some reference must be made in its analysis to the different signs used to signify the object in question. Now it is not enough just to say that the name 'Scott' and the name 'The author of Waverley' signify the same object. For regarded purely as signs it is quite arbitrary what objects these two expressions are taken to signify. Frege therefore finds it necessary at this point to distinguish between the difference of two signs simply as physical objects and their difference as signs ('On Sense and Reference', p. 57). The first difference is difference of shape, or of sound if the signs are uttered; the second is rather a difference in mode of signification. The point is subtle. It is that we cannot ignore the fact that our two signs are composed of words; it is not irrelevant what words they are composed of. The name 'The author of Waverley' is not just a *simple* sign; if it was we could use it without question to refer to Jane Austen. It contains the general term 'author of' and the proper name 'Waverley', both of which have quite definite meanings already. Frege's point is then that the meanings, i.e. the senses and references, of such component expressions are highly relevant to the meaning of the composite definite description. And this is to say that they are relevant to its manner of designation, its mode of presentation, its sense.

Therefore statements of identity such as 'Scott is the author of Waverley' are neither arbitrary nor analytic. Application of a definite description to an object is governed by real conditions, and these are contained in the various components of the description; assertion of the description therefore involves fulfilment of these conditions. So knowing that Scott is the author of Waverley really is knowing some facts about Scott and the world; Frege's own example, that of 'The morning star is the evening star', really does express the concrete result of much scientific observation and theory. In this sense it is genuinely synthetic. And it is easy to imagine how a sentence such as 'Jekyll is Hyde' can also be in this sense synthetic; it might be said as the result of a long and detailed police investigation.

(v)

I want to end with some considerations relevant to a choice between Frege's analysis of definite descriptions and Russell's. It seems that there are two general grounds on which such choice might be made; first, grounds of theoretical convenience, coherence and simplicity; second, grounds of conformity with ordinary usage and comprehensiveness of plain facts. My impression is that while Russell's analysis may be recommended by and large by grounds of the first kind, Frege's analysis is the one supported by grounds of the second kind.

There is a theoretical comprehensiveness in Russell's assimilation of definite descriptions to the rest of his class of denoting phrases. This is a merit, even though the considerations which drove Russell to make this assimilation from a previously Frege-like position are not acceptable. In adopting Russell's analysis one need not be implying acceptance of his theory of meaning and denotation nor of his theory of knowledge by acquaintance and description. Moreover, his analysis does bring out the connection between singular definite descriptions and predicative expressions; and here Frege's seems deficient.

We may not, however, agree so readily with Russell that 'The King of France is bald' is clearly false. Russell says in 'On Denoting' that if the description 'The King of France' has no denotation, then the sentence quoted ought to be nonsense, which it is not. He assumes that there is no further possibility. Now here too Frege's theory may seem to fit ordinary notions of truth-value better; are there not sentences which are neither true nor false, nor for all that nonsensical? But once again considerations of theory can be brought in. Both Russell and Frege hold that for the purposes of science, sentences must be considered as having definite truth-value. But Frege has to stipulate that sentences having neither truth-value are to be counted in with false sentences for this purpose, where Russell had already achieved the same end by disallowing a third possibility.

On the question of the truth-conditions of such sentences ordinary notions again appear to be on Frege's side. It seems to me that the conditions of existence and uniqueness are not so much implied but presupposed in the use of definite descriptions, and indeed names in general. Of course this notion of presupposition is not wholly clear; and it may be suggested that it is in fact self-contradictory. On the analysis given earlier, a proposition P is said to presuppose a proposition Q if Q's truth is necessary both for P's truth and for P's falsity. Then is not Q's non-truth sufficient both for P's falsity and for its truth? and since this is impossible, it follows that Q must be true; which is an absurd result. I think this argument errs by ignoring just that feature of the concept of truth which the theory of presupposition is in part designed to explain, namely the possibility of a third 'truth-value' which is neither truth nor falsity. For strictly Q's non-truth is sufficient only for P's falsity together with P's non-non-truth; and these two may be consistent with one another. Ordinary usage of the notion of truth and falsity appears to support Frege; but once again theoretical considerations come down on Russell's side. For the purposes of a logic which uses only the two normal truth-values, including indeed Frege's own system, the counter to the proof of contradictoriness in the notion of presupposition will not stand up; the notion has therefore to be abandoned. And in this case there seems no alternative to Russell's analysis.

However a decision on theoretical grounds cannot be made until Frege's doctrine of sense and reference, and his application of the doctrine to sentences, has been examined. This will occupy Chapters 6 to 9 below. But first we must turn to a special case of definite descriptions, namely those of the form 'The concept So-and-so'. In explaining why although they seem by Frege's criteria to be proper names yet they are not, i.e. why they signify concepts not objects, we shall be throwing further light on the concept-object distinction.

Frege's answer to this particular problem is also found to be of general application to a range of cases involving not just concepts but functions; it therefore serves also to illuminate the obscure notion of a function with which we began and to distinguish functions from objects.

SOURCES FOR CHAPTER FOUR

'On Sense and Reference'; *Begriffsschrift*, section 8; *Grundgesetze*, i, 26–32.

CHAPTER FIVE

INCOMPLETENESS AND PREDICATION

I have referred several times in the preceding chapters to the problem of the *incompleteness* or *unsaturatedness* of concepts and functions. I shall begin my discussion of the problem in this chapter by considering the apparent paradox of the concept *Horse* (see 'On Concept and Object', p. 45). I shall try to show that this paradox is in part an instance of the problem how concepts can be a kind of function. Nothing I say in this chapter is put forward as a final solution; my intention is rather to juxtapose the different elements of the problem. And I take Frege's basic problem to be the justification of construing functions and concepts as entities.

In 'On Concept and Object' Frege puts forward arguments in favour of the sharp distinction between concepts and objects. His opponent Kerry has pointed out that when we mention the concept *Horse*, for instance, we seem to be talking about what Frege must identify as an object; it seems that the concept *Horse* is not a concept but an object. Kerry concluded that Frege's distinction was not after all a sharp distinction.

Frege's answer is that we must take expressions of this form in their possible contexts. Typically they occur in sentences like 'Pegasus falls under the concept *Horse*'. Now this is simply equivalent to 'Pegasus is a horse'. This shows that 'the concept *Horse*' should be construed as an inseparable element of the complete predicative expression 'falls under the concept *Horse*', which stands for the same concept as 'is a Horse'. In the *Grundgesetze* Frege demonstrates his point more formally (vol. i, 4). We can give as equivalents the two expressions: (a) 'The Truth-value of: Δ falls under the concept Φ (ξ)', and (b) 'Φ (Δ)'. It can now be seen immediately that what in (a) corresponds to the 'Φ ( )' in (b) is the incomplete expression 'The Truth-value of: ( ) falls under the concept Φ (ξ)', and not the expression 'the concept Φ (ξ)'. Frege concludes that the expression 'The concept Φ (ξ)' does not really stand for a concept.

The paradox is simple to expound. 'The three words "the concept Horse" do designate an object, but on that very account they do not

61

designate a concept, as I am using the word' ('On Concept and Object',
p. 45). It follows that we can say 'The concept *Horse* is not a concept',
which appears to be self-contradictory, like 'The man Socrates is not
a man'. Frege says here that we are 'confronted by an awkwardness of
language which . . . cannot be avoided' (ibid., p. 46); 'language is here
in a predicament which justifies the departure from custom'. Toward
the end of the essay he goes still further. 'There is a quite peculiar
obstacle in the way of an understanding with my reader. By a kind of
necessity of language, my expressions, taken literally, sometimes miss
my thought; I mention an object, when what I intend is a concept . . .
The obstacle is essential, and founded on the nature of our language
. . . we cannot avoid a certain inappropriateness of linguistic expression,
and there is nothing for it but to realise this and always take it into
account' ('On Concept and Object', pp. 54–5).

It is some questions arising from this that we are to examine. In
particular I shall ask (i) Is this paradox peculiar to concepts, or is it a
special case of some more general paradoxical feature? (ii) Is it in fact
a genuine paradox, or does it merely seem one because of certain of
Frege's views? (iii) Exactly how does it arise from the nature of our
language, and how is language in a predicament here? (iv) Must this
paradox, or a paradoxical situation like this one, necessarily arise in all
languages, or is it peculiar to languages with a given syntactical and
grammatical structure?

Why does the paradox ever arise? Frege is quite clear about this. It
arises out of the expression 'The concept *Horse*' itself, since it is a
criterion for an expression's standing for an object as opposed to a
concept that the expression begin with the definite article. 'The concept *Horse*' is in grammatical form a definite description, that is the
name of some object. But there is a source deeper than this; for the real
question is why such an expression should ever occur. Frege is again
quite clear about his answer. We need such expressions because we
often need to make assertions about concepts, not about objects; we
need to mention concepts as well as using them. Now in an ordinary
statement about an object, it is what is said about the object that stands
for a concept. A concept is ordinarily the reference of a grammatically
predicative expression, and it is this part of the sentence that contains
what is said about its subject. It seems, then, that in statements about
concepts the concept must be made the reference of the grammatical
subject; since it is in this position within the sentence that language
places the expression for that about which the statement is made. But,

Frege says, this is impossible before the concept has been 'converted' or altered into an object, or, strictly, before we have found some object which will represent the concept for us in the statement.

Here we come upon yet another paradox. For it is one of Frege's strongest principles that the concept-object distinction is absolute. A corollary of this is, as he puts it, that a concept cannot be made into an object without altering it (*Grundlagen*, p. x). What this means is explained by a passage in 'On Concept and Object'. A sentence can be conceived as an assertion about an object and also as an assertion about a concept, 'only we must observe that what is asserted is different' (p. 49). The sentence 'Socrates is wise' can be taken as an assertion about Socrates, i.e. that he is wise, and also as an assertion about the concept *Wisdom*, i.e. that it belongs to Socrates, or that Socrates instantiates it. So now it seems not only that we must represent a concept by an object if we wish to make it the subject of our talk; but that in doing so we shall have to say something different about the object from what could have been said about the concept.

Before generalising the paradoxes so far uncovered it should be pointed out that in everything Frege says about this matter he makes his position quite clear ('On Concept and Object', pp. 42–3). He is no-where trying to define the notion of concept, he says, since the notion is so logically simple as to be indefinable. In lieu of a definition, he is trying to give an 'explanation' (*Erklaerung*) of what he means. And as means to explanation or elucidation the logician must fall back upon the more or less intuitive devices of ordinary language, such as hints, metaphorical expressions and even general appeals to the reader's goodwill. 'In such cases I was relying upon a reader who would be ready to meet me halfway' ('On Concept and Object', p. 54). This tells us that we are to exercise not only ingenuity but also charity on Frege's remarks; within the limits of logical coherence.

(ii)

If concepts are functions of a special kind, it should on the face of it follow that the particular paradox about concepts is a special case of some general paradox about the nature of functions. This is indeed so. The general paradox about functions is that they are what Frege calls *unsaturated* or *incomplete*; objects are *complete* entities. Now shortly after the *Grundgesetze* had been published, Frege abandoned the metaphor of unsaturatedness (see the article by M. Dummett in *Philo-*

sophical Review 1956; also note 2 on p. x of *Translations from the Philosophical Writings*, edited by Geach and Black). So I shall here simply deal with the problem of incompleteness; I shall not ask why Frege dropped the metaphor of unsaturatedness in favour of the other.

When Frege says that functions are essentially incomplete, he is referring to the fact that functional signs contain blank spaces or empty brackets which are ordinarily filled by the ξ- or x-notation. But he was also saying something about functions in themselves. He seems to have held two distinct views about the relations between these kinds of incompleteness. On the one hand he thought that incompleteness of the functional sign, namely the fact that a functional sign included one part which did not itself designate but was, as it were, the position for some possible designating sign, was a criterion for the real incompleteness of the function (e.g. 'What is a Function?', p. 115). On the other hand he talks sometimes as if it were because the function itself had the nature it did that a correct logical notation for the function would have some corresponding property (e.g. 'Function and Concept'). Because functions are incomplete, functional expressions must themselves be incomplete expressions; because objects are complete, proper names must be complete expressions. On the other hand sentences contain no empty places, and are complete forms of expressions; therefore they must be taken as signifying objects, namely their truth-values.

It is explained in the *Grundgesetze* why functional expressions must have this characteristic empty position. If we wrote the expressions for functions simply in the form '*f*' or 'sin', for example, we could not express generality; we could not make the transition from general to particular within our symbolism. This also explains why we must use some letter which does not only indicate the position for argument-signs, but also indicates indefinitely the arguments themselves. Frege however insists that if we wish only to talk about a particular function, we should be careful to use not the '*x*' of the generality notation, the letter usually called the variable letter, but rather the 'ξ' that simply indicates the argument positions. Now this point can be put in another way. One use of the functional notation as thus developed is that it shows where we are to place the particular signs which are names of objects taken as arguments. It also shows that it is names that are to be placed in the functional sign and not, for instance, further functional signs. Frege puts it in another way; the fact that in a correct notation functional signs '*f*' carry with them an empty pair of brackets, e.g.

'$f(\ )$', shows their need of supplementation. It is clear from all of this how closely related is the problem of the incompleteness of functions and concepts to the problem of their general applicability to objects.

If we remember how functions can be generated, we shall acquire another insight into the nature of their incompleteness. We can derive the expression for a function, Frege says, by splitting up the complex expression for an object into a saturated and an unsaturated part ('Function and Concept', pp. 24–5). We imagine the original complex name as split up into one part taken as invariant, one part treated as variable. The two descriptions are parallel. We can then regard the whole expression as made up of an argument sign and a function sign. Now if we ignore the particular nature of the argument, and replace the argument sign by an argument-indicating letter 'ξ', we shall have derived a functional sign; if we omit the letter and for example replace it by a pair of empty brackets each time it occurs, we shall have derived what is genuinely the sign that signifies the function in question. The whole expression can then be seen as if composed of two distinct parts. The signs that make up each part will be of distinct types, either a proper name as against a predicative expression, or an argument-indicating letter and a predicative expression. The functional sign is therefore incomplete insofar as it is just part of a complete expression.

This explanation is not sufficient, since the proper name or numeral, for instance, that is the remainder of the complete expression is none the less itself a complete sign. The difference comes out when we consider how we are to say which object or which function it is that is being taken as part of the complete expression. In the case of an object, e.g. a number, we can use an expression of the form 'The number 2' or 'The emperor Caesar' as equivalent to '2' and 'Caesar'. But to describe a function we must use an expression of the form 'The function $2.\xi^2+3.\xi$', or 'The function $2.(\ )^2+3.(\ )$'. And here it is essential that the whole expression should contain some empty positions, i.e. positions obviously designed still to be filled by genuine names. It is at this point that we come back indirectly to the problem of the concept *Horse*. For in line with this necessity of expression, it can be seen that a fuller and better way of referring to the concept *Horse* is by means of the expression 'the concept *x is a horse*', or 'the concept ( ) *is a horse*'. Since concepts are functions, the expressions that signify concepts should also contain the empty position or argument-indicating letter that shows where definite names are to be placed; in this case the subject position.

We can apply in a more general way some of what has been said about the incompleteness of concepts in section (i) above. We can form expressions such as 'The function ξ^2', which by Frege's criteria signify objects rather than functions. This is the first paradox; but another appears at once. For what can it mean to give the sign 'ξ^2' as the name of a particular function? This sign is essentially incomplete in that it contains a non-signifying part, a non-designating part; it cannot actually stand for anything. It follows that the expression 'The function ξ^2' must fail of signification in just that respect in which, for example, the expression 'The emperor Caesar' succeeds, namely that the apparent name does not succeed in specifying which instance of the general term is in question. In this respect 'The function ξ^2' is analogous to expressions like 'The King of ξ' and 'ξ is a horse'. Therefore it is not good enough to try to escape from the first paradox by stipulating that we are to speak of concepts and functions in the formal mode. Even so we shall not be able to say that 'ξ^2' and 'ξ is a horse' are the signs for functions; for the function is not the expression itself nor what the expression stands for. It is rather what is expressed by or indicated in the form of the expression.

(iii)

We can now give tentative answers to at least three of the questions asked in section (i). (i) The paradox of the concept *Horse* is at least in part merely a special case of a general paradox about functional expressions. The form of the paradox is that the construction of similar phrases seems to lead to self-contradiction. We can roughly ascribe the source of this self-contradiction to the fact that such constructions demand that functions should be given proper names; and this is the demand that they should be treated as objects. (ii) The general paradox about functional expressions is perfectly genuine. But perhaps the special case of conceptual expressions escapes at least part of the paradoxical situation. For surely we can refer to concepts by means of corresponding abstract nouns, e.g. 'equinity' and 'fourness'. (iii) The paradox arises because language gives different forms to terms representing the subject of a sentence and terms carrying the content of what is said about the subject. Where this is the case, there is a linguistic predicament in trying to say things about what can itself be said of objects.

We must now return to the special case of concepts and consider another aspect of their form of incompleteness that has so far been ignored. 'The predicative nature of the concept is just a special case of the need for supplementation, the unsaturatedness, that I gave as the essential feature of a function' ('On Concept and Object', p. 47, note 2). One thing Frege means can be seen quickly from consideration of the full expression for a concept, e.g. 'ξ is a horse'. Here the fact that the expression contains an indicating letter shows that the thing signified, namely the concept *Horse*, is incomplete; and the fact that the letter stands in the place normally filled by the subject terms of corresponding sentences shows what Frege calls the particular kind of supplement required. It shows that the supplement required is of a possible subject-term. And this is to say that it may itself be regarded as a predicative expression. The concept is predicative, as we have seen; it is the reference of a grammatical predicate.

Predicative expressions, i.e. those expressions which are left when the name of the subject has been removed from a complete sentence, have two peculiarities. They need complementing; and they do not designate on their own. Both peculiarities are shown by the fact that predicative expressions when written in the explicit form contain indicating letters or obviously empty positions. They have a third peculiarity too, that Frege brings out indirectly. 'The behaviour of the concept is essentially predicative, even where something is being asserted of it' ('On Concept and Object', p. 50). Instead of saying, for example, that the concept *Horse* is realised, we can say something like 'The words "is a horse" can be truly predicated of something'. Two things are significant about this. The expression 'is a horse' is still clearly predicative; and we have had to speak of the expression or mention it, rather than use it. We cannot say 'Is a horse is truly predicable of something', unless the 'is a horse' is understood somehow to be the expression mentioned above, i.e. unless for instance it is italicised; and such devices are simply equivalent to the device of using inverted commas to refer to expressions. Now I said earlier that perhaps we may say 'Equinity is truly predicable of something'. But we have to consider that in the first place equinity is specifically said in this to be predicable; in the second that a full logical analysis of this sentence would still have to put the content of the word 'equinity' into predicative position.

It is clear that Frege's claim that essentially predicable terms are sharply distinct from others is partly reducible to his claim that the method of analysing singular propositions into the form of an object's falling under a concept is both logically perspicuous and universally valid. It is for this reason that the fourth of our questions is irrelevant although fascinating. The fact that English and German contain expressions which cannot be used as they stand as the subjects of sentences, but can be so used if inclosed in inverted commas and understood as mentioned, does not of itself prove Frege's real point. Equally the possible existence of a language containing no such expressions would not of itself disprove it.

Considering functions as the residues of complete name expressions after subject terms had been removed cast a certain light on the nature of their incompleteness. We may expect that a special application of this method would work for concepts also. At the end of 'On Concept and Object' Frege says that the problem is reducible to this: 'Not all the parts of a thought can be complete; at least one must be "unsaturated" or predicative, otherwise they would not hold together' (p. 54). If the complete thought is that 2 is a prime number, Frege's meaning is that the sense of the sign '2' and the sense of the expression 'the concept Prime number' do not 'hold together' by themselves. For what we have here is simply two objects, and as Frege says objects cannot logically adhere to one another without some kind of liaison. Since the expression for a complete thought is a complete sentence, we may say that no complete sentence can consist just of a set of proper names, even where one of the names is the name of a concept. 'Aristotle wisdom' is meaningless as it stands, and so though less plainly is 'Aristotle Greek'. And the liaison cannot itself be merely another object, so that the expression for it cannot be another proper name. Frege says in 'On Concept and Object' that essentially it comes to the relation Falls under. But still we cannot say that the proposition that the number 2 is prime is expressed by the conjunction of the three expressions 'the number 2', 'the concept Prime number' and 'the relation Falls under' or 'the relation of an object to the concept it falls under'. For now this too lacks the incompleteness which allows the relation Falls under to hold together an object and a concept. If we like to regard the distinction between concepts and objects as simply a way of bringing out the distinction of logical places in this relation, we may; for the relation is asymmetrical in Russell's terminology. But we must not think that this disposes of the problem; for now the incompleteness is present in the expression 'falls under'.

This refers back to the view that all complete singular propositions can be expressed in the form 'Object A falls under the concept F'.

What is new is the insistence that there is something peculiar to grammatically complete sentences, which is not possessed either by names or general words or any less complete expressions. Concepts will simply be incomplete on this account because they are not complete in the way peculiar to sentences or rather propositions. And what remains to be discovered is why proper names and objects are not incomplete in the same way; for proper names are not complete sentences, though as we shall see Frege thought complete sentences were analogous to proper names. The answer can be given in a rough form; conceptual expressions, i.e. predicative expressions, are 'failed sentences', and therefore incomplete *as* sentences; they are incomplete sentences. But proper names do not try to achieve sentencehood, and are not therefore 'incomplete sentences'; rather, they have already a quite definite and distinct function from that possessed by sentences. i.e. to name particular objects. This must be given a clearer sense. A proper name stands for the object it names whether it occurs as part of a sentence or on its own. But this does not hold for conceptual expressions, just as it does not hold for functional signs. (This will be discussed in Chapters 6 and 7 below). On the other hand, if we start with a complete sentence or complete arithmetical expression, we can analyse it in such a way that part of the sentence or expression can be called the proper name of some object. There will then be a remaining part of the original expression, which is regarded as the sign for the functional or conceptual part. A functional sign or predicative expression may be said to stand for a function or concept when it occurs as an element in a complete sentence or expression. In the complete sentence 'Caesar is dead' the expression 'is dead' stands for the part of the complete reference of the sentence which Frege calls the 'concept'. It is important to notice that this concept is only discovered as the common part of several propositions, just as the function$( )^2$ only has meaning as what is represented by the common part of the expressions '2^2' and '3^2'. 'Is dead' stands for the concept which is the common part of the propositions 'Caesar is dead' and 'Brutus is dead'. It is in this extra dependence on previous sentence forms that concepts differ from objects.

(iv)

It is already clear that an understanding of Frege's views on meaning is involved at many points in understanding the problem of incompleteness. It is for this reason that discussion of this topic acts as a bridge between the general theory of the concept as function and the subjects to be discussed in Chapters 6 to 10 below, notably the application of Frege's theory of meaning to the case of sentences and propositions, or thoughts. But there are three further points that may here be made in connection with the topic of incompleteness; though distantly related, they are nevertheless related and therefore partially illuminating.

The first concerns the metaphor of part and whole which Frege applied both to expressions and to what expressions signify. He abandoned this metaphor soon after publishing the second volume of the *Grundgesetze*. The reason he gave was that the argument of a function could not be taken as *part* of the value of the function in any sense at all; Denmark is not *part* of Copenhagen, though it is that argument of the function *The capital of* which yields the value Copenhagen. This is one case of a wider mistake he had made himself. He had assumed that the reference of a part of an expression was itself part of the reference of the whole expression. But although the name 'Copenhagen' is part of the sentence 'Copenhagen is the capital of Denmark', it does not follow that Copenhagen itself is part of the reference of this sentence, namely in Frege's theory the truth-value The True. It will also now follow that concepts, which are in his theory the references of predicative expressions, are not part of truth-values either. Frege concluded from this that the metaphor of unsaturatedness had better go. What should remain in its place was the notion of the '*Unselbst-staendigkeit*' of functions and concepts, the fact that no function or concept can stand on its own. And this is simply the contrary of the defining characteristic of objects, their '*Selbststaendigkeit*' or ability to stand on their own.

The second concerns the presumptive opposite of incompleteness, namely completeness. Frege remarks in the *Grundlagen* that completeness often goes with one-ness. What he means is that to call something a complete such-and-such is often no more than to call it one such-and-such, or *a* such-and-such. The point of this is that we have to know what sort of entity the incomplete thing is incomplete as; it must be an incomplete pack of cards, for example. It was for just this reason that in discussing the incompleteness of concepts we had to treat them as incomplete thoughts; and in general functional expressions are incomplete regarded as expressions for objects. The expression '$()^2$' is incomplete if regarded as the expression for the number 9 taken as a value for the argument 3, or the number 16 taken as a value for the argument 4.

The third concerns a pair of Frege's doctrines of meaning. The first is the principle that in order for a functional expression to be usable in logic, some definite value must be stipulated for every possible argument; for a concept to be usable in science, it must be stipulated for every possible argument, i.e. every object, whether the value of the complete expression is truth or falsity. Frege says at one point that unless this condition is satisfied the so-called concept is not really a concept at all, but merely a 'fluid conceptual construction' (*Grundgesetze*, ii, 58; and see also *Grundlagen*, pp. 59–60). This shows that even the incompleteness of a concept must lie within sharply defined boundaries. The fact that every concept must be incomplete does not entail that concepts cannot be objective in the sense discussed above. The second doctrine is that which Frege takes as the second of his guiding principles in the *Grundlagen*, namely that we should not ask for the meaning of words on their own, but only in propositional contexts, i.e. as possible parts of complete sentences. 'It is enough if the proposition (*Satz*) as a whole has a sense; it is through this that its parts also acquire their content.' The importance of this emerges when we consider concepts as incomplete thoughts. I shall say more about these points in Chapters 8 and 9 below in discussing Frege's theory of sense and reference.

Frege himself took incompleteness to be indefinable; he said that it was a 'primitive feature of logical structure' ('Foundations of Geometry', p. 12). It is clear from this that he did not believe the problem or set of related problems discussed above to arise merely from particular forms of language, such as the distinction between nouns and verbs or adjectives, or from the interaction of syntactical position and grammatical form. The distinction between subject and predicate to which he is implicitly pointing is logical. Roughly speaking, it is the distinction between referring to and predicating of, or between mentioning something and saying something about it; these distinctions should be regarded as logical rather than grammatical.

We can now give a second form to the answers put forward in section (iii) to my original four questions. The problem of the concept *Horse* is paradoxical (a) as a special case of the general problem of functional signs; this paradox only arises if, with Frege, we interpret concepts as a kind of function. It is paradoxical also (b) as a case of the problem of predicative expressions; and here it only arises if we interpret concepts as the references of predicative expressions. This is the problem how predicates can be referred to; how what is suitable to be said about things can itself be specified as a subject for predication. And because reference and predication are not grammatical features but logical features, this problem is not peculiar to languages of a restricted class, namely languages which distinguish in grammatical form referring expressions and predicative expressions. It arises for all languages in which reference and predication are possible; Frege would probably have said that they were essential features of any language in which definite thoughts were expressible and through which definite knowledge could be achieved and communicated.

This shows too why a Russellian analysis of definite descriptions would not be enough to solve the problem. It would indeed dissolve one of Frege's own problems, namely why the expression 'The concept *Horse*' cannot refer to a concept but only to an object. But this problem is I think dealt with quite well by Frege's own method of analysing contexts in which such expressions occur. And in a way the methods are similar, since Frege's analysis may be understood to show that the object named by 'The concept *Horse*' is in a way only an apparent object; this is not to say that it is not perfectly genuine, for Frege says explicitly that it is ('On Concept and Object', p. 45), but to say that it is superfluous to logical analysis. We can if we like analyse the sentence 'Pegasus falls under the concept *Horse*' as relational; we can regard it as stating that two objects fall under a certain relation, namely the relation *Falls under*. But since *Falls under* is a relation, i.e. function of two arguments, and The concept *Horse* is an object, then 'Falls under the concept *Horse*' can be taken as standing for a function of one argument, i.e. an ordinary concept. We can then rewrite the original sentence 'Pegasus falls under the concept *Horse*' in the form 'Pegasus falls under the concept *Falls under the concept Horse*'. This redundancy explains the point made in section (iii) above; and it shows the uselessness of analysing the expression 'falls under the concept *Horse*' into a part standing for an object and a part standing for a relation. Any expression that signifies a concept, i.e. 'is a horse', can be rewritten in a form such that part of the new expression signifies an object, but need not be; and as I have argued, any expression which apparently signifies an object of this type without being accompanied by the typical expression for the relation which completes it into a concept expression can in fact be rewritten in such a form. Once we see this, we see that there is nothing mysterious in the fact that part of the expression signifying a concept can signify an object. What is mysterious is rather the nature of the relation *Falls under*; but in a way this too is an unnecessary puzzle, in Frege's analysis. For it dissolves into the question as to the nature of concepts or functions, the question how they can be incomplete or predicative entities.

SOURCES FOR CHAPTER FIVE

'On Concept and Object'; 'Function and Concept'; 'What is a Function?'; *Grundgesetze*, i, 1–4.

CHAPTER SIX

SENSE AND REFERENCE

I have referred several times in the last chapters to the notions of meaning or signification, and it is now time to go into Frege's precise theories. Frege distinguishes two elements of meaning, or two different kinds of meaning, which he calls an expression's *Sinn* and its *Bedeutung*. Now both of these terms are common and colloquial in German, and their meaning corresponds closely to the equally common English words *sense* and *significance* or *meaning*. However it is at first sight no use to translate *Bedeutung* in this way, and therefore it is customary to use terms such as *reference, denotation* or *nominatum* instead. I shall use the term *reference*, since it is the least technical of these alternative terms, but in section (vi) of this chapter I give reasons why I think *significance* may, after all, be the simplest and best translation.

The distinction between sense and reference is introduced, in part, as a later refinement upon Frege's early theory of the *content* of expressions and mental acts. For it is clear that this term confused two distinct things. On the one hand the *content* of a sign is described as that object which it signifies, represents or stands for; on the other, the *content* of an act of judgement is a thought or proposition, and Frege is clear that whatever thoughts may be they are not *objects* of thought. We may perhaps compare the sense-reference distinction to the distinction between the content and object of a mental act, e.g. the act of making a judgement; but the value of such a comparison is of course limited. Now quite early on Frege had distinguished between the actual content of a sign and the particular way in which the sign determined or introduced this content. In the *Begriffsschrift* he uses this as the solution to the problem of statements of identity. These are meaningful, because the mere difference between the two equated signs together with the fact that they signify the same object informs us of something. 'We have different designations for the same (entity), and these names ... indicate the mode of presentation; and hence the statement contains actual knowledge' ('On Sense and Reference', p. 57).

The relation between an object and its properties may be seen as another early form of, or another theory which helped to produce, the distinction between sense and reference (*Grundlagen*, sections 21–32). There is a real distinction between an object and its properties. Properties are signified by predicative expressions, whereas objects are signified by proper names. The object can be apprehended either directly by reason, if it is of the appropriate type, e.g. a number, or indirectly through apprehension of its properties; this latter being dependent on sensation and perception. From this there follows also a rough correspondence between the distinction of an object from its properties and the objective-subjective distinction. Frege certainly called *subjective* whatever depended upon conditions of sensation or perception, including in his view such properties as are sensible. But we must make a further distinction in order not to be misled. Frege remarks that 'when we call snow white, we mean to refer to an objective quality which we recognise . . . by a certain sensation'; we do not mean to refer to this subjective sensation which gives us the means of recognising the presence of an objective quality of whiteness. Although the quality of whiteness is partly dependent upon our particular forms of sensation and perception, this does not prevent statements about the whiteness of objects from being objectively true or false. The objectivity of the quality of whiteness consists in the objective truth or falsity of statements attributing whiteness to particular objects; its subjectivity consists in the existence of a relation between the actual sensation of whiteness, i.e. the nature of the quality as a phenomenon, and our forms of sensation. To the distinction between an object and its properties there also corresponds roughly the further distinction between an object and its guise, the way it is presented (e.g. *Begriffsschrift*, p. 11; *Grundlagen*, pp. 77–8; 'On Sense and Reference', pp. 56–7). If we are, for instance, talking about perception, then we may try to identify the perceived property of an object with the way it is presented perceptually. Objects can be presented in other ways than through perception; in particular, they can be presented or introduced in language, through understanding of the signs of that language.

This theory is related to the third primitive root of Frege's sense-reference theory, namely his belief that nothing prevents one and the same object from being signified by several different signs. Although the use of different signs is sometimes arbitrary and therefore superfluous, it is sometimes the case that the difference between the signs goes with a difference between the ways each sign presents the object in question, the *Darstellungsweise*. The expressions 'the teacher of Alexander the Great' and 'the Stagirite philosopher' both signify

Aristotle, but they signify him in different ways. And it is clear that in such a case the difference in the way of presentation which makes these signs genuinely distinct as signs goes with the allusion to different properties possessed by the object they signify. It is important at this point not to confuse the way an object is presented in language with any of its properties. For supposing the object A is the one and only thing which is F, then we can present it either under the name 'A' or under the description 'the F'. And it is clear that neither being called 'A' nor being described as 'the F' are genuine properties of A, since as expressions each is quite arbitrary.

I have tentatively argued that three fairly primitive and intuitive notions underlie the distinction between an expression's sense and reference. First, there is the distinction between the mental, and often subjective, content of a mental act and its non-mental and often objective, object. Second, there is the distinction between the partly subjective properties of an object and the presumably objective object itself. Third, there is the distinction between the way a sign signifies an object and the actual object it signifies. This raises the question whether the distinction between sense and reference is only grounded in traditional notions for the case of proper names, and whether it is not so supported for the case of predicative expressions and concepts. This will be discussed in section (iv) below. The general question perhaps raised in a similar way, namely whether an expression's *sense* can be objective or not, will occupy Chapter 7; in particular, section (iii) will be devoted to a comparison of the notions of sense and property.

(ii)

'It is natural now to think of there being connected with a sign . . . besides that to which the sign refers, which may be called the reference of the sign, also what I should like to call the *sense* of the sign, wherein the mode of presentation is contained' ('On Sense and Reference', p. 57). 'By means of a sign we express its sense, and designate its reference' ('On Sense and Reference', p. 61). This simple principle must be extended and qualified. In the first place the reference of the sign strictly belongs not to the sign but to its sense. There are two passages which support this qualification of the principle. The most explicit occurs in 'The Thought', where Frege says that to say a sentence is true is strictly speaking to say that its sense is true; for as we shall see, he regarded the truth of a true sentence as its reference. It is not the expression, the sentence, itself but rather the thought or proposition it expresses that can be called true or false. The less explicit occurs in 'On Sense and Reference', where Frege says that 'to the sign there corresponds a definite sense and to that in turn a definite reference' (p. 58), ending the same paragraph with the words 'In grasping a sense, one is not certainly assured of a reference'. The point seems to be similar; that it is not the expression itself which has the reference, but rather that which it expresses, namely its sense. This qualification is necessary in order to prevent our thinking that, for example, the word 'Aristotle' is just as it stands a name of Aristotle, and to show that its being a name of Aristotle depends upon our intending it to be such (*Grundgesetze*, ii, 99). It is not until an expression is incorporated into a language that it can be said to signify anything at all; before that it is simply an object like other objects.

The second qualification to the principle supports this first qualification. In the same passage of 'On Sense and Reference' Frege points out that although a given sign has unique reference, at least in an ideal language which is free from ambiguity and so forth, the converse does not hold. One and the same object can be presented by quite different signs, i.e. can be the reference of different signs. Aristotle is the reference of 'Aristotle' and of 'the teacher of Alexander the Great'. Further, the same sense can be expressed by different signs; Frege himself uses this for the case of sentences, but the application to particular words is not so clear. Frege seems therefore to say both that signs refer and have sense, as it were, through the mode of their reference, and that their senses refer, i.e. that they have reference only through their sense. Is there a contradiction in this? I think if we remember his careful distinction between sign as object and sign as sign, we see that there is not. For he glosses his expression 'as sign' by the words 'in the way it signifies something'; two signs are distinguished *as signs* by the difference in the ways they signify. And this is to say that they are distinguished *as signs* by their difference of *senses*. Therefore his apparently conflicting ideas can be reconciled as follows. To say that signs have reference only through their senses is to say that signs *as objects* have reference only through their senses, i.e. only through being incorporated into some language. To say that signs have sense only in their mode of reference is to say that signs *as signs* are essentially entities that are understood and intended to refer to objects, and that it is only insofar as they signify these objects that they have a definite place in language. I think this shows that the connection between sign, sense and reference, which might easily appear contingent or quite mysterious, is in fact neither. For an object to become a sign is to acquire a sense, and to be given a reference is the same as both.

Primarily it is proper names and signs that represent proper names ('On Sense and Reference', p. 57), i.e. definite descriptions, that have both senses and references. It appears from the two formulae quoted at the head of this section that to have a reference is much the same as to *name* an object. I shall show later how Frege appears to assimilate all referring to the case of naming. In the case of genuine proper names Frege takes their senses to be definite descriptions. For example, the sense of 'Aristotle' might be the description: the pupil of Plato and teacher of Alexander the Great. In the case of definitely descriptive expressions the matter is not so clear, unless we are to say that the sense of the expression 'the pupil of Plato' is the description: the pupil of Plato, as above. Now in 'On Sense and Reference' the distinction between sense and reference is introduced as if necessitated by the correct analysis of statements of identity; and the particular type of statement of identity that Frege is dealing with is the type in which one or two definite descriptions are applied to the same object, e.g. 'Scott is the author of Waverley' or 'The morning star is the evening star'. For the time being I shall say that the sense of a definitely descriptive expression is the mode in which it presents a certain object to us, i.e. the guise under which the object appears in language. The reference of 'the author of Waverley' is the writer Scott himself; its sense is the mode in which this expression presents Scott to our understanding, i.e. as the author of Waverley.

It is clear, in any case, that we shall find it difficult to isolate in every case some entity that is *the sense* of a particular expression; for really there are only two distinct entities in question, namely the expression, which is itself an object, and the object it signifies. And since the *sense* of the expression is simply the mode in which it signifies the object, it is obviously difficult to prise this apart from the object or some of its properties, on the one hand, and on the other hand from the expression and its properties, i.e. its *Gestalt* ('On Sense and Reference', p. 57). The reason for this peculiar indistinctness is partly given earlier in this section.

Now we have apparently to extend the terms of the formulae I quoted, since Frege speaks as if it is not only proper names that signify objects, but also predicative expressions and sentences that have reference, and therefore presumably also sense. He calls concepts the references of grammatical predicates ('On Concept and Object', p. 43, note 1). This is of course a crucial point, and there are two principal difficulties concerned. First, we must distinguish reference to an entity from naming it, contrary to the tendency of the remarks quoted at the head of the passage, since it is a cardinal principle of the concept-object distinction that the expressions which signify objects name them, i.e. can be called *names*, and the expressions which signify concepts cannot except in an analogous sense. Then we may perhaps allow that concept-words refer to concepts without, strictly speaking, naming them. But here the second difficulty appears. For reference is, it seems, essentially correlative to the possession of sense; a sign cannot refer without referring in a particular way. So concept-words should possess a sense as well as their reference to some particular concept. They should refer to their respective concepts in particular ways, or present them in various specific modes. And once more we seem to be in danger of confusing concepts with objects. I shall examine the peculiar difficulties over concepts in section (iv) below. But it should be remembered in any case that some distinction is already made in the fact that concepts are incomplete entities, unlike objects.

We should expect Frege, in line with his general policy, to extend any principle concerning signs to the case of complete sentences, and indeed he does so. The reference of a sentence is identified with its truth-value, namely the fact that it is true, if it is true, or the fact that it is false, if it is false. The sense of a sentence is identified with the thought it expresses. I shall examine these identifications in Chapter 9. This shows clearly the connection between the early doctrine of signs and their contents and the later sense-reference theory. 'In the reference of the sentence all that is specific is obliterated . . . judgements are distinctions of parts within truth-values . . . to every sense belonging to a truth-value there would correspond its own manner of analysis' ('On Sense and Reference', p. 65). Since each truth-value is an object, it can be signified by many different expressions, i.e. sentences. Further, a 'comprehensive knowledge of the reference would require us to be able to say immediately whether any given sense belongs to it' (ibid., p. 58). The particular thing to be clear about is that Frege definitely fails to identify the reference of a sentence with the fact it states.

(iii)

Before discussing the extension of the sense-reference theory to concept-words, i.e. predicative expressions, and concepts, I shall ask some more general questions about the doctrine itself. First, how is the theory for particular expressions connected with the extended theory for sentences? Frege began by totally accepting a view he later partially rejected. This was the principle that the sense of a complex expression was composed of the senses of its constituent expressions, and that the reference of the complex was composed of the references of the constituents. At first he took this principle to cover the case of complex names, such as definite descriptions; later he used it rather to apply to the relation between the senses and references of the separable expressions in a sentence and of the sentence itself. On this view part of the reference of 'Caesar is dead' would be the reference of 'Caesar', i.e. the dead emperor himself, and another part would be the reference of 'is dead', namely the concept *Death*. Part of the sense of this sentence would be the sense of 'Caesar', for instance: the first emperor of Rome. But for two reasons Frege came to modify this comprehensive theory. First, he saw that it is often false to say that the reference of part of an expression is part of the reference of the complete expression. Although 'Denmark' is part of 'the capital of Denmark', it does not follow that Denmark is part of Copenhagen. The second reason is that he came to think that the reference of an expression as a whole did not suffice to determine the reference of a part of it, given the reference of the remained. This is obviously so for sentences. Given the reference of the sentence 'Caesar is dead', namely the Truth, and the reference of 'Caesar', we cannot deduce the reference of the remainder, namely the concept *Death*. We cannot tell from the fact that a sentence is about Caesar and that it is true what it predicates of Caesar. The converse also holds. Given the truth-value of a sentence and given the concept it predicates, we cannot deduce what subject it is predicated of. Concepts hold of many different objects.

Second, there is the question of the relative independence of an expression's sense from its reference. This comes out most clearly in the case of sentences. Frege is careful to point out that we must separate the question of what thought a sentence expresses, and the question whether this is true or false. Apprehension of a thought is quite distinct from and logically prior to recognition that it is true or false, as the case may be. The same holds for definitely descriptive expressions. It is often possible to grasp the sense of such expressions without knowing what their reference is, or even whether they have any reference. To have a sense is therefore not sufficient for having a reference ('On

Sense and Reference', p. 58). We may think that the principle works in a different way for genuine proper names. Normally it is only the reference that matters in such cases; the particular sense one or another person attaches to the name does not make any difference to its use.

The relative independence of sense and reference comes out in another way too. Besides the principle that the sense and reference of a complete expression are composed of the senses and references of its components, Frege held at one time a second converse principle. The reference of a component part of an expression cannot be relevant to the sense of the whole, nor its sense to the reference of the whole. Replacement of one component part by another with the same reference but a different sense cannot affect the reference of the complete expression, but must affect its sense. Replacement of a component by another with the same sense but a different reference would not alter the sense of the whole, but would alter its reference ('On Sense and Reference', p. 62).

Third, there is the question of the possibility of different signs expressing the same sense. If we accept Frege's identification of the sense of a sentence with the thought it expresses, this possibility appears to be made out for the case of sentences, since we can obviously have different sentences which express the same thought. It is not so clearly made out for names and expressions which are not sentences. It is tempting to consider expressions like 'the King of France', which fits several different persons but never more than one at any given time, as expressions which have several different references but one and the same sense each time. But this is superficial. Frege would say that such an expression is incomplete unless the time of reference is explicitly mentioned in the expression (*Grundlagen*, p. 59). 'The King of France in the year . . .' is the full form of this expression. And when we complete the expression by adding the number of the year, it is plain that we do not even have a set of similar descriptions any longer. Another possibility is indicated by descriptions of the form 'the capital of *x*'. Here we might say that although two such descriptions stood respectively for Paris and Berlin, still the sense of each description was the same, on the grounds that the expressions 'the capital of Germany' and 'the capital of France' signify these cities in a similar way; the mode of presentation is the same in each case.

Fourth, there is the obvious question whether genuine proper names like 'Aristotle' really have any sense at all. We are naturally inclined, with Mill and Russell, to deny that they do; to say with Mill that they 'do not indicate or imply any attributes as belonging to those individuals', i.e. the individuals they denote (*System of Logic*, Book 1, ch. 2, section 5). Frege clearly believes and explicitly states that they do have sense. Knowing the reference of a genuine proper name like 'Aristotle' is simply knowing what object the word refers to. Now Frege defines the sense of a name as the contribution, *Beitrag*, made by that name to the thought expressed by the sentences of which it is a part (*Grundgesetze*, i, 32). Therefore the sense of 'Aristotle' is what this name contributes to the sense of a sentence containing this name, in particular what it contributes to thoughts about Aristotle. And it seems that the contribution which the name 'Aristotle' makes to such a thought is to identify the subject of the thought, i.e. that object about which the thought is. It seems then that knowing what the sense of the name 'Aristotle' means is more or less the same as knowing what its reference is. The same account would hold for definite descriptions, with an important difference. We want to say that knowing that 'Aristotle' is the name of the particular person who bears this name is not knowing anything informative, factual, predicable of that person. It tells us nothing about that person, and therefore we want, with Mill, to hold that the name 'Aristotle' has no sense. On the other hand knowing that the object of reference of 'the pupil of Plato and teacher of Alexander the Great' is Aristotle really does involve possessing some factual knowledge about Aristotle. So we want to hold that definite descriptions do have sense, here too agreeing with Mill. Now Frege would, I think, agree with this analysis of the two cases in terms of our knowledge. But he does not take this to mark the distinction between terms having sense and terms lacking it. For he begins with the occurrence of terms in complete sentences which make complete sense, not with the occurrence of terms on their own as isolated names, where the analysis might be thought to entail the common belief about names indicated. In analysing the 'meaning' of proper names we must begin from the fact that proper names are used typically in the context of complete sentences about the individual they name, and work from there; in this respect proper names are on a par with general words. Then we can see that proper names make a contribution to the complete sense of any sentences they occur in, just as much as definite descriptions do, though a contribution of a somewhat different kind. In Frege's terms, denial that genuine proper names have sense would amount to denial that 'Aristotle is dead' and 'Plato is dead' have different senses.

And he clearly believes that they do have different senses, i.e. express different thoughts.

Russell's theory is somewhere between Mill's and Frege's. He agrees with Mill that strictly speaking proper names do not assign a property to an object 'but merely and solely name it' (*Mysticism and Logic*, ch. X). But he agrees with Frege that most proper names are 'usually really descriptions. That is to say, the thought in the mind of a person using a proper name can generally only be expressed explicitly if we replace the proper name by a description' and concludes that 'I' and 'this' are the only genuine proper names. On Frege's account of 'I' in 'The Thought' (p. 297), even 'I' would not have been a genuine proper name. In saying that proper names have sense, Frege is not attacking Mill's and Russell's view that proper names neither assign properties to nor imply the possession of any given properties by their bearers. He is rather attacking their view that proper names could have an intelligible use in language even though their use as *names* was quite unconnected with the user's possessing any factual knowledge. He is, perhaps, attacking their implicit view that the utility of proper names does not even presuppose the possession of any properties by their bearers or any such factual knowledge in their users.

(iv)

How does the theory of sense and reference fit the case of predicative expressions and concepts? I do not intend what I say to solve the problem but rather to expose it. There seem to be four related questions to ask here. (i) Are concepts really to be accepted as the references of grammatically predicative expressions, as Frege explicitly says? (ii) If so, what are the senses of predicative expressions? (iii) Is it possible to interpret concepts as the senses of predicative expressions, contrary to Frege's words, on the grounds that only senses can be components of senses, that thoughts are senses, and that concepts appear at first sight to be components of thoughts? (iv) If so, what should we take as the references of predicative expressions, i.e. should we take as their references the properties corresponding to the concepts?

It will be useful to begin by considering the general version of the theory of function and argument in this context. Frege's most detailed application to functions of the sense–reference theory occurs in the opening sections of the first volume of the *Grundgesetze*, especially sections 26–32. He first states his definition of a name as any sign which

7

refers to, *bedeutet*, an object rather than merely indicating it, *andeutet*. This is the distinction drawn as early as the *Begriffsschrift* between names which explicitly name particular objects and letters which merely indicate objects indefinitely and functional signs which indicate their values indefinitely. He then extends the term 'name' to functions. What has so far been called a functional sign or expression is now called a 'function-name'. The name of a function of the first level may be said to have a reference, or to refer to something, or to be *referential*, *Bedeutungsvoll* (strictly, 'meaningful'), if the proper name formed by inserting some already referring proper name in the argument position always has a reference. Conversely a simple name has a reference if every proper name formed by inserting the simple name into the argument position of some function-name has a definite reference. The method of constructing function-names illuminates Frege's view. Normally we construct a function-name by removing some proper name from an expression which is already itself a complex name. If both the complex name and the simple name removed are referential expressions, then the constructed function-name will itself be referential subject to the conditions of completeness of definition.

It is clear from this that if we turn to the special case of predicative expressions, we cannot avoid concluding that concepts must be construed as the references of predicative expressions. For a concept-name, as we might call it, will be constructed by removing a proper name from a complete sentence, granted the applicability of Frege's sense-reference theory to sentences. And if the sentence has reference, i.e. a definite truth-value, and if every other sentence constructed by substituting a different proper name in place of the removed name has some definite truth-value, then the concept-name will be a meaningful, *bedeutungsvoll*, term, i.e. will refer to a definite concept.

It now becomes apparent that for this approach to work we must already assume the applicability of the sense-reference theory to sentences. For if sentences do not have reference as a whole, then they will not be analogous to complex names, and will not necessarily contain components which themselves refer. Therefore the crux of this problem is whether Frege is justified in taking sentences and indeed mathematical equations as functions of a certain type and applying the terminology of function, argument and value to them. Only if this procedure is justified can complete sentences be construed as completed functional expressions standing for values corresponding to the arguments whose names have been used to complete them.

If we allow this analogy for the time being, and construe concepts as the references of grammatically predicative expressions, then we must look for corresponding senses of such expressions. The reference of a complete sentence, i.e. its truth-value, must according to Frege's principle be composed of the references of its components. We can now take these to be respectively an object and a concept, in the case of singular propositions. The object Caesar and the concept *Death* together make up the truth-value of the sentence 'Caesar is dead', namely the Truth. Now the method of composition of object and concept is neither arbitrary nor merely aggregative. As Frege says, there is an essential difference between the composition of a set of objects and the composition of the parts of a thought; and this difference applies also to the case in hand. Caesar and the concept *Death* are compounded by the peculiar, irreducible, unanalysable logical relation *Falling under*. And it is this compound which together makes up the truth-value the Truth. Here we are very likely to be baffled; how can truth be composed of an object and a concept cemented to one another by a mysterious logical relation? Frege's answer, which will be discussed in Chapter 9, is that since truth is itself an object there is really nothing mysterious about this at all. It is no more mysterious than the fact that Copenhagen is the capital of Denmark, i.e. in his early theory that the city of Copenhagen is composed of the country of Denmark and the concept *Capital city* cemented to one another by some logical relation, or that the number 4 is composed of the number 2 and the concept *Second power* in some logical relation to one another. Moreover Frege's apparently idiosyncratic use of language need not of itself commit him to any odd views. For it is clear that we can rephrase what has been said as follows; it is true that the object Caesar and the concept *Death* are joined by the relation *Falls under*. And this is to say that it is true that Caesar is dead, which is to say no more than that Caesar is dead.

The sense of a complete sentence must in a similar way be composed of the senses of its components. Now the sense of the whole is identified with the thought the sentence expresses. In general Frege defines the sense of an expression as what the expression *expresses* as opposed to what it stands for or refers to. Clearly his identification of the sense of a sentence, i.e. what it expresses, with a thought is much more plausible than his identification of its reference, i.e. what it stands for as a whole, with its truth or falsity. Now in the *Grundgesetze* he clearly takes this identification as basic to the whole problem of the sense of names, since as we saw he defines the sense of a name as part of the thought expressed by a sentence in which it occurs. The sense of sentences is taken as prior and fundamental to defining the sense of names. The sense of a name is identified, as I said in section (iii), with the contribution it makes to the sense of the whole.

Here we come back to the puzzling point I made there, namely that it seems hard to distinguish a name's sense from its reference, if we are right in saying that the contribution a name makes to the thought expressed by a sentence containing the name is to identify the subject of the sentence. In the sentence 'Caesar is dead', it seems that the name 'Caesar' contributes to the thought that Caesar is dead by referring to Caesar. And then how does the sense of this name differ from its reference? One immediate answer is that the reference is the actual dead emperor Caesar, but the sense is not at any rate exactly this; nobody would say that the contribution made to the thought by the name was actually Caesar himself. It is rather, we might put it, the thought that it is Caesar himself who is the subject of thought. The reference of 'Caesar' is Caesar, but its sense is that it refers to Caesar. Now this distinction does not take us very far. And indeed even as it stands it needs expanding, in order to deal with the possibility of different names referring to the same object. We should say, perhaps, that the sense of a name, i.e. its contribution to the sense of a sentence in which it occurs as subject-expression, for example, is to identify the subject of the thought expressed in a particular way, to present that object to our understanding in some specific manner. Both 'Caesar' and 'The first emperor of Rome' present Caesar to our understanding, and I have argued that this is their contribution to the sense of sentences in which they occur; but they present Caesar in different ways, or under different guises. The mode of introduction differs, and therefore the sense differs.

Since the immediate answer does not seem very helpful, another may be tried; this is intended only as a suggestion of a possible line of attack. It is clear that Caesar himself is not part of any thought about Caesar, i.e. the thought that Caesar is dead. Russell would have denied this instantly, but if we reject the epistemology of direct acquaintance which led him to do so, the proposition seems true enough. Now Caesar is identified by Frege with the reference of the name 'Caesar'. I think therefore we may take the sense of this name to be something like that component of a thought about Caesar which in some sense *corresponds* to Caesar himself, but is not identical with him; a thought-counterpart of Caesar. If I am near the truth in this suggestion, then another can be made. The close relation between a sign's sense and its reference may be designed in part to explain how there can be some component of thoughts about Caesar which ensures that all such thoughts are about one and the same person, and that none is about Antony or Pegasus or Napoleon. In analysing the relations and differences between sense and reference we are in part analysing the relation between the components of a thought and the components of the corresponding fact or state of affairs. That such a way of thinking was not foreign to Frege will be shown in Chapter 10 below.

Returning to the definition of sense which Frege gives in the *Grundgesetze* we can say that the sense of a predicative expression is the contribution it makes to the sense of a sentence in which it occurs. The sense of the expression 'is dead' is the contribution made by this expression in a given sentence, e.g. in the sentence 'Caesar is dead', to the thought expressed by that sentence, e.g. the thought that Caesar *is dead*. The particular contribution of these words is to identify what is predicated of Caesar, namely the concept *Death*. We may again find it difficult to distinguish the function of contributing to a sentence's expressing the thought it does from the function of identifying some concept under which the object falls. How does the sense of the predicative expression 'is dead' differ from its reference, namely the concept *Death*? Perhaps an answer similar to that given above may be tried here. For it certainly seems correct to distinguish the actual state in which Caesar is when dead, namely the state of death, from any component of the thought that Caesar is dead. It is here that the problem of truth crops up. For Frege, as we shall see, identifies true thoughts, i.e. true propositions, with facts. What he means is, in part, that instead of saying 'It is a true thought that *p*' or 'The thought that *p* is true', we can equally well say 'It is a fact that *p*'.

Now this answer relies on a sharp distinction between thoughts and their components on the one hand, and situations or states of affairs and their components on the other. And certainly Frege made some such distinction; for example, he said that objects, taking the sun as his instance, cannot be parts of thoughts ('On Sense and Reference', p. 64). But here we get into trouble. For though we want to identify the Caesar who is the object of reference of the name 'Caesar' with the actual person who formed part of certain actual situations, we do not so readily want to identify the concept *Death* which is the reference of 'is dead' with the actual state of the dead person, i.e. some part of certain actual situations. Concepts are not properties, and we must distinguish between the redness of a rose or the redness of all red things and the concept *Red*. The general difficulty is this; should we make a distinction between the reference of a sentence, e.g. 'Caesar is dead', which is its truth-value, namely, 'the circumstance (*Umstand*) that it is true' ('On Sense and Reference, p. 63), i.e. the *fact* that it is true, and the actual state of affairs consisting of Caesar's being dead? for surely we can call this too the fact that Caesar is dead. I shall say something about Frege's attitude towards *facts* in Chapter 9.

My suggestion is that the terminology of sense and reference may be at least in part designed to deal with the problem of truth. Frege believed that the forms '*p*', 'It is true that *p*' and '"*p*"' is true' had identical truth-values while differing in some way. The theory of sense and reference seems to be designed to explain such differences.

(v)

In this section I want to bring together some of the reasons that favour a theory which like Frege's distinguishes the notion of meaning into two elements such as *sense* and *reference*, one we might say a horizontal relation and the other a vertical relation; one relating signs to one another, the other relating them to what they signify. First, there is the apparent existence of a distinction between the mental act of thinking and its content, i.e. between the act of believing, judging, inferring and the belief, judgement, inference itself. Frege adds to this his own view that thoughts, beliefs or judgements are identical with the meanings, i.e. senses, of sentences. A third component element of the same complex is the notion of the objectivity of meanings, i.e. senses. This is achieved partly by distinguishing the senses of words from ideas or mental images and the senses of sentences from complex mental images or 'floating thoughts'. Frege concludes that since we communicate and understand each other's communications, we must construe the senses of words and sentences as public entities, as opposed to such mental images, which are essentially private.

Second, there is a group of idioms (in English) employing the terms 'sense', 'sensible', 'make sense' and so on. We say, for instance, that sentences make sense or do not make sense or are nonsense; that we can grasp the sense of a sentence or not, that we understand the sense of a sentence or a set of words, or that we understand the sentence or what is being said. These idioms primarily apply to the case of sentence-sense. And we have seen how this notion is one of Frege's two plausible starting-points for the theory, i.e. the plausible beliefs that many *sentences* make sense and that many *names* signify objects. The fact that such idioms exist may be a reason behind the identification of a sentence's sense with the thought it expresses; I say more about this in the next chapter.

Third, and related in also stemming from quite common and harmless ways of talking, is the theory of judgement already briefly sketched. The facts to be accounted for are roughly these. When we speak in philosophy of a *judgement* we are speaking of what is thought, judged, believed; and it is tempting to construe the 'what' in this as the relative pronoun. Speaking of *what* is judged appears to be speaking of some entity, as it indeed is in 'He threw what he held'. And in the second place, when a man asserts '*p*' it is in some way a natural presupposition that he thinks or believes that *p*. It is perhaps this that underlies the identification of the thought expressed by a sentence with the meaning of the words it contains.

Next, there is a set of facts concerning the relations between truth and meaning. First, we can apparently express the same thing in the different forms '*p*', 'It is true that *p*' and ' "*p*" is true'. Second, there is some connection between the fact that a name refers to some definite object and the fact that a sentence of which it is the subject expression is definitely true or false, or expresses some definite thought. Third, the truth or falsity of a sentence seems to be simultaneously independent of its meaning and nevertheless closely related. For on the one hand it is possible to know what a sentence means without knowing whether it is true or false; and if G. E. Moore was right we can also sometimes know that a given sentence is true or false without knowing what it means. And on the other hand, we cannot know what a sentence means without *ipso facto* knowing in what conditions it would be true and in what false. To know what a sentence means is, as Frege says, to know what are its truth-conditions. This group of facts seems to underlie the identification of the reference of a sentence with its truth-value, and the assumption of an essential relation between the sense and reference of a complete sentence and the senses and references of its component expressions.

Finally there are two particular problems which the sense-reference distinction is meant to solve. First, there is the problem of statements of identity. As Frege sees it, the problem is how certain types of statement of *identity* can be non-analytic and informative. And his solution is that we are not restricted either to the view that statements of identity are about the signs they contain, or to the view that they are about the things or thing signified by such signs. We must distinguish between talking about signs as objects, and talking about signs as signs, i.e. about their respective modes of signification. Statements of identity can be synthetic because the sense of one sign for a given object can differ from the sense of another, and in learning that two signs with different senses apply to the same object we are learning some proposition with a definite and substantial sense itself. The second particular problem is the problem of *intensional* contexts, which constitute an apparent exception to the Leibnizian notion of identity as substitutability *salva veritate* in all contexts, as well as to Frege's principle, which is related to this, that the reference of a complete expression contains the references of its components. For the reference, i.e. truth-value, of the sentence '*p*' in the context '*A* judges that *p*' is not relevant to the truth-value of the latter. Frege's answer is to distinguish the customary reference and sense of an expression from its *indirect*, *ungerade*, reference and sense. 'The indirect reference of a word is accordingly its customary sense' ('On Sense and Reference', p. 59).

There are thus a good many *prima facie* facts with which Frege's theory manages to deal in one way or another. And this constitutes some kind of immediate justification of the theory. Therefore, in spite of the fact that certain internal difficulties have already been made evident, I shall devote the next chapter to pressing the theory harder, and to asking in particular what his puzzling notion of *sense* comes to, and what are the roots of this notion.

(vi)

As an appendix to this chapter something should be said about the common German term *Bedeutung* which Frege apparently made into a technical term. The verb *bedeuten* means pretty well the same as our verb *signify*. A possible range of senses of each includes the notions of mean, imply, be of importance, inform, point out, give to understand and portend. Similarly, the noun *Bedeutung* means much the same as *significance*, and the adjective *bedeutungsvoll* means much the same as *significant*, in the varied senses of these terms. These three German words have very little in common with the English words *refer*, *reference* and *referential*.

Two things would make the obvious translation of *Bedeutung* as *significance* troublesome. First, we must translate Frege's *Sinn* by *sense*, and in distinguishing *Bedeutung* from *Sinn* we should have to draw a sharp distinction between an expression's *significance* and its *sense*; and this distinction does not seem sharp in fact. Against this is the equivalent difficulty of drawing a sharp distinction in normal German between an expression's *Bedeutung* and *Sinn*. Second, it seems to be difficult to appropriate the word *significance* for the *object signified* by an expression. We do not normally say that Socrates is the *significance* of the name 'Socrates', or that the number 2 is the significance of the numeral '2'. Against this is an equal difficulty in the same respect as regards the ordinary term *reference*.

Now in view of Frege's assimilation of *Bedeutung* to naming, standing for or signifying, the customary translation *reference* conveys his intention fairly well. People who compare Frege's distinction between 'sense' and 'reference' with Russell's distinction between 'meaning' and 'denotation' are apt, perhaps remembering Mill, to suppose that 'sense' is roughly the same as Russell's 'meaning' and 'reference' the same as his 'denotation'. They then discover that in fact it would be truer to say that Russell's 'meaning' corresponds to Frege's 'reference'; and because of the dissimilar connotations of these terms, bewilderment arises. There is no need for this, since the term translated as 'reference' is the German equivalent for 'meaning'; and moreover Frege, like Russell, takes as his paradigm of the relation of 'meaning' the case of names, i.e. *naming*. Translation of *Bedeutung* by *significance* rather than by *reference* would help to avoid this needless difficulty.

In addition, Frege remarks in the *Grundgesetze* (i, 30) that his usage of *Bedeutung* is only meant to clarify the already existing usage of the term by reference to the common practice of recognising proper names as *Bedeutungsvoll*, i.e. *significant*. In view of all this, I conclude that Frege's *Bedeutung* should be translated as *significance*, or perhaps as *meaning*. This would serve to distinguish clearly the common usage of the term from Frege's theoretical application and interpretation of it, just as in Russell's case. My reason for ignoring my own conclusion is that this book is not intended as a translation of Frege but as a description of his writings; and that the kind of confusion made possible by translating *Bedeutung* as *significance* is initially more dangerous than the misinterpretation possibly caused by the translation *reference*.

SOURCES FOR CHAPTER SIX

'On Sense and Reference'; 'On Concept and Object'; *Grundgesetze*, i, 26–33.

CHAPTER SEVEN

THE NOTION OF SENSE

THE notion of an expression's sense breaks down into several distinct components. First, there is the notion of the *contribution* made by an expression to the thought expressed by a sentence in which it occurs. Now it seems that one and the same expression, e.g. a proper name like 'Aristotle', may quite well make different contributions to different thoughts. And Frege realised this when he said that as things were the senses of names tended to differ for different persons; since the thought that occurs to me when a sentence containing the name 'Aristotle' is uttered differs from the thought that occurs to you, we may say that I attribute a different sense to the name. But Frege thought that ideally sense would not be variable; ideally the same name would make exactly the same contribution to thoughts in whatever sentence context it occurred. Next there is the bunch of notions which fall under the heading of *ways of* doing so-and-so ('On Sense and Reference', p. 57; 'On Concept and Object', p. 44; 'Function and Concept', p. 23); the way an expression refers to an entity; the way it presents the entity referred to; the way it designates; the way it introduces a term into discourse and understanding. Related to these notions is a set of similar notions connected with the activities of users of language rather than with the functions of linguistic expressions. There is the way of analysing an expression; the way of looking at an entity; and the way of treating an entity, which extends to include its treatment in language. Finally there is the way in which an entity occurs, once again both in general and in language. Frege is never explicit about such expressions, and in order to relate the notions expressed to his idea of sense we should have to press them beyond the permissible limits of exegesis. But their chief defect is that on the face of it they apply only to the case of proper names. And even if we allow that the language of 'referring' can be extended from this central case, still this extension amounts to the drawing of an analogy between proper names and other expressions. This analogy is, indeed, explicit in the description of complete sentences as names of a certain type.

We have to distinguish an expression's sense from any property

92

possessed by the expression's object of reference. For the sense of the expression is closely connected with the relation between the expression and its object of reference, and this relation is independent of the object's properties or of its altering the properties it has. And we must not confuse the sense of a sign with the type of which the particular sign in question is a token, or with the shape and other physical properties of the sign itself. For difference in sense between signs is, as we saw, difference insofar as they are signs, rather than just difference as objects. The two are of course related, since difference in physical properties, i.e. difference as objects, is usually a sufficient condition for difference as signs. If the signs for two different objects were physically similar, they could not serve the purpose of signifying just this or that object. Still what is essential to the signs' differing as signs is a difference in their modes of signification.

The sense of an expression may be confused with what Frege at first called its *conceptual content*. But in this early use of the term 'content' Frege undoubtedly still confuses the sense and the reference of expressions. And it seems that by using this particular phrase Frege commits himself to a view he later rejected. For if we suppose that proper names have conceptual content, then we shall have to suppose that this is their sense, i.e. some concept, since their references are to objects. And then thoughts, which are composed of senses, will contain nothing but concepts. Now this is a common view of the nature of thoughts, and was held for example by Kant; but Frege certainly rejects it after writing the *Begriffsschrift*.

The notion of the sense of a sentence too can be broken down into a set of related notions. First there is the notion of a sentence's making sense, or of its being a significant sentence, as opposed to its being nonsensical. It is here that the identification of sense with thought becomes plausible. Next, there is the idiom of a sentence's asserting something or saying something definite. Close to this is the notion of its being something that can be seriously asserted. This in Frege's view, distinguishes sentences of fiction, sentences in poetry, and metaphorical sentences, from those which state factual truths in literal terms. Related to this is the notion that the assertion of a sentence should have some point. We say 'What's the sense of saying that?', and similar idioms with the word *Sinn* can be found in German. It is here, perhaps, that Frege's notion of the 'cognitive purpose' of science can be introduced, together with his idea of the 'cognitive value' of non-analytic sentences.

Finally a few oddities should be mentioned, since they show how easy it is to say things about *sense* that can be taken to fit both particular words and complete sentences. There is the notion of the amount of information or knowledge conveyed by a sentence, or by a sentence containing some given expression, or by the occurrence of a given expression in a sentence; or, in the last resort, by the isolated use of a word on its own. Now Frege never thought that words by themselves in isolation could give information or express thoughts, unless they were taken as conventional proxies for complete sentences, e.g. as the words 'Yes' and 'No' are when given as answers to questions. And in the second place there is the notion of an expression's use, *Gebrauch* or *Anwendung* (*Grundlagen*, pp. 22–3; p. 59; p. 97; *Grundgesetze*, ii, 95–96 etc.). Frege distinguishes the *use* of an expression from its sense and reference, as he distinguished the *application* of a sentence from its sense. He spoke of using words in certain senses; he said that the basic use of words could be brought out perspicuously in certain forms of sentence, and believed that in coming to understand a word's basic use we should get a better grasp of its meaning. But he seems to have taken *use* to denote an activity of the speakers of language; justifying the use of an expression is therefore usually the same as justifying the assertion of a sentence that contains this expression.

I think the notions of the *sense* of a sentence and of the *sense* of an expression such as a proper name which is not a sentence are clearly shown to be distinct notions by such considerations. In section (v) below I shall discuss some parts of the assimilation of sentences to proper names which this extension of the notion of *sense* appears to imply. And in Chapter 8 the question of Frege's analysis of sentences will be opened.

(ii)

The notion of sense is explicitly related by Frege to a set of terms which seem to denote mental activities, especially 'expression', 'understanding', 'communication' and 'knowledge'. Primarily it is the notion of sentence-sense which is related to such activities, but as we have seen Frege extends the notion in such a manner that anything sayable about sentence-sense can be said of word-sense and vice versa.

The sense of a sentence is identified with what the sentence expresses, i.e. a thought. Now at one point Frege says that expression is an activity performed by the person who utters a sentence, rather than a function of the sentence itself ('The Thought', p. 294). In uttering a sentence the speaker is expressing a thought. Is expression then to be taken as a function of language or of our use of it, i.e. of speech? Frege would probably have said that insofar as the speakers of language can do some particular thing in uttering a sentence, it is because the sentence itself already possesses the logical function of doing whatever it is; e.g. insofar as we can express thoughts in sentences, it is because sentences themselves already possess the function of expressing thoughts. Only sentences can express complete thoughts, and complete thoughts can only be expressed by complete sentences, or in special circumstances by expressions that are conventional substitutes for complete sentences. But this is not all. Frege distinguishes the sense and reference of an expression through a distinction between what the expression expresses and what it designates. This as it stands is not helpful; for one thing the distinction is not introduced as anything more than illumination; for another, we are still in the dark about what a word on its own could 'express'. And if this distinction is to explain the sense-reference distinction, we still have to justify Frege's applying the term *designating* (*bedeutet oder bezeichnet*) to sentences. We can certainly agree that language contains some expressions that express and some that designate. For example, sentences are expressions that express thoughts; proper names are expressions that designate. It is by no means clear that every separable expression in language has both functions. Of course there is more than the possibility of a kind of pun underlying Frege's view; the fact that all words, including proper names, can be called *expressions* itself shows that they *express* (*Ausdruck, ausdruecken*). Frege seems to me to have been susceptible to such pun-like pressures from within language and its idioms; we might say that he took language too seriously, too literally.

A second element in the theory of sense is the notion of understanding. For Frege identifies understanding a sentence with grasping or apprehending the thought it expresses, i.e. its sense. ('The Thought', pp. 307–9.) Here we may construe the terminology of *sense* as merely a way of stating familiar facts in such a manner as to uphold Frege's belief in the objectivity and publicity of meanings; Frege takes a harmless notion and refines or objectifies it. For by translating the idiom of understanding a sentence into the terminology of grasping a sense, Frege provides himself with an entity which is objective and public, and which therefore itself contains the guarantee of the objectivity and publicity of our understanding one another. Understanding also has a subjective element, since we may say that what a person understands by a given expression is something private to him. This explains why Frege says that different people can take one and the same expression to have different senses and that consequently they will attach different senses to any sentence containing that name. According to Frege this is a defect of language; and in a perfect, scientific language there could be no such private and subjective element in the sense of an expression.

The third such notion is that of communication. In the late essay 'The Thought' Frege argues that we do actually communicate and that this entails the presence of some common and objective factor with which communication is carried on. In general the existence of communication is presupposed by Frege; here his explicit argument is that if thoughts were not communicable entities, then my thought that p and your thought that p might have different truth-values. This itself is an absurd supposition; and how could we justify our use of the same expression 'p' in both cases? Thoughts must be communicable if the notions of truth and falsity are to be objectively applicable, rather than being simply characteristics of certain states of mind. Communication comes about through our understanding; Frege describes it as the deliberate causing of certain changes in the environment with the intention of getting another person to understand the required thought. Communicating with one another is therefore the other side of one coin to understanding.

The fourth such notion is that of information or acquisition of knowledge. Apprehending a true thought and recognising its truth, i.e. grasping the sense and reference of a sentence, is simply acquiring knowledge. Frege analyses knowledge into only two elements. For the truth of 'A knows that p' we need the truth of 'A judges that p' and the truth of 'p'; if a thought is true and thought to be true, then it is known. Further, Frege's explanation of statements of identity is in terms of the information that they convey; it is because statements of the form '$a=b$' are not necessarily *apriori* and may therefore sometimes be synthetic that the problem arises. And he solves this problem by distinguishing sense from reference; in learning that two signs with different senses both designate the same object, one grasps a genuine thought.

These four notions apply in analogous forms to the case of word-sense. It is Frege's view that isolated expressions, e.g. proper names, can *express* just as well as complete sentences. And it is clear that he also believed that such expressions can, as much as sentences, be understood, i.e. that their senses can be common public property, and that sometimes the fact that a certain object is signified by a certain name itself 'contains knowledge'. Now in all these cases it is important to distinguish the objective sense from the subjective elements which accompany the understanding, expressing, communicating or informing; these are associated ideas, mental images, and various other psychological occurrences. It is perhaps here that Frege's technique of deriving word-sense from sentence-sense is most useful. For although it is quite easy to fail to make the necessary distinctions between the objective and subjective elements in word-sense, it is by no means so easy to be confused in the same way about sentence-sense. Here, as he insists, anybody who wants to deny the objectivity of thoughts must either deny the objectivity of truth and falsity or produce a quite different account of the relation between a sentence's truth and its meaning; and it is one of the great strengths of Frege's theory that he manages to give a reasonably comprehensive account of this relation.

(iii)

It seems that Frege held certain fairly crude beliefs which unconsciously helped to form the mature doctrine of sense and reference, so that by examining them one may get the doctrine itself clearer. I have already mentioned three primitive metaphysical beliefs of this kind, namely the theory that mental acts have contents distinct from the acts themselves and objects distinct from both, the theory that objects possess properties that are partly objective, partly subjective, and the theory that signification is a many-one relation, i.e. that any object may be signified by more than one sign and that different signs may sometimes present the object signified in different ways. The analogy of the telescope ('On Sense and Reference', p. 60) underlies all three beliefs.

Frege drew a sharp distinction between an object and its properties; in traditional terms he accepted the distinction of the categories of substance and quality. Corresponding to this distinction is a distinction between the modes of apprehending objects and properties. Frege speaks of the apprehension of properties as direct, and the apprehension of objects as in general indirect, since they are generally apprehended through or by means of their properties. The characteristic mode of apprehending an object is recognising it as the same as an object already identified, and we recognise it by the presence of the same set of properties or a sufficiently similar set. Some objects can be apprehended by reason as opposed to sensation and perception, but even here it is not evident that Frege believes them to be directly apprehended. For even 'rational objects' such as numbers can perfectly well have properties.

Together with the object-property distinction goes a set of distinctions between reality and appearance, the thinkable and the actual, the public and the private, the objective and the subjective, the physical and the mental. Not all of these coincide. Properties can be just as real, thinkable, public, objective and physical as objects; conversely there appear to be objects which are private, subjective and mental, e.g. ideas. We must be careful at this point, however, since Frege says in the *Grundlagen* that 'objective ideas (*Vorstellungen*) can be distinguished into objects and concepts' (p. 37, note 1). Ideas are what he calls the contents of mental acts rather than their objects. As the content of an act it is something subjective; but of course it can itself be the object of another mental act and can then be treated as objective.

The central example of a sentence was for Frege the simple singular predicative judgement, in which a concept is predicated of an object, e.g. 'Socrates is wise'. To say that the object Socrates falls under the concept *Wisdom* is simply to say that Socrates is wise. Now if we bear in mind his identification of the sense of a proper name with some definite description of its bearer, we can see how this set of primtive distinctions gets carried over. For given the name 'Socrates', there is some object which is the reference of this name, and there are certain properties possessed by this object, which yield various alternative possible senses for the name. Socrates possessed the property of being Plato's teacher, and correspondingly we may take: the teacher of Plato as the sense of 'Socrates'. It may seem that in order to fulfil Frege's demand that a proper name should have only one fixed sense we must identify this ideal sense with the complete description of its bearer. There is no doubt that Frege accepted the Identity of Indiscernibles as giving an account of the notion of identity of objects, and that he believed objects were individuated by the complete set of their respective properties. The proof of this is that if we consider the class of all true predicative sentences of the simple form described above, we see that Frege assumes that the possibility of placing two different names in the subject position of exactly the same set of such sentences would guarantee the identity of their bearers. To fall under the same set of concepts is to be identical. Therefore 'comprehensive knowledge of the reference would require us to be able to say immediately whether any given sense belongs to it' ('On Sense and Reference', p. 58); complete knowledge of Socrates necessitates knowledge of all his properties.

This theory seems to carry something over from Frege's early view that thoughts are just sets of concepts. For on this later theory thoughts will contain not the objects of reference of the names in corresponding sentences but their senses. And it is easy to move from this view to the view that a thought about Socrates will contain corresponding to the name 'Socrates' in the sentence that expresses it a set of concepts under which Socrates falls, e.g. the concepts *Teacher of Plato* and *Philosopher*. And on this view thoughts will still apparently be composed of concepts, and thus one point of Frege's analogy between thoughts and completed functions will be lost.

Frege says several things which seem to go with the idea that the senses of expressions are subjective, and these fit well with the tentative derivation of the notion of sense from the notion of property. The notion of sense is correlative with the notions of understanding and attaching meaning to expressions. If we take different descriptions of an object as the sense of its name, we shall attach different senses to any sentence in which the name occurs, and therefore up to this point will fail to communicate. This is shown very clearly in the case of personal pronouns ('The Thought', p. 297). If Socrates says 'I am Greek' and Plato agrees 'Socrates is Greek', do they express the same thought, i.e. is the sense of Socrates' remark accessible to Plato? If Plato and Alcibiades both understand by the name 'Socrates' the same thing, for instance the description: the cleverest man in Athens, then they will understand 'Socrates is wise' in the same sense. But if Alcibiades knows Socrates under some different description from that under which Plato knows him, their thoughts will differ. Frege goes so far as to say that if two people are in possession of entirely distinct descriptions of one and the same individual, or object in general, then as far as the name of that individual goes they speak different languages, since although they do in fact refer by the name to the same individual they do not know that they do. In such cases they can never understand each other's remarks about this individual. 'With a proper name, it depends on how whatever it refers to is presented'. Now Frege also believed that there was a 'primitive way of self-presentation' in which each person is necessarily and inaccessibly presented to himself. It follows therefore that all statements made in the first person express incommunicable thoughts unless the speaker 'gives "I" a graspable

8

sense'. This theory is remarkably similar to Russell's theory that while knowledge of oneself is direct acquaintance, knowledge of others is always by description. Russell too says that others 'are not acquainted with the proposition itself', i.e. that they cannot make the judgment which only I myself can make ('Knowledge by Acquaintance and Knowledge by Description'). This is the only such case discussed by Frege. But obviously the same difficulties arise on such an account for all private entities, e.g. ideas and sensations. Only the person who actually has an idea can attach a sense to a sentence about it.

Just as sensible properties seem to be partly objective and partly subjective, so too do senses. 'Even a colour-blind man can speak of red and green, in spite of the fact that he does not distinguish between these colours in his sensations' (*Grundlagen*, p. 36). The sense of a name is subjective insofar as it depends upon our particular natures and experiences what sense we actually attach to a name, and the thought expressed by a sentence containing this name is subjective in a similar way. But the sense of a sentence is objective in that once presented it is independent of the constitution of our minds what the thought-content is and whether it is true or false. The sense of a name is objective in that the concepts that compose the particular description we attach to the name are objective. The meaning of the description does not depend on my understanding. In the passage of the *Grundlagen* quoted above Frege distinguishes the meaning (*Bedeutung* in the loose terms of this work) of a word from the intuitions, *Anschauung*, of its users; a distinction which seems to foreshadow the reference-sense distinction. 'What is objective . . . is what is expressible in words. What is purely intuitable is not communicable'. Frege supposes that there are two rational beings who can intuit only projective properties and relations, e.g. the lying of points on lines and planes, such that whatever one intuits as a point the other intuits as a plane. 'In these circumstances they could understand one another quite well, and would never realise the difference between their intuitions . . . We can therefore still say that this word has for them an objective meaning, provided only that by this meaning we do not understand any of the peculiarities of their respective intuitions'. They would agree about the truth-values of all geometrical theorems, and more besides, e.g. they would agree about the methods of proof, since every theorem in projective geometry has a counterpart and every proof also.

As roots of the theory of sense and reference we should compare with this primitive object-property distinction another set of distinctions which Frege accepted, namely the distinctions between fact and fiction, between sciences and games, between knowledge and imagination, and between reason and sensation or perception. The importance of this disparate set of distinctions is that they serve to show the kind of thing Frege meant when he distinguished the objective from the subjective. They show that the principal criterion for objectivity is that the notions of truth and falsity apply within this realm. Neither works of fiction nor poems nor metaphorical and figurative remarks can be true or false. The rules and results of games are not the sort of thing which can have a truth-value. The products of imagination, sensation and perception are incapable of being true or false. Frege believed however that fictional and metaphorical remarks could express thoughts and therefore possess senses. 'In hearing an epic poem ... we are interested only in the sense of the sentences and the images and feelings thereby aroused. The question of truth would cause us to abandon aesthetic delight for an attitude of scientific investigation ... It is the striving for truth that drives us always to advance from the sense to the reference' ('On Sense and Reference', pp. 62–3). These distinctions relate to the sense-reference distinction when it applies to sentences; here it amounts to the distinction between thought and truth-value or thought and fact. And what distinguishes one set of members of the contrasted pairs mentioned is that they are concerned with truth-values and not merely with thoughts, i.e. with the references and not merely the senses of sentences. This means too that they are concerned with the references and not merely the senses of proper names. It is a mark of the boundary between science and what is not scientific that we begin to inquire whether there really was someone called 'Odysseus'.

It has been suggested to me that the ordinary meanings of *Sinn* and *Bedeutung* would also naturally tend to go with the contrasts between imagination and reason, or between works of fiction and poetry and metaphorical utterances on the one hand, and on the other the language of fact and science. The *Bedeutung* of an expression would be understood as something amenable to processes of reasoning, expression and communication. The *Sinn*, like the drift or import of a remark, would be accessible to the hearer's or reader's interpretation and intuition, related to his emotions and sensations rather than to his intelligence. It is also idiomatic to use the term *Sinn* to denote the content of poetry, rather than the term *Bedeutung*. And a German could well speak of an expression's having *Sinn* but no *Bedeutung* or as having *Bedeutung* but no *Sinn*. Many of Frege's remarks may be taken in two ways, either as truisms about the ordinary meanings of these terms or as philosophical remarks about their technical meanings; of course he would not have seen a distinction here, since he believed that he was simply clarifying ordinary use.

(iii)

One of Frege's strongest principles is that the meaning of a word should not be looked for on its own but in the context of propositions. This is most explicitly stated in the *Grundlagen* (Introduction, p. x), where however Frege had not yet drawn a distinction between *Bedeutung* and *Sinn*. This raises a question. Does he mean that the sense of a word is dependent on its propositional contexts or that its reference is? And does he mean this principle to apply to proper names or to concept-words? And further, does he mean that what meaning, i.e. sense or reference, a word has depends on its context, or does he mean that a word does not have any meaning, i.e. sense or reference, except when it occurs in such contexts?

As a first approximation to answering these questions the following can be said. The sense of a proper name is not constituted by its contexts. But it is true that what a particular person understands as its sense will depend upon his accepting some statement of identity, e.g. 'Socrates is the teacher of Plato'. The reference of a proper name is not given by its context. But it is partially determined by the set of true sentences of which it is subject, i.e. determined insofar as the object of reference is determined by the set of its properties. For concept-words the case is a little different. The reference, i.e. the concept referred to, is given by the true sentences of which the concept-word is predicate and the false sentences of which it is predicate. This will be qualified below.

The reference of a proper name, i.e. an object, is clearly not dependent for its existence on the occurrence of the name in a sentence. The sun would exist none the less if there was no name for it or no people to utter the name. But to say that an object, i.e. the reference of a proper name, exists is to say that there is some concept of which it is an instance. This is to say that there is some true sentence in which its name is subject term. 'Odysseus' is not the subject of any true or false sentence. The reference of a proper name is not affected by its contexts, but is the same in whatever sentence the name occurs. But what the particular object named by a given name is, is given implicitly by the set of true sentences of which the name is subject. Given this set of sentences we can identify the object of reference of the name, granted that the Identity of Indiscernibles holds.

The sense of a proper name is dependent for its existence and thus for being the particular sense it is on the true statements of identity into which the name can enter. The particular sense that I attach to a given name depends on the particular set of statements of identity containing that name that I accept, and thus far its sense is dependent on its occurring in contexts. Ideally there is just one complete set of statements of identity into which the name enters, and we might say that the true or ideal sense of the name is defined by this set of statements. If no statement of identity of the form in question, e.g. 'Socrates is the teacher of Plato', could be made about the object of reference of a genuine proper name, then even for Frege it would be senseless. 'For every object there is one type of proposition which must have a sense, namely the recognition-statement, which in the case of numbers is called an identity' (*Grundlagen*, p. 116).

The case is different for predicative expressions. The reference of a predicative expression, namely a concept, is defined if and only if the truth-values of all sentences of which it is the grammatical predicate are defined, i.e. if it is determined for every object either that it falls under this concept or that it does not. As things are, this requires us frequently to stipulate truth-values. There are many names which when attached as subjects to given predicative expressions do not yield sentences with definite truth-values. This means that knowledge of the reference of a concept-word is essentially different from knowledge of the reference of a proper name, since an object can be known in many different ways, i.e. under many different descriptions, whereas a concept is not known at all if it is not known completely. In strict science there can be partial and incomplete knowledge of objects but not of concepts.

It is clear that the reference of concept-words is also dependent on their occurrence as predicates of sentences. For it is only because we start with a complete sentence having a definite truth-value and subtract from it a part having reference, namely a proper name, that we can speak of the remaining predicative expression as referring. And, at least on Frege's earlier view, the reference of the predicate is determined by the reference of the subject term, in the case of singular sentences, and the reference of the whole. What is not clear is whether concept-words only refer to concepts when they occur as predicates in complete sentences. There is no doubt about this point in the case of proper names, since these signify their bearers even on their own. Now Frege says that functional signs do not refer to complete entities but rather indicate them indefinitely. Concept-words must therefore do the same; what contributes to the false view that they refer in isolation is the tendency to isolate them and consider them on their own. For in this way it can come to seem that the word 'red' need not differ essentially from a name like 'Socrates'. But if we remember that the complete expression should rather be 'x is red', then this temptation is weakened. Concept-words must be said only to indicate indefinitely in isolation, and to refer only in context. What they indicate indefinitely are their possible values, i.e. the two truth-values truth and falsity. Now surely there are what Frege calls function-names, i.e. signs that signify functions, and therefore surely there are isolated signs that signify concepts, namely concept-words? This is indeed true; but it is not helpful, since the function or concept signified can be identified only as what is represented by the common part of a set of complete expressions. The concept *Red* can be identified only as what is represented by the common part of all sentences containing as predicate the expression 'is red'.

The senses of concept-words are extremely puzzling and mysterious entities. Whatever they may be, it is at least clear that they depend for their existence on the occurrence of the concept-word in question in a sentence ('Foundations of Geometry', p. 13). Since concept-words are essentially incomplete sentences, they cannot have complete thoughts, i.e. thoughts, as their senses. When a concept-word occurs as predicate in a complete sentence, then the sentence as a whole expresses a complete thought, and the sense of the concept-word is part of this thought. And just as the concept-word and the concept are each in its own way incomplete, so, Frege says, the sense of the concept-word is also incomplete or predicative in its own way ('On Concept and Object', p. 54). Conversely the sense of a proper name, like the name and its bearer, will be complete. This suggests forcibly that it is mistaken and a grave misunderstanding of Frege's outlook to go on asking what the sense of a predicative expression can be, and what are the conditions for the existence and identification of such an entity. We should rather turn to the analysis of complete sentences. This conclusion is reinforced by another consideration. Just as for concept-words, the sense of a proper name is determined by its being part of a complete thought expressed by some sentence, or rather by its being a common part of a set of complete thoughts. Now this throws light on the question of the isolated reference of concept-words. For if the sense of a concept-word is somehow not a complete entity, yet is identified with the word's mode of introducing the concept or of signifying it, it follows simply that the word's mode of introducing or signifying or referring to the concept is essentially incomplete. And whatever exactly this means, it surely means at least that its referring to the concept is incomplete, i.e. that it somehow fails of complete reference to the concept. Presumably when the concept-word occurs as grammatical predicate of a complete sentence, then it achieves complete reference to the concept.

There is a strong temptation to construe the *senses* of predicative expressions as concepts. This would satisfy all that Frege says about their incompleteness; moreover it would square with his early view that thoughts, i.e. the senses of complete sentences or in his early terminology their *contents*, were conceptual, and that scientific thinking was conceptual thinking as opposed to intuitive. This, however plausible, would be a bad confusion; for concepts are certainly the references of predicative expressions, and therefore not parts of thoughts but rather, like objects, parts of truth-values. The concept *Red* is part of the fact that strawberries are red, not part of the thought or proposition that strawberries are red.

It therefore seems best to interpret the *Grundlagen* principle of meaning in terms of the sense-reference theory as follows. Since general words are essentially predicative, in asking about their meanings, i.e. senses and references, we should begin from complete sentences in which they occur as predicates. Such sentences express thoughts, so the sense of a general word will be the predicative element in a thought or set of thoughts. Since sentences signify truth-values, the concept that is the reference of a general word will be the predicative or incomplete element in a truth-value. We can put this in another way. The concept is what is predicated through a singular sentence of the object named in it. It is that which is true of its subject when the sentence is true and false of it when the sentence is false. We must therefore ask about concepts by way of determining which sentences are true and which are false. The second view is a general view of the sense of words in isolation, namely that we must begin from an investigation into the thoughts expressed by sentences. And since Frege identifies the thought expressed by a sentence with the thought that its truth-conditions are fulfilled, both views come to the view that inquiries about the meanings, i.e. senses and references, of words must begin with investigations into the truth-values and truth-conditions of sentences. 'We can inquire about reference only if the signs are constituent parts of sentences expressing thoughts' (*Grundgesetze*, ii, 97). It is significant, too, that the doctrine of sense and reference is discussed by Frege only as it applies to proper names and to complete sentences. It is sometimes argued that since he never discusses its application to concept-words, he never envisaged its extension to apply to them. I think this view is wrong, but it is right in implying that discussion of the application to complete sentences is enough; we do not then need, nor could we have, a separate doctrine of its application to concept-words.

(v)

Frege held a certain view of the nature of language and thought and their essential relation, which will be discussed above all in Chapter 10 below. Roughly speaking, he held that though the correspondence theory of truth is false, or perhaps since it is false, we must accept a kind of correspondence theory of meaning in its place, in order to guarantee that our thoughts and utterances can represent reality. His view is essentially that adopted by Wittgenstein in the *Tractatus*, namely that there is a structural correspondence between thoughts and their expressions in a logically adequate and perspicuous notation. I should like to link what I have so far said about sense and reference to this theory.

It seems to me that the principal ground for such a theory lies in the assimilation of sentence-sense to word-sense. Frege simply carried over into his discussion of the sense of sentences his views on the sense and reference of words. And in turn he assimilates the meaning of all words to the kind of meaning characteristic of what he calls proper names, i.e. genuine proper names together with singular definite descriptions. The ultimate spring of the sense-reference theory may therefore lie in Frege's construing definite descriptions on the model of genuine proper names.

The process of assimilation can be brought out in the reverse way. Frege first construes naming, i.e. the function performed by genuine proper names, as a kind of referring. Next definite descriptions, because they have the function of identifying objects, are said to be referring expressions and therefore to be a kind of name; referring is here identified with naming. But a distinction between reference and sense has already been imposed for definite descriptions in order to deal with the logic of their appearance in non-analytic statements of identity. Since descriptions are construed as names, the theory of sense and reference is finally taken to apply to genuine proper names also.

Next the multiple analogies concerning function, argument and value are brought into play. Expressions containing proper names are taken as a kind of functional expression, such that the object named is the argument and the reference of the complete expression is the value. Such expressions may now be regarded as complex names. Then complete equations are construed as functions on the grounds that they contain variable letters; possible substitutions are construed as possible arguments, and for the value of the resulting arithmetical equations, truth and falsity respective to the equation concerned. Finally complete sentences are taken as functions, since like arithmetical equations they state facts. The proper name that is subject term, if the sentence is singular, is taken to refer to the argument and as value we take once again the truth or falsity of the complete sentence.

In the third place the theory of sense and reference is extended from proper names in Frege's sense to arithmetical expressions, which are taken as names of numbers. And generally any expression in whatever notation that signifies an object of whatever kind is taken as subject to the theory. From complete expressions signifying objects the theory is finally extended to cover complete sentences. The object named by the subject-term of a singular sentence and the truth or falsity of the sentence are construed as the references of the subject expression and the complete sentence respectively. The complete sentence is taken as a kind of complex proper name.

And finally the sense which the extended theory demands for sentences is located in the thought it expresses. This identification is the easier for Frege, since the German *Sinn* has a cognate verb *sinnen* which means 'think', or 'consider', 'have in mind' and the like. The assimilation of sentences to names is then as it were reversed, and the sense of an expression is construed as part of the sense so defined of a complete sentence.

The second ground for Frege's general theory of meaning appears to be the existence of a group of contrasting pairs; thing and fact, object and property or relation, noun and adjective or verb, subject and predicate, name and description, standing for and being about what is stood for, naming and stating, designating and expressing. Each of these contrasting pairs contains one member which might be called simple and one which might be called complex and also contains the first as a component or presupposes the existence of the first in some other way. Moreover the complex also contains or presupposes the existence of something that is characteristically incomplete and characteristically completed by or only found in conjunction with the first. This account is deliberately vague, in order to bring out the real but vague analogies between different pairs of this group.

Perhaps the process of assimilating expressions into the theory of sense and reference is by itself sufficient to generate a belief that these contrasted pairs are genuinely analogous, and that the pairs can be arranged into two columns. It is also clear that Frege was much impressed by certain facts of grammar and syntax, notably by the singular subject-predicate sentence and by the simple descriptive assertive sentence in the indicative mood and containing the ordinary copula *is*. The form 'Socrates is wise' lurked at the back of Frege's mind as a paradigm, as it has lurked at the back of many other philosophers' minds. For in a sentence of this form the contrasted pairs mentioned above do seem to fall pretty closely together. There is an object named 'Socrates' that possesses the property of wisdom, and the whole makes up a complex fact. 'Socrates' is a proper name and has a grammatically substantival form; 'is' is a verb and 'wise' an adjective. 'Socrates' is the sentence's subject, 'is wise' its predicate. The name stands for the subject of the proposition expressed, the predicate says something about the subject. 'Socrates' serves to refer to Socrates, 'is wise' adds an element which makes the whole into an assertive sentence.

Before making any further general comments on Frege's theory of meaning I shall discuss his theory of the judgment and application to this theory of the sense-reference distinction.

SOURCES FOR CHAPTER SEVEN

'On Sense and Reference'; 'On Concept and Object'; *Grundgesetze*, i, 26–33; *Grundlagen*, sections 58–60.

CHAPTER EIGHT

THOUGHT AND JUDGEMENT

IT is impossible to understand Frege's theory of truth and its relation to meaning, i.e. his application of the sense-reference theory to sentences, without getting his notion of a judgement quite clear. Now Frege himself did not achieve his later clarity without passing through typical early confusion, and a brief account of this early position can throw much light on his later achievement. Already in the *Begriffsschrift* Frege was distinguishing the judgement itself from its *content*. The content of a judgement is here described as a 'complex of ideas', and it seems that the difference between possible contents of judgement and ideas which are not possible contents is just that the former are complexes of ideas. The sign for a complex of ideas, e.g. perhaps a complete sentence, is 'combined . . . into a whole' by a horizontal stroke prefixed to the sign. This stroke is called the *content-stroke*, and can only be prefixed to signs for possible contents of judgement. The complete sign can then be read as 'the circumstance that . . .' or 'the proposition that. . . .' To symbolise the actual *judging*, i.e. 'recognition or non-recognition of the truth of this', a vertical stroke is fixed to the left-hand end of the content-stroke. This is the *judgement-stroke*, and it expresses the *assertion* of the whole formed by the sign for the content and the content-stroke. The composite prefix may be taken as the common *predicate* of all judgements, since any proposition can be rewritten in the form '. . . is a fact', e.g. 'Caesar's death is a fact'. Here then 'the subject contains the whole content, and the only purpose of the predicate is to present this in the form of a judgement' (p. 3). This symbol is the only predicate of judgements that logic need take account of. *Negation* is expressed in the *Begriffsschrift* symbolism by attaching a smaller vertical stroke to the lower side of the content-stroke. The whole will therefore express the assertion '. . . is not the case'. Negation thus attaches to and is 'a mark of a possible content of judgement', rather than of the act of judgement.

Frege's mature theory can be seen as a progressive distinguishing of elements confused in this early account. In particular, the *Begriffsschrift* is not clear about the nature of assertion and its relation to the sentence asserted; it confuses more than one activity under the name of *judgement*; it gives a muddled account of what it is to be a content of judgement; and it fails to explain just what is the relation between the symbols used and the entities they symbolise.

(ii)

In the final version of his theory ('The Thought', especially pp. 291–296) Frege distinguishes three separate components of the *act of judgement*; the apprehension of a thought, or *thinking*, the recognition of the truth-value of the apprehended thought, or *judging*, and the manifesting or expressing of this recognition or judgement, the *asserting*. We can make an assertion only where we have already made an act of judgement, but the converse does not hold. It is possible to perform the inner and subjective act of judgement without expressing this in an outer act of assertion.

Corresponding to these three distinct acts are three distinct kinds of entity as their respective *contents*. The content of the act of thinking is a *thought*; the content of the act of assertion is a *sentence* expressing this thought; the content of the act of judgement proper is an identity judgement, namely a thought of the form 'The thought that *p* is true'. Asserting a thought is uttering the sentence that expresses the thought. Making an assertion and expressing a thought are one and the same. Not every sentence uttered, however, is thereby asserted. Imperatives and questions are uttered as sentences but they are not asserted, and they differ from indicative sentences in just this respect. For the indicative sentence or declarative sentence falls into two halves, namely thought and assertion; questions fall into thought and request for a decision as to its truth-value; imperatives fall into thought and command as to its realisation.

It is very easy to confuse *assertion* with predication. One obvious reason for the confusion is that assertion is connected with the indicative form of the sentence. But language does not contain any special word or symbol, as Frege's *Begriffsschrift* and Russell's *Principia Mathematica* notations do, to express the fact of a sentence's being asserted. Instead, the assertive force is supplied in the form of the assertoric sentence, namely the indicative form of the verb. And the verb is essentially part of the predicate of the sentence. It is easy then to think that assertion is contained in predication. But assertion is an act of the speaker relative to the whole sentence or thought, while predication is not treated by Frege as an act at all, but rather as an element of the sentence or thought to be asserted. Predication is indeed logically prior to assertion, but only because only what is already in part predicative can be asserted.

The *indicative* form of the assertive sentence combines several quite different functions. First there is the fact of the sentence's being asserted. This is shown by the fact that the verb is in the indicative mood rather than the imperative or subjunctive. Other moods than the indicative are used to show that the given thought is presented for decision or realisation, for instance. Second, there is the implicit recognition of the truth of the thought expressed by the sentence. It is presumably this that causes Frege to say that a false thought 'may not' be uttered assertively ('Negation', p. 122). To assert something is to imply belief in its truth; if I judge that a thought is false, then I cannot express this judgement of mine by simply asserting the corresponding sentence. My assertion '*p*' expresses my recognition of *p*'s truth, and recognition of *p*'s falsity is expressed by my asserting 'not-*p*'. Next there are the factors of tense in the indicative verb. If the indicative sentence is in the present tense, then the verb will according to Frege contain two distinct tenses. It contains a genuine present tense appropriate to express the thought in question and to indicate the relation between the time of assertion and the time at which the conditions for the thought's being true are said to hold. It also contains a tenseless present that expresses the recognition of the truth of this thought. Frege says that the 'is' in a sentence like ' "*p*" is true' is timeless, if '*p*' is made fully explicit. It is this 'is' that is implicitly contained in the indicative form of the verb.

The relation of the act of asserting a sentence to its truth is very puzzling. It is clearly wrong to conflate the assertive utterance of a sentence with the realisation that the thought it expresses is true. Frege, however, still wants to say that the assertion expresses or contains the realisation of truth, and surely he is right. But the converse does not hold. Prefixing a sentence with the words 'It is true that' does nothing to give the sentence assertive force. For this, only what he calls 'seriousness' is sufficient ('The Thought', p. 294). There seem to be two distinct elements in this notion. The first is that the sounds or shapes which constitute the sentence should be produced with the intention of expressing the thought they really do express. The second is that the context of production itself should be serious, i.e. that we should not be writing fiction or speaking dramatic parts. The speaker should be making the assertion *in propria persona*, and the act should really be in Frege's words the subjective possession of the agent. What makes it easy to confuse assertion of a sentence with asserting its truth is the tendency to get the relation between the sentence and its truth wrong. For if we take this to be the relation of a subject to its predicate, in the manner of Frege's early theory, we shall perhaps think that asserting the thought is identical with saying that it is true.

(iii)

Frege restricts the term *judgement* to denote the act of recognising the truth of a thought. But judgement is not just *supposing* a thought to be true. Frege sharply distinguishes supposing from believing. Thoughts which are merely supposed to be true and not believed to be true cannot be asserted in fully declarative sentences. They occur appropriately in the clauses of hypothetical sentences, for instance, where the whole is asserted but the parts are not. ('Function and Concept', p. 34 and 'Negation', pp. 119 ff.). It seems that supposing or assuming, *Annahme*, must also be distinguished from thinking, i.e. the apprehension of a thought. For Frege defines supposition as 'the putting of a case', *das Setzen eines Falles*, and this is surely distinct from and posterior to the grasping of the case.

The act of judging is said to be indefinable ('Negation', p. 126). But as an act, says Frege, it must belong to a definite agent each time it is performed, and occur at a particular time. It is because of this that it is not perfectly clear that the 'is' of 'is true' is timeless. For recognition of a truth is itself an act which occurs at one or another specific time. Frege gives some equivalents for this term; recognising the truth of a thought, realising that it is true, seeing that it is true, admitting that it is true, deciding that it is true. But he takes *recognition* as the basic term and analogy. Judging a thought to be true must not be confused with grasping it. It is quite possible to grasp a thought, to understand the sense of a sentence, without passing judgement on its truth-value. Indeed, more than this, we must be able to understand the senses of sentences, to grasp thoughts, before we can make any judgement as to their truth-values. This comes out clearly in the case of questions. If to grasp a thought were already to judge its truth or falsity, then it would not be possible to ask questions. For one could not ask a question without knowing the answer to it. And it would not be possible to answer questions, since a question cannot be answered either way until its sense is understood.

The third act which makes up the complete act of assertion is the original *apprehension* of a thought. If we are given a sentence, we apprehend the thought that it expresses by grasping the sense of the words or by understanding what is said. It is to this act of comprehension that Frege gives the name *thinking* ('The Thought', p. 294). He seems to take this notion also as indefinable. In 'The Thought' he speaks in metaphorical terms about it. We must distinguish thoughts from sense-impressions, which are had or borne by particular persons, and from things, which are seen or otherwise perceived. Thoughts, we should say, are 'apprehended'. 'A particular mental capacity, the power of thought, must correspond to the apprehension of thoughts . . . In thinking we do not produce thoughts, but we apprehend them' (p. 307). He tries to point to one distinction by saying that something in the thinker's mind is 'aimed at the thought'.

(iv)

We must now turn to the distinctions drawn by Frege within the contents of the various acts discussed. A different element in the whole complex corresponds to each of the three different elements in the complete act of assertion. To the thinking there corresponds a *thought*; to the judging the recognition of its truth-value; to the assertion the *sentence* that expresses the thought.

Frege calls a sentence a 'series of sounds having sense' ('The Thought', p. 291). This is not a complete definition, since not every series of sounds having sense is a *sentence*. Some complex expressions have sense but are not complete sentences; names have sense; questions and commands have sense but are not strictly sentences. They are not assertoric and declarative. Commands do not express thoughts, although they have senses ('The Thought', p. 293); questions, *Satzfragen*, although they have sense and contain thoughts, do not express the thoughts they contain. Rather, they express a request to the hearer to decide on the truth-value of the thought they contain.

In the *Grundgesetze* Frege distinguishes two forms of propositional expression. A sentence on its own, e.g. '$2+3=5$', just designates a truth-value and expresses a thought. It is simply a name of a peculiar kind. But the same sentence when prefixed with the composite vertical-and-horizontal stroke expresses the assertion of this thought. It is therefore quite possible to write down the expression for a thought, i.e. a sentence, without asserting its truth.

Since a sentence is a kind of expression, every complete sentence must have both sense and reference. It is fundamental to Frege's analysis of sentences that he identifies the sense with the thought expressed by or contained in the sentence, and the reference with its truth-value. Strictly speaking it is not the sentence, but rather the thought expressed by it, which has the truth-value in question. A sentence, then, is the *name* of a truth-value, but does not say which truth-value it is the name of (*Grundgesetze*, i, 5). When prefixed by the composite sign of judgement and assertion, the whole sign expresses the thought that the name-sentence refers to the truth, i.e. that the thought expressed by the sentence is true. Without this sign, or without the seriousness of utterance which confers assertive force on an uttered sentence, the expression only expresses a thought, without saying that this thought is true.

A thought is thus defined as the *sense* of a sentence. Now in his last years Frege came to distinguish between the *sense* that a sentence expresses and its *content, Inhalt*, although earlier he had identified them. He came to see that the forms of language do not always enable us to express thoughts exactly or to make a precise identification of the thought expressed by a given sentence. Not every thought can be precisely expressed, and not every sentence precisely expresses some thought. There are several reasons for this. First, language serves not only to express definite thoughts, but also to express feelings and emotions, or to give vent to the workings of the imagination. 'It makes no difference to the thought, whether I use the word Horse or Steed or Carthorse or Mare. The assertive force does not extend over that in which these words differ' ('The Thought', p. 295). Because there is an essential connection between assertion and the truth-values, such that only what is true can be asserted, these emotional and imaginative components though expressible in some sense cannot be asserted. Second, language is filled with metaphorical and figurative expressions, and therefore intrinsically subject to the defects that poetry and fiction possess as modes of expression in comparison with the sober, direct language of science. Science cannot avoid such expressions, but they should only be used in trying to approach a precise thought by means of guesswork (ibid., p. 295; see 'On Concept and Object', p. 43). Third, language contains many expressions which are simply aids to the mutual understanding and communication between speaker and hearer, e.g. words like 'but' and 'although', whose peculiar content as conjunctions cannot be reproduced distinctively in a logical symbolism

(*Begriffsschrift*, p. 10; 'On Sense and Reference', pp. 73-4) but which 'illuminate (a clause) in a peculiar fashion', or 'place it in a (certain) light'. The grammatical distinction between subject and predicate, too, merely serves to arrange in order of intended importance the elements of a speaker's communication (*Begriffsschrift*, p. 3). Further, devices such as stressing of particular words and syllables, peculiarities of intonation and possibilities of altering normal word-order all play similar parts. Sometimes, therefore, the thought expressed may 'go beyond' the actual content of the sentence; conversely, sometimes the content may go beyond the thought expressed. In the former case we need more than just understanding of the words in order to grasp the complete thought. We need knowledge, for instance, of the conditions in which the words are uttered, including information about the speaker's personal idiom, his beliefs and the facts of the situation. The latter case typically occurs when the speaker stresses part of the sentence in order to convey his meaning more accurately to the hearer. The stressing does not affect the actual thought expressed by the sentence, but it may confer more *content*, *Inhalt*, upon the sentence. And perhaps a sentence with more *Inhalt* may be described as more *inhaltlich*, meaningful. Stress makes a sentence more meaningful without affecting its meaning.

The sense of a sentence is a thought. In the *Grundgesetze* Frege says that it is the thought that the conditions in which the expression refers to the truth are fulfilled, where it is taken as already laid down what these conditions are (i, 32). This goes some way to explain why the truth-value attaches to the thought rather than to the actual sentence. But it may seem to contradict the earlier distinction drawn by Frege between grasping the sense of a sentence and judging it to be true or false. This is not the case. The conditions in which the sentence '*p*' is true are simply that *p*; so that the sense of '*p*' will be the thought that these conditions are fulfilled, i.e. the thought that *p*. Grasping a thought is merely understanding what must be the case for it to be true; it is not knowing that it is true. Frege distinguishes its being laid down what the truth-conditions of a particular sentence are from these truth-conditions actually being fulfilled. It may seem that he assimilates grasping the sense of a sentence to grasping that its truth-conditions are fulfilled, but there is a subtle distinction still to be drawn. Grasping the sense of 'Caesar is dead' is not simply understanding the thought that 'Caesar is dead' if and only if Caesar is dead; it is understanding the thought that Caesar is dead; and we could not grasp the

9

former without grasping the latter. But the thought that Caesar is dead is identical with the thought that it is true that Caesar is dead. Here lies the possibility of confusion, and here the further distinction must be drawn. For the truth-value of the thought itself is identical with the truth-value of the thought that this given thought is true. Therefore, just as we must distinguish between grasping the thought that Caesar is dead and judging this to be true, so also we must distinguish between grasping the thought that it is true that Caesar is dead and judging this to be true. Understanding what 'It is true that Caesar is dead' means is not understanding that Caesar is dead; but it is understanding what 'Caesar is dead' means.

This explains why Frege said that the sense of every complete sentence was either true or false, i.e. why he takes thoughts as what are either true or false ('The Thought', p. 291), although he does not offer this as a definition of the notion of *thought*. In order to get his meaning still clearer we must turn to his theory of negation.

'Of the two thoughts: *A*, and the negation of *A*: there is always one and only one that is true. Likewise, of the two thoughts: the negation of *A*, and the negation of the negation of *A*: there is always one and only one that is true . . . Thus of the two thoughts: *A*, and the negation of the negation of *A*: either both are true, or neither is' ('Negation', pp. 134 f.).

Negation is a function of thoughts. It is therefore a possible component of the senses or contents of sentences, and neither part of sentences nor part of the acts of asserting or judging. The act of denial is the opposite of the act of assertion; positive sentences can be denied, and negated sentences can be asserted. Negation has nothing to do with denial, therefore, except that when a sentence may be asserted the corresponding negative sentence may be denied. Just as the act of asserting a sentence implies belief in its truth, so the act of denial implies belief in its falsehood; and as we shall see a sentence is false if and only if the corresponding negative sentence is true. Negation does not affect the act of judgement, i.e. recognition of truth, either. This is one and the same act, whether the sentence be positive or negative ('Negation', p. 129).

Negation should not be identified with negative expressions such as 'not', 'nothing' and so forth, nor with so-called negative terms such as 'nonsense', 'not red' and possibly 'immortal'. Rather, negation is part of what is expressed by sentences containing such terms. Even this is not quite adequate. If we take two sentences such that one differs from the other only in containing a negative expression or negative term corresponding to a positive term, then we can say that one of these is negative and the other positive or affirmative. This formulation is inaccurate, since it fails to deal satisfactorily with sentences containing words like 'every' and 'some'. But it will cover sentences such as 'Caesar is dead', and this will do to illustrate Frege's point. Frege assumes, as we have seen above, that every thought has a negation; the relation of negation to thoughts is governed by the laws of Excluded Middle and Contradiction. Now the relation between a thought and its negation is that the one is true if and only if the other is false. The expressions for a pair of such thoughts will be two sentences of the forms '*p*' and 'not-*p*'. Now the thought expressed by '*p*' is the thought that the truth-conditions of '*p*' are fulfilled; so that 'not-*p*' will express the thought that the truth-conditions for 'not-*p*' are fulfilled. 'Caesar is not dead' expresses the thought that the conditions in which 'Caesar is not dead' is true are fulfilled. And Frege takes this to be the thought that the conditions in which 'Caesar is dead' is false are fulfilled. For, as he frequently says, there are only two truth-values, true and false, and false in his view is identical with not-true and true with not-false. The relation between two opposite thoughts: *p* and not-*p*: is simply that one is true if and only if the other is false and false if and only if the other is true, and that one must be true and the other false. The conditions for the truth of one are identical with the conditions for the falsity of the other, and the conditions for the falsity of the first identical with the conditions for the truth of the second.

In view of the close relation between negation and falsity, the two are often confused. For if '*p*' expresses a true thought, then 'not-*p*' will at the same time express a negative thought and a false one. But there are two clear distinctions. First, it is obvious that sometimes it is the negative of a pair of thoughts which is the true one, e.g. the thought: Caesar is not alive. Second, the negative-positive dichotomy is arbitrary in a way that the true-false dichotomy is not arbitrary. As Frege says, there are no criteria in general for telling which of a pair of opposite sentences is the negative and which the positive. Even the example I gave above is not clear: Caesar is not alive; I said that this was a negative sentence, but it seems to be equivalent to: Caesar is dead, and why should this not be called a positive sentence? On the other hand, there are criteria for telling which of such a pair is the true and which the false thought. In view of this lack of criteria it may seem plausible to abolish the negative-positive distinction altogether and reduce it to the distinction between falsity and truth and the distinction between sentences of the forms '*p*' and 'not-*p*'. But this would be a mistake. For it would prevent us explaining the distinction between a pair of opposite thoughts when neither truth-value was known. And generally, since we must know the sense of a sentence before we can know its truth-value, we should not be able to say how the senses of '*p*' and 'not-*p*' differed, if we did not possess the negative-positive distinction.

(v)

Frege calls the senses of certain sentences *thoughts*, and I have used the term as if it expressed something familiar. In one way it does. The *thought* that *p* is simply *what* is thought, the *content* of thinking, when it is thought that *p*. But since Frege put a strong interpretation on these italicised terms, it is necessary to be more specific. His terminology is unfamiliar, and it may therefore be helpful to take his 'thought' as equivalent to the 'proposition' of Moore and Russell. There are two points to be borne in mind, however. First, Frege sometimes used the word *Satz*, translated as 'proposition', without this meaning, e.g. in the *Grundlagen* when his mature distinctions had not yet been worked out. And second, the terminology of 'thoughts' brings out the relation between these entities and the psychological processes of *thinking*; in this respect, the terminology of 'propositions' falls down.

I have said that the later theory of sense and reference serves in part to replace an earlier theory of expressions and their *contents*. Now a serious problem arises from this. In his earlier terminology Frege often drew a contrast between form and content, and spoke of the content of expressions as 'conceptual'. In the *Begriffsschrift* he cites two sentences, saying that they agree pretty well in sense; and he then continues, 'I call the part of the content that is the same in both the conceptual content' (p. 3). And he calls thoughts, at this early period, the contents of judgement. The analysis into function and argument, for example, is said to concern our way of looking at the conceptual content and not this content itself. Ordinarily it is quite arbitrary what function-argument analysis is applied to a given conceptual content. In the *Grundlagen* too he describes his method as one of taking a given *content* of judgement and dividing it up into different sets of component *concepts*. Further, his early theory of identity judgements contains the view that the symbol of equality '=' expresses the fact that two signs have the same conceptual content, 'so that *A* can always be replaced by *B* and conversely'. It is clear from this that Frege in these early works confused what he later distinguished as an expression's sense and its reference; and that sometimes, as in the last case cited, he takes as the conceptual content of a symbol what he later called its *reference*, but more often, and particularly when the symbol in question is a sentence, he takes its *sense* as its conceptual content. The problem that arises from this is what relation Frege conceived to hold between the *thought* contained in a sentence as its *sense*, and the *concepts* referred to by the expressions of the sentence. Surely it is natural to think that a thought can be composed of concepts, and Frege's own talk of conceptual thinking supports this? And then concepts may well appear more like the senses of certain expressions than their references; alternatively, thoughts might plausibly be construed not as the senses but as the *references* of sentences, just as objects are the references of names and concepts the references of predicative expressions. This is helped by the way Frege discusses thoughts, so that it often seems simpler to construe thoughts as *objects* of thinking, as Russell at first construed propositions. But this is not how Frege relates thoughts and concepts. This relation will be discussed in the next chapter.

In 'The Thought' Frege argues at length that thoughts are objective entities. This implies, for instance, that they are not essentially parts of psychological events or acts, and so are not private and thus subjective. They are independent of our faculties of sensation, perception and imagination, but dependent on the faculty of reason. Sentences and thoughts about thoughts are capable of objective truth and falsity. Thoughts cannot be subjective ideas or presentations, *Vorstellungen*, since if this were the case my thought of Pythagoras' Theorem might differ from your thought of the same theorem, and then the one might be true while the other was false. 'The words True and False . . . could be applicable only in the sphere of my consciousness if they were not supposed to be concerned with something of which I was not the bearer, but were somehow appointed to characterise the content of my consciousness' (p. 301). If truth-values were subjective there could be no dispute about truth and therefore no 'science'; Frege takes this to be an absurd conclusion.

Using a metaphor, we may therefore say that there exists a third realm besides the subjective realm of psychological phenomena and the objective realm of actual physical phenomena. Thoughts 'obviously' do not belong to this external world, to such external entities. Frege thinks Idealism must concede this point directly. Thoughts belong to this third realm (p. 302). Like ideas they are not sensible objects; like external things they are not possessed privately and do not depend for their being upon anyone's consciousness of them. If different people utter the same sentence assertively, then what is subjective is merely the act of assertion. The thought that this 'same sentence' expresses is really one and the same, and it is this that is common to the different acts of assertion. It is this that guarantees the possibility of science and communication, and even according to Frege of thought itself (p. 307).

A further factor in the objectivity of thoughts is that they have truth-values, and these truth-values are objective. A thought is 'true independently of whether anyone takes it to be true . . . It is not true for the first time when it is discovered, but is like a planet, which, already before anyone has seen it, has been in interaction with other planets . . . When one apprehends or thinks a thought, one does not create it, but only comes to stand in a certain relation . . . to *what has already existed beforehand*' (p. 302; my italics). Later in the same essay he adds that 'the work of science does not consist of creation but of the discovery of true thoughts' (p. 307). Moreover, 'what I recognise as true, I judge to be true quite independently of my recognition of its truth, and of my thinking about it'. At one point he even defines a true thought as a *fact* (p. 307). The pressure generated by such language to construe thoughts as objects of thinking is very strong. It must be resisted; we must realise that there are not just two types of objective entity, namely objects and concepts, but three, objects, concepts and senses. The objectivity of senses must not be explained away as the objectivity of concepts or of objects of a certain kind.

Another factor in the objectivity of thoughts is that every thought must be capable of being recognised as the same thought again as some previously identified thought. Frege stresses this point. It may be seen as an indirect consequence of the quite general requirement that, if we use a symbol to signify an object, we must have some criterion for deciding in all cases whether the object signified by another symbol is identical with the first object or not. We must have some criterion for deciding whether any two sentences express the same thought or not. For Frege takes it that even here the same sense, i.e. the same thought, can be expressed in different ways, and can be recognised as what is common to these different expressions. 'If all transformation of the expression were forbidden on the plea that this would alter the content as well, logic would simply be crippled; for the task of logic can hardly be performed without trying to recognise the thought in its manifold guises' ('On Concept and Object', p. 46, footnote). And this would also make definition impossible in many cases. For often the problem of defining the sense of a sentence, i.e. a thought, is simply the problem of reproducing the content of the sentence in other words.

Why should thoughts not be construed now as objects of a certain kind; surely the terminological evidence is piling up? The answer will emerge fully in the next chapter. It is, briefly, that because Frege treats truth and falsity as objects, he cannot also treat thoughts as objects. Truth and falsity are the objects of reference of sentences; sentences are their names. Thoughts, on the other hand, are the senses of sentences. Sentences, and expressions in general, do not stand for or signify their senses, but as Frege says they rather express them. And senses are not objects. It is true that expressions of the form 'the sense of "Caesar"' and 'the sense of "Caesar is dead"' are proper names, and that therefore they stand for objects of some kind. This is exactly parallel to the case of expressions like 'the concept *Horse*'. And it is no more proved by the existence of expressions of the former kind that senses are themselves those objects than it is proved by expressions of the latter kind that concepts themselves are these objects. It is also true that in certain peculiar cases expressions *refer* not to the objects they usually refer to, but to their usual *senses*. But this too does not prove that senses are objects, since such expressions have 'indirect reference' or are 'used indirectly' ('On Sense and Reference', p. 59).

Not every expression like a sentence contains a thought. Besides hypotheticals, questions and imperatives, there are two other kinds of expression to which the simple analysis of thought as sense does not apply ('On Sense and Reference', pp. 58-9 and 65-78). The first is the kind just mentioned, where the expression does not have its usual reference but refers to what is usually its sense. This indirect reference to an expression's sense occurs typically in indirect speech, *oratio obliqua*. Here the subordinate clause introduced by the word 'that' refers not to a truth-value but to a thought. Its sense is therefore not the sense of the words themselves, but rather the sense of the words 'the thought that . . .', where the expression for the original thought fills the gap. In the sentence 'He says that Caesar is dead', 'Caesar is dead' does not stand for a truth-value nor express the thought that Caesar is dead. Rather, it stands for the thought that Caesar is dead, and its sense is the sense of the words 'the thought that Caesar is dead'. Similar contexts are clauses dependent on verbs like 'seem that', 'think that', 'hope that', 'regret that' and 'remember that'. Another similar kind of expression is exemplified by the sentence '*A* inferred from the fact that *p* that *q*'. Final clauses, clauses after verbs of command and clauses after verbs of request are also, says Frege, further contexts of the same general nature.

The second kind of expression for which the simple identification of thought contained and sense expressed is inadequate comes in two fairly distinct species. First, we sometimes associate 'subsidiary thoughts', *Nebengedanken*, with a sentence, although these thoughts are not actually expressed in the words of the sentence. 'And since the subsidiary thought appears to be connected with our words (in accordance with psychological laws), . . . almost like the main thought itself, we want it also to be expressed. The sense of the sentence is thereby enriched, and it may well happen that we have more simple thoughts than clauses . . . It may be doubtful whether the subsidiary thought belongs to the sense of the sentence or only accompanies it. This may be important for the question whether an assertion is a lie, or an oath a perjury' ('On Sense and Reference', p. 75). Second, sometimes 'the clause expresses more through its connection with another than it does in isolation'. Frege's example is this. We must analyse the sentence 'Because ice is less dense than water, it floats on water' into three, not two, thoughts; (1) Ice is less dense than water, (2) If anything is less dense than water, it floats on water, and (3) Ice floats on water. Neither (1) and (2) without (3), nor (2) and (3) without (1) would be sufficient. Here, in fact, the clause 'Because ice floats on water' expresses not only thought (1) but also part of thought (2); therefore we must say that the clause 'it floats on water' expresses not only thought (3) but also the remaining part of thought (2). And of course this clause only expresses a definite thought at all in virtue of being attached to the former clause. Another example of the same context would be given by the sentence '*A* wrongly thinks that *p*'. Here two distinct thoughts are expressed, namely that *A* thinks that *p*, and that not-*p*.

(vi)

It remains to say a little about the activity of *thinking* and how thoughts are related to this activity. Frege took thinking to be indefinable, and spoke of it in metaphorical terms ('The Thought', p. 307); nevertheless it can be distinguished from some related mental activities. Earlier we distinguished *asserting* a thought to be true, *recognising* a thought to be true and *apprehending* a thought, which Frege also calls comprehension or the grasping of a sense. It is this last that is properly called 'thinking'. Thinking might also be confused with the activity of *inferring*; but this is, rather, the act of moving from one thought to another. It is important, while on this point, to distinguish thinking from *calculating*. Frege treats this as an external activity, for instance as the writing of various sets of figures in order is an external activity; but it is not the being external that is essential. The point is rather that true thinking is not simply the manipulation of symbols irrespective of their content according to certain rules, and it does not make any difference whether this is done on paper or in one's head. This theory of thinking disregards the thought-process, *Denkprozess*. What is meant by calling calculation an external activity is that it is not essentially an internal activity, since it can actually be done externally. But thinking, in Frege's view, cannot be performed externally, but can only be *expressed* externally; what is external can never be more than the expression of thinking. It cannot replace it. (See *Grundlagen*, pp. III–IV; *Grundgesetze*, ii, 101–102).

Thinking must equally be distinguished from *intuition*. In part this results from a distinction between the possible objects of thought and of intuition. For Frege seems to construe intuition, *Anschauung*, as something very closely related to imagination and perception, the having of ideas or sensations. This contrast between thinking and intuition is sometimes drawn as the contrast between conceptual thought and intuition; for Frege wishes, it seems, to say that concepts cannot possibly be the objects of intuition. In the Introduction to the *Grundlagen* he describes thinking as 'in essentials the same everywhere . . . such differences as there are consist only in this, that the thought is more pure or less pure . . . and further to some extent too in the finer or coarser structure of the concepts involved'. Concepts and intuitions in the wide sense, i.e. mental presentations, are explicitly contrasted (ibid., p. 37, note 1); conceptual thinking is also contrasted with intuition roughly as the ability to make assumptions and inferences is contrasted with the ability to have mental pictures. Finally, it is only because in some way thinking is essentially conceptual that it is possible to confuse the laws of logic with the psychological laws of thinking. For in Frege's view the laws of logic certainly treat of concepts among other things. 'We have only to try denying one of (the fundamental propositions of the science of number), and complete confusion ensues. Even to think at all seems no longer possible . . . The truths of arithmetic govern all that is numerable. This is the widest domain of all; for to it belongs not only the *actual*, not only the *intuitable*, but everything *thinkable*. Should not the laws of number, then, be connected very intimately with the laws of thought?' (*Grundlagen*, p. 21). And he characterises the task of mathematics in the words 'the proper object of reason is reason' (ibid., p. 115).

SOURCES FOR CHAPTER EIGHT

'The Thought'; *Begriffsschrift*, sections 2–4; 'On Sense and Reference'.

CHAPTER NINE

TRUTH AND MEANING

THE crucial step in Frege's whole theory of meaning appears to be his identification of a sentence's truth or falsity with its reference or value. There are three distinct steps in this identification. First, sentences are taken as referring expressions, as expressions that refer to certain objects. Second, truth and falsity are construed not as predicates of sentences, i.e. as concepts, but as objects of a peculiar type. Third, sentences are so analysed by means of the application of the technique of function, argument and value, that the value signified by a complete sentence can be identified with its truth or falsity. I shall try, therefore, to show how Frege connects his sense-reference theory of expressions with his theory of concepts as functions, and how he makes these two distinct theories support one another.

Frege's process of identification seems to have begun with the application of the function theory to sentences and their predicates. For it is part of this that a complete sentence must be taken as the sign for something. It must be construed as the sign that signifies some object. 'A statement (*Behauptungssatz*) contains no empty place, and therefore we must regard what it stands for as an object' ('Function and Concept', p. 32). Now it seems clear that Frege construed signifying and standing for on the model of naming, so that to say something is a sign that signifies an object is to say that it is a name of that object. Therefore applying the notion of value of a function to complete sentences amounts to saying that they are names of objects of some kind. In order to get the sense-reference theory fully working, it is now necessary to show that there is something we can take as the sense of a sentence, and that this is not the same as its reference. Frege identifies the sense of a sentence with the thought it expresses. Besides the natural help given by the ambiguities of the root *sinn-* and by the existence of idioms in German that are similar to idioms of the word 'sense', Frege gives an explicit argument in favour of this identification.

This argument rests on a principle which plays a very important part in determining the application of the sense-reference theory to sentences, namely the principle that the sense or reference of a whole expression is determined by and determined only by the senses or references, respectively, of its component expressions. Now it is necessary, in order for this principle to apply to sentences, that they should be construed as expressions to which this principle is primarily applicable, i.e. complex names such as 'The King of France'. The process can go in either of two ways. Either the analogy with names can be brought in simultaneously with the analogy with functional expressions, on the ground that completed functional expressions are already thought of as names of some kind. Or the analogy with names can be brought in with the application of the sense-reference theory, on the ground that this theory is derived from and primarily applicable to proper names. There seem to be three distinct elements compounded in this principle. First, it is assumed that all complete expressions, i.e. all expressions that contain only referring expressions and not expressions whose function is rather to indicate, are themselves as a whole referring. Second, it is assumed that if all the components of a complex expression refer, then the whole expression must itself refer as a whole; and conversely, that if a complex refers as a whole then all its components must also refer individually. Third, it is assumed that the reference of components is irrelevant to the sense of the whole, and that the sense of components is irrelevant to the reference of the whole. The principle as I have expounded it is not identical with, and does not entail, the principle later abandoned by Frege that the references of components are themselves components of the reference of the whole, and that the senses of components are components of the sense of the whole. This latter doctrine can be abandoned without abandoning the principle expounded.

The explicit argument for identifying sense and thought is this. If we replace a word in a given sentence by another word having the same reference but a different sense, our replacement cannot affect the reference of the whole but must affect the sense. This is derived directly from Frege's interpretation of the axiom of the Identity of Indiscernibles. If two different signs both signify the same object, then in normal contexts we may use either without affecting the truth of the whole. Frege argues, then, that such a replacement is discovered to affect the thought expressed by the sentence, but not to affect its truth or falsity. Therefore the thought expressed by the sentence can be identified with its sense.

Frege also has an argument to show that the sense as so located, i.e. as identified with the thought expressed, must be distinguished from what his theory calls 'reference'. This shows that in attributing sense to a sentence we are simply applying part of the complete sense-reference theory, and that we are therefore justified in applying the rest of the theory. If we consider, for instance, the two equations '$2^4=4^2$' and '$4.4=4^2$', we are led perhaps to ask in what respect they are alike, or what they have in common; for it is clear that they express different thoughts, i.e. have different senses. The difference between them is that where one contains the expression '2^4' the other contains the expression '4.4', which is to say that the two equations differ by containing two components with different senses but the same reference. Applying the general principle described above, Frege concludes that this shows the reference of the two equations to be the same; what they have in common is the same object of reference. And this is enough to show that the sense and reference of sentences must be kept sharply distinct. A further implicit argument can be derived very simply from the principle stated above. Since the logical components of a sentence are referring expressions, it follows that the whole they compose is itself referring. But this argument is dangerous, since it uses the fact that predicative expressions refer as a premiss. Frege's line of thought can be exposed more clearly if we argue, rather, from the fact that sentences refer to the fact that predicative expressions refer.

(ii)

Frege now identifies the 'reference' of a complete sentence, whose existence only has been demonstrated by the kind of argument given above, with the sentence's truth, if it is true, or falsity, if it is false. This is probably the most important single step in the whole complex structure of theories. There seem to be two main arguments that Frege relies upon in making this identification.

The first is given very briefly in 'Function and Concept', and can be reconstructed quite easily from Frege's words. The question has arisen in this essay of treating complete algebraic equations as functional expressions. What can be their *values*? Now we can say two things. We can say first that when such equations are 'completed' by substituting definite numerals for the x's and y's we get equations that are either true or false. If the analogy with functions is to be satisfactory, such equations and indeed sentences too must refer to something, namely the value for the functional equation corresponding to the argument whose sign was substituted. Frege omits a central step. There must be some essential relation between a sentence and its truth-value; there must be essential relations between a sentence, the thought it contains and its truth or falsity. Alternatively we can say that for Frege the proposition ' "*p*" is true' must either be predicative or identificatory. But since truth is not a concept, it must be an object. This means that the only possible essential relation between a sentence and its truth is the relation of a sign to what it signifies, namely the referential or naming-relation. Therefore a sentence must be said to refer to, *bedeuten*, its truth-value. In terms of the analogy with functions its truth-value is the value signified by the complete sentence, and this consists of a functional part, i.e. the predicative expression, completed by a proper name.

The second argument relies more closely on the principles quoted earlier ('On Sense and Reference', pp. 62 f.). Frege first shows how we may construe the contained thought as the 'sense' of a sentence. Then he asks the obvious question, whether this identification commits us to looking for some reference also. For perhaps sentences are not referring expressions at all. Indeed, he begins his proof by admitting that certain types of sentences are not referring, namely fictional sentences, and other sentences containing non-referring names. He does not however now rely directly and solely on assimilating sentences to complex referential expressions, whose referring is guaranteed by their components' having references. He argues, instead, that considering such non-referring sentences, we see that the attempt to ascribe a truth-value amounts to the attempt to ascribe a reference to their non-referring names. Roughly, finding out whether a sentence is true or false involves in such cases finding out what object it is about. When we are not interested in the question of a sentence's truth we need not and often do not bother about the actual references of its components. Frege distinguishes two attitudes, which he calls the aesthetic and the scientific. For he is clear that it is quite proper and common to be interested in sentences without being concerned about their truth-values. But it is precisely when we move from considering the question of the thought contained or expressed to considering the question of the truth of the sentence, that we turn to considering the hitherto ignored references of the components of the sentence. Moreover, we turn to considering these references from a previous consideration of the sense of the sentence and its components. This argument, Frege concludes, justifies us in identifying the reference of a sentence with its truth-value. Now it is clearly not a logically compelling argument;

it is merely persuasive, and to be accepted only together with the kind of argument sketched in the first section of this chapter. For it does not prove that the sentence as a whole has any reference. All it shows is that the questions of the truth of a sentence and of the references of its components are identical or at least essentially connected.

The first argument presupposed that truth is an object since it cannot be a concept. 'Is true' is not predicative but rather identificatory. Frege gives two arguments in favour of such a view. The first occurs in 'On Sense and Reference'. Because we can construct sentences of the form 'The thought that p is true', we may be tempted to think that the relation of truth to thought is that of predicate to subject. This was precisely Frege's early view in the *Begriffsschrift*, where he says that any proposition 'p' can be rewritten in the form 'p's being the case *is a fact*'. 'The subject contains the whole content, and the only purpose of the predicate is to present this in the form of a judgement. Such a language would have only a single predicate for all judgements, 'is a fact' ' (p. 3). But he came to see that the contents of the sentences 'p' and 'The thought that p is true' are identical. 'p' and 'It is true that p' have the same sense, and this shows that 'It is true that' cannot function as a predicate. If it were predicative, something would be added by adding to the 'p'. Further, if it was predicative then even adding it to 'p' would not help us to move away from the 'level of thoughts', *der Stufe der Gedanken*, to the level of references, the objective ('On Sense and Reference', p. 64). Logical predicates are parts of thoughts. 'By combining subject and predicate one reaches only a thought, never passes from sense to reference, never from a thought to its truth-value' (loc. cit.). Similarly in 'The Thought' he shows that it is the indicative form of the verb which combines the assertedness of the thought with the express recognition of its truth. The words 'It is true that . . .' do nothing to give a sentence assertoric force that did not previously possess it.

Besides these arguments there is a play upon the word 'value' which is not of itself an argument, but rather indicates one of those connections in the language which seem to have directed Frege's thought so often. He says during his comparison of fictional or metaphorical and literal sentences that 'The thought *loses value for us* as soon as we recognise that the reference of one of its parts is missing', *Der Gedanke verliert für uns an Wert* . . . ('On Sense and Reference', p. 63; my italics). But the same word is also used in the general theory of functions to denote the object signified by a completed functional expression;

therefore to say a thought has no value may be taken to mean that there is no such object. This is not a one-track play of terms, since precisely the same ambiguity affects the word *Bedeutung*, significance, and Frege's point and possible punning misinterpretation could be put with this word just as well. 'The thought *loses significance for us* as soon as we realise that the *reference* of one of its parts is missing'. Thoughts can perfectly well be said to have value or significance; Frege believed that only true and false thoughts were significant for science; he also construed 'value' and 'significance' to denote certain objects signified by expressions and their senses. Therefore in the case of thoughts 'being significant' means both being true or false and signifying some object. And it is easy to identify these.

(iii)

It is disagreeable that truth and falsity should be called objects, even logical objects. Nevertheless it should by now be clear what this means. It must be construed in the context of Frege's general theory of functions and concepts, and the application of this theory to sentences can be taken simply as expressing the possibility of analysing sentences and thoughts by the techniques of the general theory of functions. It is not so much calling truth and falsity objects that is peculiar, as identifying these objects with the references of sentences. But we must still be clear how Frege understands the expression 'truth-value of a sentence'. If a sentence 'p' is true, then the truth-value of 'p' is the fact that 'p' is true, i.e. the fact that p. If 'p' is false, the truth-value of 'p' is the fact that not-p. Instead of writing 'It is true that . . . .' we can write 'It is a fact that . . .'. This shows in a way that there is no independent problem of truth; the problem is rather a problem about the expression 'it is a fact that', i.e. the problem of assertion.

Why people often think it strange and disagreeable to call truth and falsity 'objects' is that in the context of the sense-reference theory they come to seem objects of a most peculiar kind. There are only two of their type, they are in some way mutually exclusive and together inclusive, and they are signified by all assertible sentences. 'All true sentences have the same reference . . . in the reference of the sentence, all that is specific is obliterated . . . One might also say that judgements are distinctions of parts within truth-values. Such distinction occurs by a return to the thought. To every sense belonging to a truth-value, there would correspond its own manner of analysis' ('On Sense and

Reference', p. 65). This way of talking is strange, since it applies very literally the notion that sentences are proper names of truth-values.

But it need not be made stranger than it is. One point is simply this. When we ask about a sentence whether it is true or false, we are not asking about anything peculiar to and dependent on its being the particular sentence it is. 'True' is not ambiguous between ' "p" is true' and ' "q" is true'. This point is similar to another more familiar point. To say 'it is true that' cannot be to give a private characterisation. There cannot be a true 'p' in my mind and a false 'p' in yours. Similarly, if 'p' and 'q' are both true, then they cannot be true in a different sense, though they can be true in different ways. What makes each true, i.e. some quite general relation between the senses of the sentences and particular facts in the world, is the same for each. 'Is true' may be thought of as analogous to a functional sign such as 'x^2'. For 'multiplied by itself' sometimes comes to 'multiplied by two' and sometimes to 'multiplied by three', and what it comes to depends on the argument of this function. Similarly 'is true' sometimes comes to p's being the case, sometimes to q's being the case, and what it comes to in any particular instance depends on what proposition, i.e. thought, is taken as its 'argument'. In Frege's terms, 'is identical with the truth' is a one-place predicate taking thoughts as its arguments; every true thought satisfies this function in a distinctive way, i.e. through a distinct sense.

Both points relate to the characteristic objectivity of the truth-values. Saying that truth and falsity are objective is in the first place saying that the question of a sentence's truth-value is distinct from all questions as to its psychological relations, e.g. its being believed or its being justifiably asserted. The fact that you or I utter or believe that p can have no relevance to the question of p's truth. In the second place, questions of truth and falsity are themselves factual questions. This is simply to say that the notions of truth and falsity apply to the questions whether a given thought is true or false. To say that the truth of 'p' is objective is partly to say that it is objectively true that p, and this is to say that it is true that it is true that p. The objectivity characteristic of truth and falsity is in this way the characteristic each term possesses of being indefinitely applicable in a familiar way. If 'p' is true, we can say 'It is true that p' is true, and 'It is true that it is true that p' is true, and so on. At each stage the questions of truth and falsity arise, arise in precisely the same way, and are to be answered in precisely the same way.

This helps to show why Frege does not try to give a helpful definition of truth and falsity. It seems that so far we have been operating within a tight circle of closely related notions, so that for instance in pointing out that 'It is true that' and 'It is a fact that' are interchangeable no illumination is given. And if we can replace 'It is true that p' by simply 'p' and 'It is false that p' by simply 'not-p', then these notions appear to be empty. The denial that truth is a predicate takes on another significance here. For it now appears that the peculiar predicate of thoughts 'is identical with the truth' is an empty predicate. In the *Grundgesetze* Frege treats as a *function* what he had formerly called the 'content-stroke'; '$- \Delta$ is the True if Δ is the True, and the False if Δ is not the True' (i, 5). This function-sign may be read as 'is identical with the truth'. And if '$-p$' stands for the truth, then 'p' stands for the truth, i.e. is true; if '$-q$' does not stand for the truth it stands for the false, and then 'q' does not stand for the truth, i.e. either is false or possesses neither truth-value.

Frege actually argues that truth is indefinable ('The Thought', p. 291). For any definition of truth would itself involve the notion it was intended to define. Frege firmly believed that definitions were truths; therefore of any attempted definition of truth we can always ask 'Is this definition true or false?' This method will remind readers of Moore's method of showing the impossibility of defining goodness. Another objection to defining truth is that unless one understood what a definition was, one could not grasp what had been achieved; but one cannot understand what a definition is unless one already possesses the notion of truth, among others. Therefore one could not understand any definition of truth unless one already possessed the notion of truth; so that any definition of truth would be either useless or unnecessary. Frege says that if we want something like a definition, there is a possible kind of explanation. For 'the meaning of the word "true" is explained by the laws of truth' ('The Thought', p. 290). The laws of truth are, in the first place, the fundamental axioms of logic, and in the second place the derived theorems. The notion of truth is 'explained' by the law of excluded middle, the law of contradiction and the axiom of the identity of indiscernibles, i.e. the law that substitution of signs for identical objects does not affect truth-values. But these fundamental laws are nowhere explained or justified.

A certain insight into the absence of definitions can be gained, perhaps, by looking at the traditional term 'laws of thought'. Frege certainly began by accepting the view that these fundamental laws stated the conditions under which thought was possible. And since his position in the *Grundlagen* is largely Kantian, we may give a Kantian sense to this view. The fundamental laws of logic state the necessary conditions under which objective thought, i.e. thought concerning objects and concepts, is possible. They state the necessary conditions to which objects and concepts must be thought to conform. Therefore it seems that they might be described not so much as laws of truth as 'laws of objectivity'.

(iv)

The immediate objection to Frege's theory of truth is its apparent incompleteness. It does not seem to account for the fact that truth and falsehood are in part dependent on actual states of affairs, on how things in the world are. I shall explore such objections in section (v) below. Meanwhile I shall discuss Frege's attitude towards one theory of truth which tries to provide a clear connection between truth-value and fact, namely the correspondence theory. In 'The Thought' Frege explicitly attacks the notion that truth properly belongs not to sentences or thoughts but to *pictures*. This attack has several functions. First, since the picture-theory is one common variety of the correspondence theory of truth, and was that adopted by Wittgenstein in his *Tractatus*, Frege's attack on it destroys one possibility of showing how truth-values are related to facts. Second, since he applies the notion of truth to thoughts, it follows that for him thoughts cannot be any kind of picture, as Wittgenstein made them. Third, it seems that though Frege rejected a picture-theory of truth, he was working towards a picture-theory of meaning; this will be dealt with in Chapter 10.

Frege agrees that we do sometimes call pictures 'true'. But for this it is necessary that the picture should be a representation of something, and should contain an intention that it represent this thing. A picture-like object which either lacks all human intentions or is executed without any intention of representation cannot be called either true or false. A picture is called 'true' with respect to the intention that it should correspond to its subject in some way. Now when we consider this, we see that some more fundamental notion of truth is involved. For some notion of truth applies to the judgement that a picture corresponds with a given situation; and this cannot be in turn a kind of picture-truth or correspondence, but a kind of truth appropriate to sentences. This argument may seem alright as far as it goes. But if sentences were pictures of some kind, then all that the argument would show would be that the problem of picture-truth in general is reducible to the particular problem of the truth of sentence-pictures. However it is easy to see a reason for distinguishing sentences from pictures. In considering the 'truth' of a picture one need compare with the situation represented only the picture itself. One must also know what the painter's intentions of representation were, but when this is known the intentions play no further part. On the other hand in considering the truth-value of a sentence matters are quite different. We cannot decide the question of a sentence's truth merely by inspecting it and comparing it with some fact. For the sentence itself does not show us which fact to compare it with. Here we have to compare not so much the sentence as the thought it is intended to express with the fact; moreover understanding the thought does show us of itself what situation we are to look for.

It is also easy to see two respects in which thoughts cannot be called pictures, on an account such as Frege's. For if thoughts were a kind of mental picture of facts, then on his account of picture-truth we should have to say that the truth of thoughts consisted in their intentionally corresponding with the requisite situations. But this is nonsense. Thoughts are not related to situations in such a way that they would not be so related unless it were our intention that they should be. Thoughts are essentially thoughts that such-and-such, i.e. that a situation of a specific kind obtains. The relation between a thought and the situation it is about is internal and necessary. Moreover, Frege would say that there could be no possible 'correspondence' between thoughts and facts. For two entities to correspond there must be some 'coincidence' between them, and Frege denies any coincidence between reality and the ideal ('The Thought', p. 291).

We might infer that since pictures are 'true' or 'false' with respect to some intention that they should correspond to a given situation, picture truth is identical with the relation of correspondence itself. Frege argues against such an identification. First, 'true' is not a relation-word. This follows from his view that 'is true' is not a predicative expression. Second, to call a picture 'true' is not to say what to compare the picture to in order to discover if it really is true. Third, since the relation of correspondence involves some coincidence, such a view would tend towards the confusion made by Idealism between reality and our ideas. If things and ideas can share some properties, then there would seem no contradiction in the hypothesis that they share all properties.

Fourth, if truth were correspondence, it would have to be either a complete correspondence, in which case we are involved in a full-blooded Berkeleyan Idealism, or a partial correspondence. And in either case the notion of corresponding presupposes the notion of truth.

The distinction between thoughts and mental pictures can in general be inferred from Frege's view that it is not only subjective and private entities that are the possible objects of awareness. Not every object of awareness is a content of the subject's consciousness. Frege is not arguing that there is nothing private and subjective about, e.g. our awareness of physical objects. He would have agreed with the principle of the sense-datum theory, namely that all outer perception is mediated by something private, namely some presentation, *Vorstellung*, which is related to the outer object with being identical with it. He is arguing rather against solipsistic idealism. If the 'outer entity' were itself a content of my consciousness, then it would follow not only that it could not be a content of yours, i.e. perceived by you, but also that it would be senseless to speak of it as an 'outer entity'.

But I can, according to Frege, be an object of awareness to myself. Now either I am the bearer of my ideas or I am just one more idea among others. But if everything is an idea, then nothing can be the bearer of ideas, since no idea can 'bear' another idea. All ideas will exist independently of any bearer. Frege takes this to be self-contradictory, since it is essential to ideas that they be contents of consciousness, i.e. that their existence depend on being 'borne'. He concludes that the self is both a possible object of awareness and something that cannot itself be just a content of consciousness. And if this is the case, then outer entities and thoughts too in their 'third realm' can be taken as objects of awareness without being *ipso facto* just contents of consciousness.

(v)

It may be useful to give at this point a general summary of the apparent objections to Frege's theory of meaning and truth, and to describe what he achieved despite the details of his theory. Much of this has been said earlier, and I shall therefore try to be concise.

There seem to be three main defects in Frege's account of truth. In the first place it is strange to call truth and falsity objects, and our discomfort at this survives the kind of explanation I gave above. For from what Frege says no sharp distinction emerges between these two objects and objects of other and more easily acceptable types. One is led naturally to ask which particular objects truth and falsity are. Now truth sometimes seems to be much the same as 'what is the case'; we might say that The Truth is another name for Reality. The totality of true sentences refers to the total state of the world. If we interpret Frege in this way, then we get some understanding of his notion, and moreover some explanation of the fact that Truth and Falsity are mutually exclusive and mutually inclusive objects. Further, this interpretation would link Frege to Wittgenstein. Wittgenstein said that sentences referred to certain facts, and not to their truth-values; true sentences referred to facts about the world or facts in the world, since the world was composed of facts. This view is usually taken as an attack on Frege's theory of truth as object of reference, but on the interpretation advanced above would be nearer to an expansion of that theory. However this may be, the interpretation of The True as Reality must be rejected simply because no hint of such an interpretation is found in Frege's own writings. Frege's theory of truth therefore fails to satisfy us, since the only plausibility it possesses is given to it by our ordinary understanding of the notions of truth and falsity, and no explanation of these ordinary notions is provided within the theory.

In the second place the theory is incomplete, since not enough is said about the relation of sentences to facts and facts to things and their properties. I do not think much of this objection, however, since the notion of a fact is very obscure, and the idea that facts are somehow in the world and that therefore explaining the relation of true sentences to facts is explaining their relation to the world and actual objects may well be mistaken. I said earlier that Frege mentions facts at one point, namely when he calls true thoughts 'facts'. I said there that this could be taken as a partial definition of the notion of a thought; but it can equally well be taken as a partial definition of the notion of fact. Therefore I am inclined to say that this second objection comes to little, since if a theory explains truth-values by referring to things and properties of things, there is no need for it also to refer to facts. Facts are not another type of object over and above the things they concern.

In the third place the theory of truth depends on an extension of the theory of sense and reference to cover complete sentences, and this extension cannot be defended. We can grant Frege his view that general words refer to concepts without also granting him the view that complete sentences refer as wholes. This objection was earlier put in terms of a distinction between typically referential expressions and typically expressive ones, but can be put independently of this distinction. I tried earlier to show that Frege's arguments do not succeed in identifying the reference of a sentence with its truth-value, and this gives us two possible ways of attack. We can say either that sentences simply do not refer as a whole, and that they are not names of any kind nor even analogous to names, or that although they are referential they do not refer to their truth-values, but, e.g., to the facts they state. Now it may seem that the former, stronger objection can hardly be upheld without the destruction of a large part of Frege's theory, and particularly his analogy between predicates and functions. So this valuable analogy cannot be preserved without also preserving Frege's view that sentences are referring expressions. I do not think this is the case. We can hold that predicates are functions which do not yield 'values' although they take arguments. If this seems to destroy the analogy, there is another way out. The value of the function 'x^2' for the argument 3 is the number 9, i.e. the second power of 3. Now we can adopt a Russellian approach to expressions of the latter type instead of Frege's; we can hold that definite descriptions of this form are not names. Similarly we can say that the value of the function 'x is wise' for the argument Socrates is the being-wise of Socrates, yet refuse to construe 'the being-wise of Socrates' as a kind of name. Therefore I think that we can preserve Frege's analogy between predicates and functions without necessarily preserving his view of sentences as referring expressions.

This objection to Frege's account of truth conveniently leads on to objections to his account of meaning and in particular sense. I have dealt with these above and shall only summarise them again here. First, Frege gives several different explanations of the notion of sense, and it is not at all clear that these explanations coincide, i.e. that it is just one notion that is being explained. Why, for example, should we identify the way a term refers to its bearer with the contribution it makes to a sentence in which it occurs? What are we to make of this identification? Second, there are great difficulties in applying the distinction between reference and sense to proper names and general words. In the case of general words it seems that their reference collapses into their sense; it is difficult to distinguish the two. In the case of proper names, there is a natural reluctance to ascribe any sense at all, and though this can be partly overcome it does appear to point to a real difference of function between names and sentences, which typically do have sense. Third, Frege does not tell us what kind of entities senses may be, and this is made more serious by the fact that they are neither objects nor concepts. And fourth, not enough is made of the dependence of the sense of sentences on their use in discourse, or of the dependence of the sense of a word upon the conditions of our learning and teaching its use in sentences. Frege does admittedly mention factors of discourse, but in such a way that our understanding, communicating and expressing, for instance, still seem to be directed towards certain entities, i.e. senses. It is arguable that the introduction of these entities does nothing to explain such factors of discourse, but instead makes them quite inexplicable and unjustifiable notions.

Although Frege's theories of meaning and truth are open to these objections as well as to others, they are not valueless. On the contrary, they explained a great deal that earlier theories could not explain, and in so doing gave a new impetus to philosophy. Most of what is valuable in Wittgenstein's early work is derived either directly or by opposition from these Fregean theories, and since contemporary philosophy descends largely from the *Tractatus*, Frege may be seen as one of its originators. Frege's achievement may be divided into three parts. First, he explains the relation between a sentence's truth-value and its meaning; second, he explains the relation between a sentence's truth-value and the meaning of the terms it contains; and third, he explains the relation between a sentence's meaning and the meanings of the terms it contains. By 'explains' I mean 'explains, granted the sense-reference theory'.

The truth-value of a sentence is distinct from its meaning, i.e. *sense*; a sentence can have meaning although it is false. We can sometimes know the meaning of a given sentence without knowing whether it is true or false. But the truth-value of a sentence though distinct from is dependent on its sense. If a sentence has no sense then it cannot be either true or false, and conversely if it is either true or false then it must have a sense. In the *Grundgesetze* Frege identifies the sense of a sentence with the thought that the conditions for its truth are fulfilled. It follows that if there are no conditions in which a given sentence would be true then that sentence expresses no thought, i.e. has no sense. Frege did not accept, however, the similar principle that if there are no conditions in which a sentence would not be true then it has no sense, i.e. the view that tautologies are just as senseless as contradictions and for a similar reason. It also follows that if there are conditions in which a given sentence would be true, even though it is in fact false, then it expresses a sense. 'Ulysses was clever' would be true if there had in fact existed a man named 'Ulysses' and satisfying the usual descriptions of Ulysses. And since there is nothing impossible in this supposition, the sentence 'Ulysses was clever' does have a sense. If a sentence could be true or false, we may put it, then it has a sense.

A sentence is true if and only if its predicate is true of its subject, false if and only if its predicate is false of its subject. This basic principle must be extended to apply to sentences not of the form of subject and predicate, e.g. universal, existential and hypothetical sentences. It remains the case that questions of truth-value are simply questions about the applicability of predicates to objects. The truth-value of a sentence, given a certain state of the world, depends completely and solely upon what objects and properties of different levels its terms refer to. The truth-value of 'Socrates is dead', given a certain situation, is determined by the reference of 'Socrates', i.e. what person it names, and of 'is dead', i.e. what property is predicated of this person.

Most important of all, it is primarily complete sentences that have meaning, i.e. sense, and not isolated words or expressions. 'We ought always to keep before our eyes a complete proposition. Only in a proposition have the words really a meaning . . . It is enough if the proposition taken as a whole has a sense; it is this that confers on its parts also their content' (*Grundlagen*, p. 71). These may be the best words Frege ever wrote. A word or isolated expression has a meaning, i.e. sense, if and only if there exist meaningful sentences in which it can occur. Conversely, a sentence is only meaningful if it is composed of expressions which are themselves meaningful, but for this all that is needed is that the expressions should possess definite reference. The sense of a sentence is determined by the references of its component expressions, and determines in turn the senses of these expressions.

My conclusion is that both the analogy between predicates and functions and the distinction between sense and reference are valuable and illuminating, and therefore should not be rejected. There are defects in both which make them unacceptable as they stand, but further distinctions may well clear these up. Frege's theory of meaning and truth was a definite step in the slow progress of philosophy towards accuracy.

SOURCES FOR CHAPTER NINE
'On Sense and Reference'; 'The Thought'.

CHAPTER TEN

LANGUAGE AND SYMBOLISM

ALTHOUGH Frege never expressed his views as explicitly as did Russell and Wittgenstein, he too possessed at least the outlines of a general theory of symbolism. Indeed his theory is remarkably similar to the theories of the *Tractatus* and *The Philosophy of Logical Atomism*. Before trying to give an account of his view of the relation between thought and its symbolic expression, I shall discuss his views on the nature of symbols themselves. I do this largely by means of extending what he says about mathematical notation in his *Grundgesetze* attack on Formalism (see vol. i, sections 86–137; the whole passage is translated). These remarks can easily be generalised to cover the case of linguistic expressions, i.e. sentences and words. And in this way I shall also try to make clearer the distinction between genuine thinking and formalistic calculating, and therefore to cast light on Frege's whole notion of thought.

I shall begin with a brief description of Frege's distinction between *form* and *content*. In the *Grundlagen* he says that 'what is of concern to logic is not the special content of any particular relation, but only the logical form' (p. 83); and he goes on to gloss 'logical form' as the 'general form of a judgement-content'. The general form of a judgement-content which deals with an object *A* is '*A* falls under the concept *F*'. In the *Begriffsschrift* he describes the function of logical symbolism in a slightly different way. Two contents of judgement may differ in that different inferences can be drawn from the two contents when combined with others. If the inference-possibilities of two judgement-contents are the same, then they have the same conceptual content. 'Only this has significance for our symbolic language . . . Whatever is needed for a valid inference is fully expressed; what is not needed is for the most part not indicated either . . . In this I follow absolutely the example of the formalised language of mathematics' (p. 3). These two views seem to be opposed, but if we remember that Frege later characterises logic as the science of the laws of truth, they can be reconciled. For the laws of truth are what the truth-tables indicate; and these laws can be summed up in the law that 'only true sentences can be derived from true' (*Grundgesetze*, ii, 91). This explains why the laws of truth are laws of inference, and so why logic is concerned only with the possibilities of valid inference. And since only meaningful sentences can be either true or false, in discussing the inference-possibilities of a sentence one is also indirectly discussing its 'conceptual content'. Frege believed that only so much of its particular conceptual content as could be expressed in some general form was relevant to its inference-possibilities. '(My concept writing) is designed . . . to be capable of expressing not only the logical form, like Boole's notation, but also the content of a proposition' (*Grundlagen*, p. 103, note 1).

The relation between Frege's notion of *form* and his theory of functions has been described earlier. Given a definite singular sentence, we can derive a certain logical form which it exemplifies by substituting for the proper name a letter which merely indicates; or equally we can substitute for the concept-word a sign which merely indicates functions. The sentence 'Socrates is wise' can be construed as exemplifying the logical form 'x is wise' or the logical form 'Socrates is $f(\ )$'; these in turn are examples of the logical form '$f(x)$'. Sometimes the grammatical form imposes a certain logical analysis upon us, e.g. where as above the subject-predicate analysis coincides with the logical analysis. But usually there is a choice of possible different logical forms exemplified by a given sentence. Frege's notion of form can be extended in this way; we can say that the logical form of all objects is the argument position; that what is common to all objects is their being indefinitely indicated by the letter 'x' in a functional expression. Similarly the logical form of all concepts is their being indefinitely indicated by the sign '$f(\ )$'. Although this is not in Frege, it may help to bring out the points of the notion of form; namely its connection with the theory of functions, its dependence on the idea of 'what is common' as distinct from what is peculiar in an expression, and its relevance to logic and especially to the notion of a valid inference. All these points are by now familiar; a good explanation of them is given, for example, in David Mitchell's *An Introduction to Logic*, Chapter 1.

In terms of the later sense-reference theory, the earlier notion of *content* splits into two halves. Sometimes what Frege at first called a sign's *content* must be identified with its reference, i.e. the object it signifies; sometimes it must be identified with the sign's sense. Perhaps the *content* of individual expressions and names becomes their reference, while the *content* of sentences becomes their sense. But this distinction is only of heuristic value.

(ii)

Frege distinguishes between signs that genuinely signify and signs of the kind his Formalist opponents believed themselves to be dealing with in their mathematics, namely pure signs with no reference, i.e. marks or objects of a certain type designed simply to be manipulated according to given rules. Frege calls these *figures* and reserves the term *signs* for those which genuinely signify objects other than themselves. What other differences between signs and figures accompany this initial distinction?

The greatest difference is between the respective statuses of the signs and figures themselves with respect to the theories of which they are an element. For if the theory simply deals with rules for manipulating figures, then 'they are no longer external aids . . . but are instead an essential constituent of the theory itself' (*Grundgesetze*, ii, 87). This is not so for signs. What we intend to speak about when we use a sign is usually not the sign itself but rather the object it signifies. 'The sign itself is really a matter of indifference . . . only an arbitrarily chosen means of expression that is not itself to be considered. The utility of the sign consists in its representative capacity' (ibid., ii, 98). Frege explains his meaning by saying that normally signs 'serve only for communication between men, including the case of self-communication during reflection'.

We must therefore be quite clear about the distinction between using a sign to speak of the object it signifies and using it in order to speak about the sign itself. This latter kind of use does sometimes occur, namely when we are talking about a given theory or symbolism or language. Here we must provide some intelligible mark to show that what we are doing is speaking about the sign mentioned rather than using it. Now the distinction cannot arise in this form for Formalism, since no sign in this view ever stands for another object. And Frege tries to show how his contemporary Formalist opponents did in fact make the confusion between *use* and *mention* of a sign. Now this distinction becomes particularly important when the same signs as occur in the theory are used in talking about the theory. In this case the signs have a double role, and it is therefore no longer clear how we are to set up consistent rules which will govern both roles. Frege realises that the existence of a distinction between using and mentioning a sign does not entail that in mentioning a sign from a given language we are entitled to say anything about it, i.e. to ignore its use within that language. If we are talking about the word 'red', we cannot say that it is a verb or that it denotes a particular shape. For already in talking about a word we are talking not just about a figure but about a sign, i.e. something that has a definite signification that must be taken into account.

There are further differences between figures and referring signs. It is because signs refer to objects and concepts that they can be used in sentences that assert and express *thoughts*. For this reason Frege distinguishes Formalist from 'meaningful' arithmetic. So a further difference between signs and figures is that the *rules* for constructing sentences containing figures are arbitrary in a way in which the rules for constructing meaningful sentences are not arbitrary. If a sign has a definite reference, then this reference is relevant to the rules for constructing meaningful sentences containing the sign; 'it is necessary that formulas express a sense and that the rules be grounded in the reference of the signs' (ibid., ii, 92). This cannot apply to non-referring figures. It is in a way, therefore, misleading to speak of there being 'rules' for manipulating signs at all, since this seems to imply a distinction between what is given to us in the reference of the sign and the possibilities of its meaningful use. The only arbitrary stipulations that can apply to referring signs are those that lay down the reference of these signs, i.e. that attribute definite references to certain figures and thus convert them into signs. Once these 'rules' of reference are laid down, the 'rules' governing the construction of sentences containing the signs follow from the references of these signs. This is not so for figures, where the rules governing the construction of 'sentences' containing the figures are arbitrary and ungrounded in any reference of the figures themselves.

It follows from this difference between the types of rule appropriate for signs and figures that the *sentences* constructed with them will be of different logical natures. Where the signs are genuinely referring and the sentences into which they enter are grounded in these references, there the sentences will be genuine theorems. They will be meaningful, i.e. have sense or content; they will contain genuine statements about whatever objects the signs refer to. In meaningful arithmetic, where the numeral signs are taken to refer to numbers, arithmetical theorems are about these numbers and express genuine thoughts about them. This does not hold for formalist arithmetic, where there are no numbers, or if there are they are not the subject-matter of the theorems. Frege even says that formal arithmetic can contain no theorems, although the theory of formal arithmetic can. It can contain genuine theorems about the numeral signs which occur as pure figures in formal arithmetic itself.

Frege sometimes expresses this kind of thing by saying that the activities with figures which occur in formal arithmetic are 'external', while those which occur in meaningful arithmetic are simply the external manifestations of inner processes of thought. In the *Grundgesetze* he describes how we could, if we liked, operate a logical notation such as his *Begriffsschrift* gives us purely as a formal calculus. But 'what we took to be the external representation of an inference would then be . . . merely the transition from one configuration to another . . . although intellectual labour would thus be expended, there would be wholly lacking that train of thoughts which accompanied the affair for us, and actually made it interesting. It might be possible, but scarcely profitable . . .' (ii, 90). Later, in discussing a similar theory of formal arithmetic, he says that 'once we have designated the numbers by numerical signs, the properties of the numbers are mirrored in corresponding properties of the signs, and we obtain procedures in the domain of signs which serve to solve problems arising in the domain of numbers . . . The rules of this calculation have their foundation in the nature of the numbers themselves and their relations to one another . . . We may now, however, completely disregard the reference of the numerical signs, treat them as mere figures, and consider the rules of manipulation as arbitrary rules without demand for justification. And we can now calculate according to these rules . .' (ibid., ii, 101). But there is still a criticism of such a formalism, namely that it makes unintelligible the nature of operations which before formalisation had been quite intelligible and justifiable. The procedure is both useless and incomplete.

A final difference that follows on these others is that formal theories cannot add to the body of knowledge. A formal theory cannot be a science, since no theorem in the theory expresses a thought of which we can have knowledge. It is this that makes formal theories into something analogous to a game. But 'it is applicability alone which elevates arithmetic from a game to the rank of a science' (ibid., ii, 91). It is only because the signs of meaningful arithmetic have reference to objects, and because the sentences that are its theorems therefore express genuine thoughts, that meaningful arithmetic can concern itself with truth and falsehood. And it is this belief that explains Frege's distress in the face of the paradox of the class of all classes that are not members of themselves. For in accepting the existence of the paradox Frege abandoned one of his fundamental laws, namely that law which, he thought, alone guaranteed the status as objects of the natural numbers. The paradox seemed therefore to strike at the root of the whole conception of arithmetic as meaningful.

In all the respects mentioned Frege quite clearly took language to be on the side of the meaningful rather than the formal. Words and expressions are not just figures, but they are genuine signs standing for objects and concepts. The normal use of words is therefore to speak about the things they signify. It also follows that we must make a theoretical distinction between the use of language to speak about these things, and its use as a kind of meta-language to speak about the words and expressions of language itself. Expressions in language will nevertheless be arbitrary in one way. It does not matter what simple name is chosen as the name of a given object; but once chosen, the behaviour of the word is governed by its reference. This is to say that the use of words in sentences is governed by their references. Sentences will then be capable of expressing thoughts and will make genuine statements of fact about the things signified by their components. It will also be seriously misleading to speak of 'rules' for the construction of sentences from particular expressions. For such rules of construction are already given in the particular references of these expressions. Since sentences express thoughts, the activities of speaking and writing them will be only external expressions of inner processes of thought. The only point of having such means of expression is to enable people to communicate with one another, and as Frege says with themselves. It follows too that sentences in language and language itself can be called scientific. There can be a scientific language, though Frege did not believe that the natural languages of everyday use had achieved this status. It seems sometimes that he believed that certain logical stipulations would turn everyday language into a proper instrument of science. True sentences do however give us genuine information and extend our knowledge of the world. It also follows from Frege's description of the theoretical possibility of transforming a meaningful theory into a formal one that language itself could be treated as it if were a purely formal theory, i.e. a sort of calculus of verbal symbols having no relation to reality and operated according to now inexplicable rules. But he would have said that this procedure would be both uninteresting and unhelpful; it would make unintelligible things that are easily intelligible and justifiable when language is considered in its ordinary applications to things. He would have made this kind of attack on those who try to set up theories of language as formal systems, or to describe a language by reference to its vocabulary and grammar alone.

(iii)

Frege drew a sharp distinction between the meaning or content of a sign and its behaviour with respect to the rules of the theory it occurs in. He thought that there were two things wrong with this confusion. First, it does not follow from a sign's being given and from the stipulation of rules for manipulating this sign, that it acquires or has any content. Chess pieces have to obey the different rules of chess, but this is not to say that they have or acquire any meaning in the game of chess. The sign itself, or rather the figure, does not acquire any new properties by the rules for manipulating it. Second, it is misleading to say that signs 'behave' in particular ways in a game or theory. Strictly it is we who behave in certain ways with respect to the rules, and our behaviour consists either in correctly applying the rules in various ways or in applying them incorrectly. And if we disobey them then we are no longer properly playing this game, since it is defined by the pieces or figures and the rules. But besides these faults of formulation there is a serious confusion in saying that a rule can give content to the figure it deals with, since 'the relation of a piece (sign) to a rule is not at all to be compared with the relation of a sign to its sense or reference' (*Grundgesetze*, ii, 96). There is still some sense in the notion, however. Only what sense there is is precisely the opposite sense to the one this theory attributes to it. Insofar as we can speak of rules at all when it is genuine signs that are in question, the rules are grounded in the references of the signs. The content of the signs, we might say, determines the rules and not the other way about.

There are two views of meaning which Frege strongly opposed. The first is the notion that although the figures in a formal theory do not have reference, they may be said to have a 'formal reference' in virtue of being subject to a given set of rules (ibid., ii, 97 and 112). Frege answers that it is merely a gratuitous confusion to use the word 'reference' in this case; 'the formal reference . . . cannot be recognised'. Moreover, it would follow that all numerical figures have the same 'formal reference' since, on the Formalist theory, the rules hold indifferently of all of them. The second is the notion that the meaning of an expression is simply its use or application, *Anwendung*. There is indeed a certain connection between the use of an expression and its meaning (e.g. *Grundlagen*, pp. 13, 22–3, 59, 97 and note 2; *Grundgesetze*, ii, 142 and 91). Instead of trying to perceive a mental image corresponding to a given word what we ought to do in inquiring as to its meaning is to 'imagine a situation (*Sachlage*) where some proposition in which the word occurs would be called for'. In investigating the concept of number, he tells us that 'it should throw some light on the matter to consider number in the context of a judgement which brings out its basic use, *Anwendungsweise*'. I shall say more about the notion of applicability in section (iv).

There are two kinds of rule that are demanded by a formal theory, namely prohibitive and permissive rules. These are logically distinct. 'No prohibition restricting a permissive rule can follow from a set of exclusively permissive rules' (*Grundgesetze*, ii, 113); a principle of importance not only to the logic of mathematics but also to the logic of moral behaviour. Their functions differ. Permissive rules are those normally identified as the formation rules of a theory, i.e. those that lay down possible combinations of signs into which given signs can enter, and as transformation rules, i.e. that lay down possibilities of replacing simple and complex signs by one another. They state what is permitted, not what is obligatory nor what is forbidden. It is however understood in an explicit system that if something is not explicitly permitted it is to be taken as prohibited. There can also be explicit prohibitive rules. These are needed, for instance, when new figures are introduced into a theory, for which the existing rules make no provisions. It is because of the existence of these two kinds of rule that contradictions can occur even in formal theories. For prohibitive rules are essentially restrictions on permissive rules, and must be construed as overruling them in force. It is then possible that one prohibitive rule may explicitly prohibit what another permissive rule explicitly permits. Such contradictions can be avoided by the stipulation of relative forces just mentioned, but it is still necessary to state all the rules of either kind (*Grundgesetze*, ii, 119).

The difference between rules of these kinds and the 'rules' under which expressions function in meaningful systems is clear. The permissive rules can 'give nobody a liberty he did not previously have . . . The rules of formal arithmetic, as patterns for action, are more closely related to the laws of morality than to the laws of meaningful arithmetic, which can be unrecognised but never broken' (ibid., ii, 110).

There are in general two quite different kinds of laws, including rules. There are those which ought to be obeyed but to which events do not necessarily conform, and those which are generalisations of natural occurrences. To this division of kinds corresponds roughly the distinction between genuine rules of a formal system and those rules 'established in the name of reason or nature' which describe the uses of expressions in language. For it is clear that once the signs of language have been given reference, no legislator can lay down permissions and prohibitions about their uses. Given that the purpose of language is what Frege calls 'cognitive', i.e. that at least one use of language is to express and exchange knowledge, then because knowledge is of truths and because sentences composed of referring signs depend for truth-value upon the references of these signs, no linguistic legislator can have anything to say about the construction of sentences.

Does not Frege's assertion that the 'rules' for meaningful sentences are grounded in the references of expressions contradict his principle that the sense of a sentence is independent of the references of its components? It shows that this principle must be qualified in two ways, both already mentioned. First, an expression's sense is dependent on its reference in that its sense is its mode of referring to this particular object; the attribution and possession of reference is prior to the possession of sense and might be said to 'ground' the sense. Second, and more important, the sense of a sentence is not independent of the references of its components; there is a necessary relation between a thought and its truth-value, even on Frege's theory, although this fact is not evident. The references of the components determine the reference of the whole But the sense of the whole is, says Frege, the thought that the conditions under which the thought is true are satisfied. And once the references of the parts and the whole are given the conditions of truth are determined, and therefore the sense is determined. It is possible to know a sentence's sense without knowing its truth-value, but it is not possible to know its sense without knowing what would make it true, i.e. in what conditions it would be true.

Rules must be distinguished from genuine 'theorems', i.e. meaningful sentences, and operations, activities or processes. Whether or not the theorems of a system express anything, i.e. whether or not they are genuine theorems, they are not themselves about the signs they contain. But rules are about the signs used in the system. Moreover, they are logically distinct from the theorems, since they prescribe what theorems may and may not be written. Since it is possible to use the same signs both in the theorems of the theory and in the rules of the meta-theory, confusion may ensue. People may think that one and the same set of signs can be treated now as a rule, and now as a theorem. Frege attacks Formalists who tried to do this. Rules are not operations either. 'Heine further writes; Rules according to which two numbers joined by the operator sign can be replaced by a single sign are called arithmetical operations. . . . One might as well say: The rule according to which one makes socks from thread by means of knitting needles is called the knitting of socks . . .' (*Grundgesetze*, ii, 104). Nobody would think of confusing the rules of chess with moves in a game of chess on the one hand and positions reached by such moves on the other. In language and meaningful theories in general what corresponds to an 'operation' would perhaps be the activity of inferring together with its appropriate expression, or perhaps the activity of uttering a sensible remark. It is clear that rules for the construction of meaningful sentences cannot be confused with activities with meaningful sentences. Rules essentially govern such activities. The laws of logic govern the construction of sentences we utter, but do not govern our assertions of sentences; far less are they generalisations about our utterances.

(iv)

Frege compares a pure formal system to a *game* (*Grundgesetze*, ii, 90 etc). In such a theory the figures, not being referring signs, are analogous to the pieces which are moved according to the rules of a game. Games must be contrasted with *sciences*. The difference is that since the positions of the pieces in a game express nothing, they cannot be regarded as theorems or sentences. Equations in formal arithmetic are simply sets of figures analogous to distributions of the pieces on a chess board. To the distinction between positions and genuine theorems corresponds another distinction between 'moves' and genuine expressions of inferences. 'It is true that the moves of chess are made in accordance with rules; but no position of the chessmen and no move expresses a rule; for it is not the job of chessmen to express anything; they are rather to be moved in accordance with the rules' (ibid., ii, 107).

There will also be some difference between the methods of justifying the 'rules' of sciences and games. The rules of a science are directed by considerations of truth. In general they fall under the laws of logic;

their criteria may be called criteria of truth. But the only criterion for rules of a formal theory is consistency. If a rule permits a given particular operation there must not be another rule which prohibits the same operation. Frege also demands that the rules of a formal system should be complete, and finds this condition to be one of the strongest objections against the possibility of a Formalist theory of arithmetic. 'A list (of rules of play) could never be completed, for in addition to the permissive rule, prohibitory rules would also have to be established, leading to uncertainty concerning what is permitted—an uncertainty which apparently could never be wholly removed' (ibid., ii, 137; and see 111, 115–16 and 119).

An important difference between the rules of a meaningful theory and the rules of a formal theory concerns our understanding of the rules. This is related to the difference in point between sciences and games. The purposes of science are 'cognitive' (ibid., ii, 104). Once we realise that theorems in this kind of system are meaningful, we can see the point of judging them by the criteria of truth. This is not the case for formal systems. There does not seem to be an obvious point in a 'game' as such; though one possible point is to avoid metaphysical difficulties, e.g. the kind of difficulty about the nature and definition of the natural numbers with which Frege struggled for so long. But Frege, as is evident, does not think this kind of difficulty can be avoided, and so this particular point is a worthless one (ibid., ii, 89 etc.). There is a general point in formalisation, however, and Frege makes it himself in support of his introduction of a new logical notation. The point is to bring out clearly the logical features of propositions, and therefore to bring out proofs and inferences. It is to make clear just what is being said at any given point and just where the logical transitions are taking place; it is also to make clear what kind of logical transitions are occurring. In this kind of formal system the 'rules' will be justified, first, by conforming to the fundamental laws of truth; indeed they will include these laws among themselves; and second, by the degree of perspicuity and explicitness with which they bring out the logical form of theorems or sentences. But the rules of a purely formal system cannot intelligibly be justified in either of these ways.

With this difference between sciences and games goes another. 'Why can arithmetical equations be applied? Only because they express thoughts . . . It is applicability alone which elevates arithmetic from a game to the rank of a science. So applicability necessarily belongs to it' (ibid., ii, 91; and compare 'On Sense and Reference', p. 63: 'It is the striving for truth that drives us always to advance from the sense to the reference'). Frege did not, however, think that the applicability of theorems in meaningful arithmetic, or of sentences in language, exhausted their content. 'In any application a large part of the generality (of propositions constructed from referring signs or words) is always lost, and a particular element enters in, which in other applications is replaced by other particular elements' (*Grundlagen*, p. 23). In the *Grundgesetze* too he draws a sharp distinction between 'the questions about the truth of a thought and its applicability' (ii, 137, note 2). This is a typical mistake of empiricist philosophers, e.g. Mill, who 'always confuses the applications that can be made of an arithmetical proposition, which often are physical and do presuppose observed facts, with the pure mathematical proposition itself' (*Grundlagen*, p. 13). What is wrong with such theories is that they do not realise that 'I can very well recognise the truth of a proposition without knowing whether I will ever have a chance to make use of it' (*Grundgesetze*, ii, 137, note 2).

It is this that Formalists ignored. 'If we stay within its boundaries (e.g. those of pure arithmetic), its rules appear as arbitrary as those of chess. *This applicability cannot be an accident*—but in formal arithmetic we absolve ourselves from accounting for one choice of the rules rather than another' (ibid., ii, 89). From the purely formal point of view it is arbitrary which rules we choose for the arithmetic-game. Then we notice that with one particular set of rules the arithmetic-game can be applied usefully to the world around us. And it cannot now help appearing quite extraordinary that it is *this* particular set of rules which allows arithmetic to be applied; the relation between the applicability and the particular set of rules now appears quite contingent. But 'this applicability cannot be an accident'. Given the nature of the world, we can explain why meaningful arithmetic has the rules it does by pointing to facts about the world; and equally we can explain why certain sentences are true and others false in the same way. But this justification is out of the question for a pure Formalist.

Language, being the paradigm of a meaningful system of signs, must be sharply distinct in all these ways from a mere game with words as its counters. 'It is possible of course to operate with figures mechanically, just as it is possible to speak like a parrot; but that hardly deserves the name of thought' (*Grundlagen*, Introduction, p. IV). Words are referring signs, and therefore language is an instrument of scientific knowledge and not a kind of game. Admittedly, Frege distinguishes the scientific use of language from its poetic and fictional uses, for example; he might have called these 'language-games'. There seems to be some parallelism between the advance from calculation to application and the advance, discussed in 'On Sense and Reference', from sense to reference. Sentences are not mere sets of words, but expressions of thoughts about the world. Moves from one sentence to another can express genuine inferences and processes of thought. And the 'rules' of language are to be judged by the criteria of truth, i.e. the laws of logic.

(v)

Frege has a remarkable paragraph in his attack on the view that negation 'dissolved' thoughts or split them apart into their components ('Negation', p. 123). 'How indeed could a thought be dissolved? How could the interconnection of its parts be split up? The world of thoughts has a model in the world of sentences, expressions, words, signs. To the structure of the thought there corresponds the compounding of words into a sentence; and here the order is in general not indifferent. To the dissolution or destruction of the thought there must accordingly correspond a tearing apart of the words . . . the connection is dissolved, the original order can no longer be recognised. Is this what happens when we negate a thought? No . . . What we do is insert the word 'not', and apart from this leave the word-order unaltered . . . The order may not be altered at will. Is this dissolution, separation? Quite the reverse! It results in a firmly-built structure'.

The account of the relation of language to thought that we have already is roughly as follows. Complete sentences express thoughts and manifest thought-processes. Thoughts are about objects and concepts; they are capable of being true and false, though some thoughts are neither, and true thoughts are facts. A singular sentence that corresponds to a thought contains one part which represents this object and one part which represents what is said about the object. If the thought is true, this is something that is true of the object. Usually the part which represents the object stands in the grammatical subject position, the part which represents the rest in the grammatical predicate position. Now this paragraph just quoted adds to the account. Both thoughts and sentences have *structures* or forms. Frege alludes in the *Grundlagen* to the 'logical forms which have gone into the shaping of our language' (p. 103). It appears that the structure of a sentence is the order of its components. Now thoughts too are said to have components, although Frege does not apparently think they have any 'order'; the structure of a thought is not the ordering of its components but something different. Thoughts are firmly-built structures, and that is to say they are complete senses. Nevertheless the form or order of a sentence is said to correspond in some way to the structure of the thought; we may interpret the *Grundlagen* passage as saying that particular meaningful orderings of words into sentences depend upon and are derived from particular thought-structures.

I do not think there is a great mystery here. All we need to bear in mind is that the subject-predicate analysis can be related to the analysis into argument and function. If we consider a completed functional expression, two things are plain on Frege's theory. First, the expression itself has components which are separable arranged in a certain order; second, it stands for some entity which is complete but consists of separable components joined in a manner more 'internal' than mere ordering in space or time. The structure of both sentences and thoughts is the general structure of function and argument. In the world of expressions this structure is shown by the arrangement of a set of objects, i.e. signs; in the world of thoughts it exists in its logical purity (see 'Foundations of Geometry', p. 12). Since the structure of function and argument is a logical structure, a 'logical form', applying the theory of functions to sentences is one way of bringing out and dealing with the logical form of sentences. And if one believes with Frege that the terms 'function', 'argument' and 'value' denote objective entities, then at least this kind of structural correspondence between the expression and what is thought to be signified by it is guaranteed.

I have already discussed Frege's strictures on the picture-theory of truth ('The Thought', pp. 290–1). The fact that he attacks it is perhaps another reason for not being over-impressed by the apparent correspondence theory of the passage from 'Negation' quoted above. It makes it clear that he did not hold a correspondence theory of truth, but rather what might be called a correspondence theory of meaning. The structural correspondence, in his view, is not between sentences and facts nor between thoughts and facts, but between sentences and thoughts; though admittedly in calling true thoughts facts he implies that a true sentence will correspond in structure to a fact. But still it is correspondence between an expression and its *sense* that Frege points out, and not correspondence between an expression and its *reference*. Even pictures do not correspond with their references, since they do not have any; they do not signify what they represent, even though they are like signs intended to represent things other than themselves. For the type of representation is different; and pictures are not, though they could be, used as proxies for what they represent. Of course pictures could be used as a language for talking about things, if the conventions of pictorial representation were defined so that we should no longer need knowledge of the painter's intentions in reading his picture. But still it would not be in virtue of representing things unmistakably that a picture was a kind of sentence; it would be in virtue of the existence of these conventions of representation, i.e. conventions of reference, which made pictures capable of expressing thoughts.

Frege speaks of the 'properties' of signs. Usually in speaking there is 'no intention of saying anything about the symbols . . . except in so far as some property of theirs directly mirrors some property in what they symbolise' (*Grundlagen*, p. 32). We have already seen some examples of such mirroring. Since functions are essentially incomplete, the signs for functions must themselves be incomplete in some corresponding way. Since concepts are incomplete, predicative expressions must be themselves incomplete; by being complete sentences with the subject-expression omitted they 'mirror' the nature of concepts. It is important to be clear what is meant by a sign's properties. Signs are objects and therefore their properties are physical, e.g. shapes, sizes, sounds, and relative positions. The rules under which they are operated in a given theory are not 'properties' of the signs. It is not a property of the word 'brown' that it denotes the colour brown; nor that it can stand in certain meaningful sentences in certain positions. If these are properties of anything, they are likely to be properties of the concept *Brown*.

The idea that a sign's properties can mirror the properties of what it signifies was adopted implicitly from Frege's Formalist opponents. 'Once we have designated the numbers by numerical signs, the properties of the numbers are mirrored in corresponding properties of the signs, and we obtain procedures in the domain of signs which serve to solve problems arising in the domain of numbers . . . The rules of this calculation have their foundation in the nature of the numbers themselves and their relations to one another' (*Grundgesetze*, ii, 101). Frege's objection to this seems to be chiefly that if one ignores the numbers signified by the numerals, the rules of calculation will need to be multiplied in order to deal with every possible case. If one ignores the references of signs, then one must fall back on their properties in constructing rules for their manipulation. But it seems impossible to give a complete and consistent set of rules on this basis. Although the functional expression '$f(x)$' does mirror in its properties a thought like the thought that Socrates is wise, still we can only see this structural correspondence because we already know what the elements of the expression signify. Otherwise, for instance, one might take the 'f' as signifying 'It is said that', the 'x' as indicating some thought or proposition, and the brackets as signifying the negation of this thought, and read the whole as 'It is said that not — '. Here too a definite structural correspondence, a mirroring of properties, is clearly visible.

(vi)

Frege considered that ordinary language suffered from several defects from the point of view of the principles of an adequate logical notation. Most of them have been mentioned, but it is worth while bringing them together at this point. First, there are the principles of assigning proper names to definite objects. No name should be permitted that either fails to refer to any object or that refers to more than one. Similarly, no name should have more than one sense; though Frege allows 'natural languages' to contain such names as have only one sense in each given context. This condition is parallel to the laxer condition of reference, namely that a sign should refer only to one definite object in any given context of occurrence. Names should differ only insofar as they present an object of reference in different ways; for it is both legitimate and necessary to assign different names to one and the same object. Ordinary language is defective in each of these respects. It contains apparent proper names of fictional beings, mythical places, names which fail to refer to any object and which therefore are not really names at all, although they have the appearance of being names. It contains name-like expressions which in fact designate several objects, e.g. 'The white horse'. And such genuine names as it contains usually have many different senses attached to them. Further, the differences between names for one and the same object do not always go with differences in their modes of introducing the object.

Next there are general words. Frege requires that these be completely defined, i.e. that every sentence properly constructed from a given general word should have a definite truth-value. This is to say that all properly constructed sentences should at least express a definite thought, i.e. have a definite sense. Now we can achieve this for ordinary language by means of stipulating truth-values in cases where they are not already determined, as Frege does. But he would not have regarded this as entirely satisfactory for a genuinely scientific language. Here we are concerned with definite knowledge, and the mere stipulation of truth or falsity is not an increase in our knowledge, although it is one means of defining our knowledge.

In general there should be some correspondence between the properties of things and of their signs. Signs for objects must be 'complete' and able to stand on their own; signs for concepts and functions must be 'incomplete', and their inability to stand on their own must be reflected in a grammatical incompleteness that does not characterise proper names. It follows that grammatical and syntactical features should reflect and not distort logical features. For example the grammatical subject-predicate form should correspond to the logical subject-predicate form. Ordinary language is at fault here, e.g. negating and quantifying expressions often accompany the grammatical subject of a sentence.

Frege sometimes attributes to language itself the power of 'fooling' us or of 'laying traps' for us. 'Languages are unreliable on logical questions. It is indeed not the least of the logician's tasks to indicate the pitfalls laid by language in the way of the thinker' ('Negation', p. 126). Compare with this emphatic remark what he said earlier about the utility of language to the logician. 'We cannot come to an understanding with one another apart from language, and so in the end we must always rely on other people's understanding words, inflexions and sentence-construction in essentially the same way as ourselves' ('On Concept and Object', p. 45). The point here is that much in logic is indefinable, since what is logically simple or logically fundamental cannot, Frege said, be defined. And this includes such notions as object, concept, function, thought, act of judging, truth, identity, definition and incompleteness. What cannot be defined has to be 'explained' or 'elucidated'. The reader must be got to understand such a notion by means of figures of speech, hints, the 'general feeling for . . . language'. Even in a scientific language much of this work has to be done by 'guesswork'. It follows that a great deal of Frege's own most important writings, including nearly all the essays, are to be interpreted as elucidating rather than defining his characteristic notions. Apparent definitions of object, concept, incompleteness, truth and the rest are not really definitions. Not everything can be said; not all understanding can be achieved by direct methods. And this reminds one of Wittgenstein's description of his own work; 'my propositions serve as elucidations

. . .' (*Tractatus*, 6.54; and see 3.263). But Frege's point is not at all 'mystical', but rather akin to Moore's (see 'Negation', p. 134).

Apart from these general defects in logical form ordinary language differs from a genuinely scientific language in another way. It is said to be irreducibly metaphorical and 'sensible'. This is closely related to its power of expressing not only thoughts but also emotions. Besides the thought and its assertion there is a 'third component' over which assertion does not extend ('The Thought', p. 295). It is presumably this third component that characterises, for example, poetic uses of language, and what are now called 'value-judgements'. There are correspondingly three levels of difference between expressions ('On Sense and Reference', p. 61). There is difference in reference and sense, difference in sense but not in reference, and difference of 'ideas' but not sense. To this last difference corresponds our possession of different mental images, and the different associations a sentence or word may have for us. 'Here belong also the colouring and shading which poetic eloquence seeks to give to the sense. Such colouring and shading are not objective, and must be evoked by each hearer or reader according to the hints, *Winken*, of the poet or speaker . . . it can never be exactly determined how far the intentions of the poet are realised'.

Frege does not make it clear how far these apparent defects in ordinary language are really defects in the knowledge of its speakers and writers. Sometimes it must be our knowledge that is at fault; it is because our knowledge is defective in some way that our use of certain expressions is logically improper. There is nothing inherently improper in the expressions themselves. Names should have unique and objective senses; yet it is we who attach senses to names, and frequently we attach different senses to one and the same name. Now if we had 'comprehensive knowledge' of the reference, we should know just which senses really attached to a name ('On Sense and Reference', p. 58). Here it is clearly our knowledge that is defective. The same point is made in Frege's defence of identity statements as sometimes informative. Their utility is in extending our knowledge or registering an extension of knowledge. If our knowledge were complete they would be of no cognitive value. A third case is the definition of concepts; Frege admits that 'for us men, with our defective knowledge, the question may not always be decidable' (*Grundgesetze*, ii, 56). On this account it follows that our use of certain kinds of expression must always fail of logical propriety. So the real justification of banning such expressions from a genuinely scientific language is not anything defective in the expressions, but simply the fact that we are, as it were, never justified in using them. It is not clear how much would be left, i.e. what could be said by us in a genuinely scientific language; it seems at first sight that formal logic and mathematics, with perhaps certain scientific theories, are all that remain. And this conclusion too is reminiscent of Wittgenstein.

We can roughly distinguish three points in our use of expressions; (1) to communicate thought and achieve common knowledge; (2) to express truths and register knowledge; (3) to construct valid proofs and arguments. Corresponding to these three uses are (1) ordinary language with its metaphors and defects; (2) scientific language; and (3) a symbolic notation. The latter is peculiarly well designed to achieve brevity and accuracy. Its expressions are more logically explicit and perspicuous, and fit the logical facts more closely than ordinary words; and because they are shorter, what they express is more easily comprehensible. For Frege, the need for a logical notation arose when he tried to show that arithmetic was analytic, i.e. how its theorems could be derived from logical propositions alone. For if something is not explicit, it will appear that certain inferences and transitions can be performed although they do not seem to conform to the limited number of logical principles of inference. We then think that because nothing seems to justify such apparently non-logical transitions they must really be justifiable by some intuition of validity. The point of a symbolic notation is that it enables us to split up apparent transitions into sets of component transitions, and thus to replace reliance on intuitions by reliance on the specified modes of logical inference. It is therefore necessary to set out such logical rules in advance, and the possibilities of a good logical notation are restricted by this purpose.

Frege did not think that either word-language or logical notation could replace one another. Logical systems seem to depend in two ways on the prior existence of a word-language. First, explanations of the system must often be given in ordinary language, both to convey understanding of the notation and to give the necessary elucidations where definition is out of place. Second, a symbolic notation can only express truths which are already known in verbal form or which can be expressed in words. Understanding a symbolic notation rests on understanding some word-language. Also what the two types of language express differs. Symbolic notations are restricted to the expression of logical relations between thoughts of definite truth-value. They are intrinsically adapted to the expression of inferences.

But inferring truths from one another is only a small part of the things we can do in ordinary language, and for the rest we need words.

It is however true that Frege sometimes seems to succumb to the temptation to treat ordinary language as if it were a kind of symbolic notation like formal logic. For our typical relation to symbolic logic is that we write down theorems in the symbolism. But this is not at all the typical, central or primary relation we have towards ordinary language; here it is, rather, that we utter and understand sentences. The primary use of ordinary language is in speaker-hearer contexts. Together with this misapprehension goes another. Frege certainly distinguished the function of language to express from its function to communicate; but he made communication something derivative from expression. Now when we consider logical calculi it seems that here expression may be said to be the primary function, granted that such theorems express thoughts at all. But on the other hand the primary function of ordinary word-languages appears to be communication. The function of the expression of thoughts in speech or writing, and the similar function of 'self-communication', are essentially dependent upon the function of communicating thoughts.

SOURCES FOR CHAPTER TEN

Grundgesetze, ii, 86–137; 'The Thought'; 'Negation'.

CHAPTER ELEVEN

SCIENCE AND KNOWLEDGE

IN the preface to the *Grundgesetze* Frege describes his 'ideal of a strictly scientific method'. His words are worth quoting *in extenso*, since they can be taken as a justification of his own procedures both in his later work and in the earlier works, the *Grundlagen* and the *Begriffsschrift*; indeed they largely define Frege's intellectual position. 'It cannot be required that we should prove everything, because that is impossible; but we can demand that all propositions used without proof should be expressly mentioned as such, so that we can see distinctly what the whole construction rests upon. We should, accordingly, strive to diminish the number of these fundamental laws as much as possible, by proving everything that can be proved. Furthermore I demand—and in this I go beyond Euclid—that all the methods of inference used must be specified in advance. Otherwise it is impossible to ensure satisfying the first demand' (p. 137).

In this chapter I shall try to explain briefly the salient points in this ideal of a strictly scientific method, and to show how Frege applied it to mathematics. This ideal is not original; it is largely derived from the methods of Euclid and Descartes. For this reason I shall only give a brief sketch of the essentials of the idea, and describe Frege's particular deviations and applications when they arise.

Proof must be distinguished from the description of what makes us believe a proposition, since a proposition's being true is quite independent of its being believed to be true. Therefore the description of the way we come to believe or know a proposition to be true is also not a proof of it. These confusions arise when people think that their beliefs are self-evidently true, and that self-evidence is a criterion for the truth of a belief. But Frege thought this too was confused. First we must distinguish two kinds of *self-evidence*, namely ordinary and 'logical' self-evidence. Laws of logic, for instance, need not be ordinarily self-evident if they are extremely complicated theorems, but nevertheless they may be called 'logically' self-evident insofar as they are deducible from more fundamental logical laws. Following from fundamental logical laws is therefore itself a kind of self-evidence. And it can now be seen that what is important in the notion of self-evidence is the need for some further criterion to enable us to decide in which cases self-evidence proves the truth of the self-evident proposition, and in which cases it does not. In Frege's view self-evidence is a criterion of the truth of the self-evident proposition only when it is either logical self-evidence, in the sense defined, or when it is the kind of self-evidence that characterises the fundamental laws of logic themselves; logical propositions are the only propositions whose truth is proved by their self-evidence.

The need for proof therefore arises where self-evidence is not sufficient to prove the truth of the proposition in question. It also arises because self-evidence and intuition can be deceptive. For in Frege's view proof has two aims; first to give us certainty of the truth of propositions, and second to give us insight into the relations between true propositions. The first aim of proof can be expressed in another way. Proof serves the end of knowledge; so since the sciences are bodies of known truths, the method characteristic of science must be proof. The second aim comes to this; so long as our insight into the nature of relations between truths is incomplete, we shall continue to accept certain transitions in the proofs of propositions as valid even when they do not appear to conform to known laws of logic. We shall then come to think that there are valid *modes of inference* or valid forms of implication which do not conform to known logical laws; and this is to put our trust in intuition. But so long as we do this, and so long as we fail to specify exactly the mode of inference to be used, the question of the proof of our theorems must remain in doubt. For we still demand certainty that the theorem in question has been proved to be true; and we cannot have this certainty unless we know that the 'laws of truth' have been obeyed at every step, which is just what we do not know. Another reason for specifying the methods of proof in advance is that until this is done we cannot know the logical nature of what has been proved; we cannot know 'the ultimate ground upon which rests the justification for holding it to be true' (*Grundlagen*, p. 3). In particular, we shall not know whether arithmetical truths are deducible from laws of logic alone and thus analytic truths, or whether their proof rests on special assumptions which lie outside the realm of logic, as is the case according to Frege with geometry.

Three things are necessary for the correct application of this theory of proof or deduction. First, all modes of inference must be exactly specified in advance of their employment. This includes mentioning explicitly all the basic propositions which are to be used as premisses for the coming deductions. Second, the modes of logical inference must be completely analysed in order to see where our chosen methods diverge, and, if necessary, to correct them. Third, the unproved premisses must not only be mentioned but must be reduced to a minimum in number. Frege recognises that there may be a conflict between the two requirements of minimising the basic premisses, i.e. the *axioms*, and of reducing the modes of inference. His own preference is for a small set of modes of inference, though not the smallest possible such set; he realises that an increase might permit his system to be more flexible and brief, as he puts it. But the conflict between the requirements of a notation's brevity and of the ease of reading it is not something which can be settled except by individual choice (*Grundgesetze*, i, Preface pp. 137–8).

A science for which this theory of proof or deduction is appropriate may therefore be divided into two parts; the proved propositions, i.e. theorems, which are truths known to be true and to stand in known logical relations with one another, and the unproved propositions, i.e. axioms, which serve as the premisses from which the theorems are deducible. Now there are at least four different kinds of basic proposition. First, there are the genuine *axioms* of the particular science in question, i.e. propositions which genuinely predicate something of the objects of the science, namely their essential properties, or which genuinely specify marks of the concepts peculiar to that science. Second, there are the specified *modes of inference* or rules of proof; these are, according to Frege, propositions in the theory of the system in question, the theory of the science, rather than propositions of the science itself. They are about possible theorems in that they state conditions to which theorems of the science must conform, but they are not themselves theorems. Third, there are the general *laws of logic*. Since these are the laws of truth, they must be obeyed in any science, since all sciences are concerned with achieving knowledge of truths. They lay down the general conditions to which any study that purports to increase or certify knowledge must conform. Fourth, there are the *definitions* of the objects and concepts peculiar to the science in question, or of the expressions for them in the selected symbolic notation. The whole of the *Grundlagen* is concerned with defining the objects and concepts peculiar to the science of arithmetic.

Frege believed firmly that not all propositions are provable (see *Grundgesetze*, i, Preface). We can prove many propositions that are true, but since every proof relies upon unproved assumptions, and some of these must be used as axioms in every possible proof, there can never be a proof in which these axioms are deduced as theorems from some more fundamental axioms. They are presupposed in the notion of a valid proof.

It is here that sciences divide into two kinds, according as their axioms include particular truths or merely general laws. But since 'from mere individual facts, nothing follows unless it be on the strength of a law' (*Grundlagen*, p. 4, note 1), even sciences of the former kind involve general laws. Frege believed that there were two quite distinct types of *general truth*; the laws of logic were of one type, the laws of nature, namely statements that any object fulfilling one condition thereby fulfilled another, were of the other type. Frege actually describes the laws of logic at one point as 'laws of the laws of nature' (*Grundlagen*, p. 99); the distinction in this example is that the laws of nature state connections between phenomena, while the laws of logic state connections between judgments. Later Frege modified this view of the difference between laws of logic and laws of nature. He came to think that the laws of logic are more radically distinct from the laws of nature than this, since they are not really descriptive truths at all, but normative propositions. Laws of nature are simply generalisations about natural phenomena with which particular events necessarily conform; laws of logic are not generalisations about anything, and particularly not about our actual modes of thought and inference. They are rules which must be obeyed in thinking and inferring if we are to achieve knowledge of truths by those methods and to be justified in claiming knowledge of truths. They are the rules we must follow if we are to construct a 'science'.

The connection between general and particular truths of fact is roughly this. The expression of a general truth of fact does not mention any particular object, situation or event about which something is stated. Instead of a proper name it therefore contains an indefinitely indicating letter which serves to indicate the position where the names of particular phenomena should be inserted. Frege describes the form of all general truths in the *Begriffsschrift*; 'the function . . . is a fact whatever we take its argument to be' (p. 16). Now the most common kind of general truth is a proposition stating a relation between two such functions or concepts. An example given by Frege is the proposition 'All whales are mammals'. The form of a general truth of this kind is 'whatever is taken as argument, the case in which 'x is an F' is false and 'x is a G' is true, does not occur'; or 'whatever object is argument, 'x is an F' implies 'x is a G''; or 'whatever is an F is a G'. The first formulation is the explicit one given by Frege in the *Begriffsschrift*; the others are commonly given as equivalent formulations.

I mentioned necessity. Now in Frege's view there is no intrinsic difference between contingent judgements and necessary judgements, as he puts it in the *Begriffsschrift*, i.e. between contingent truths and necessary truths (p. 4). A judgement, i.e. truth, is necessary if its logical grounds are general truths, that is if it follows from general truths alone. The notion does not play a significant part in Frege's thought.

The distinction between *analytic* and *synthetic* propositions was much more important to Frege. It was here above all that Frege rejected Kant's view, and in rejecting it explains why he regards arithmetic as a body of analytic truths not, as it was for Kant, a body of *apriori* yet synthetic truths. The prime difference is that Kant's definition of an analytic judgement is concerned with the content of the judgement, while Frege's is concerned rather with its justification, or its logical grounds. Frege also rejects the Kantian definition of an analytic judgement as one where the subject concept contains the predicate concept, since it is not exhaustive (*Grundlagen*, p. 100). For not every judgement contains a subject *concept*; Kant's definition only applies in the Fregean system to universal affirmative judgments. If a judgement is singular or particular, Kant's dichotomy cannot apply to it. Moreover Kant's theory takes no account of the possible difference of level between the concepts contained in a judgement.

'These distinctions . . . concern, as I see it, not the content of the judgement but the justification for making the judgement . . . When a proposition is called *a posteriori* or analytic in my sense, this . . . is a judgement about the ultimate ground upon which rests the justification for holding it to be true' (*Grundlagen*, p. 3; and see pp. 17 ff.). It follows that the distinctions analytic-synthetic and *apriori a posteriori* apply only to true propositions. It is nonsense to speak of an analytic falsehood, since no falsehood can follow logically from any truth; and the logical nature of its grounds is irrelevant. It is also important to be clear that no reference is being made to any facts of psychology. To call a proposition analytic or *apriori* is not to say anything about our attitudes towards the proposition, any more than to call it true or singular in form is.

'If, in (following the proposition back to the primitive truths) we come only on general logical laws and definitions, then the truth is an analytic one, bearing in mind that we must take account also of all propositions upon which the admissibility of any of the definitions depends. If however it is impossible to give the proof without making use of truths which are not of a general logical nature, but belong to the sphere of some special science, then the proposition is a synthetic one' (*Grundlagen*, p. 4). This distinction does not coincide with the further distinction between *apriori* and *a posteriori* truths. 'For a truth to be *a posteriori*, it must be impossible to construct a proof of it without including an appeal *to facts, i.e. to truths which cannot be proved and are not general*, since they contain assertions about particular objects. But if, on the contrary, its proof can be derived exclusively from general laws, which themselves neither need nor admit of proof, then the truth is *a priori*' (ibid., p. 4). Therefore all *a posteriori* truths must be synthetic; but it is still possible in Frege's view for there to be synthetic *apriori* truths; here he agrees with Kant.

Frege's whole energy was devoted to showing that arithmetic was a body of analytic truths; that its axioms contained no truths peculiar to any special science or body of knowledge, but only truths of logic. He was therefore attacking in the first place the empiricists, e.g. Hume and Mill, for whom arithmetic was a body of *a posteriori* truths known inductively and in the second place the formalists, e.g. Thomae and Heine, for whom it was not a body of truths at all. But in the third place he had to meet the position of Kant, who agreed with him that arithmetical theorems were truths and were *apriori*, but held that they were synthetic. The *Grundlagen* is largely devoted to defending his position against Kant's; the *Grundgesetze* is largely devoted to defending their common view of arithmetic as a science against the formalists.

It is his disagreement with Kant that explains why Frege regarded the notion of *intuition* as dangerous to a true conception of arithmetic and science. For he agreed that geometry consists of synthetic *apriori* truths, and that what makes geometrical truths synthetic is simply that among the axioms of geometry must occur some propositions about the nature of space or about our intuition of space. 'The truths of geometry govern all that is spatially intuitable, whether actual or product of our fancy . . . the truths of arithmetic govern all that is numerable . . . not only the actual, not only the intuitable, but everything thinkable (*denkbar*)' (*Grundlagen*, pp. 20–1). By 'intuition' here Frege means 'intuition of Euclidean space', since he says that we can only picture a space of this kind to ourselves. Frege was of course, unlike Kant, aware of the recent development of non-Euclidean geometries obtained by replacing the axiom of parallelism by some alternative axiom. But he took this possibility of developing alternative geometries as a sign of the synthetic nature of geometry. 'For purposes of conceptual thought, we can always assume the contrary of some one or other of the geometrical axioms, without involving ourselves in any self-contradictions when we proceed to our deductions, despite the conflict between our assumptions and our intuition. The fact that this is possible shows that the axioms of geometry are independent of one another and of the primitive laws of logic, and consequently are synthetic. Can the same be said of the fundamental propositions of the science of number? Here we only have to try denying any one of them, and complete confusion ensues. Even to think at all seems no longer possible. The basis of arithmetic lies deeper, it seems, than that of any of the empirical sciences, and even than that of geometry' (*Grundlagen*, pp. 20–1). The whole passage shows that Frege agreed with Kant that Euclidean geometry had a special status among possible alternative geometries; it was the only system which represented the space that can be intuited. But in saying that other types of space may be conceivable although not intuitable he seems to have gone beyond Kant.

Arithmetic has like logic a peculiar character of generality; both sciences are fundamental to all other sciences. 'To apply arithmetic in the physical sciences is to bring logic to bear on observed facts; calculation becomes deduction' (*Grundlagen*, p. 99). The relation between logic and arithmetic is similar to the relation between the axioms and theorems of geometry; 'each (truth of arithmetic) would contain concentrated within it a whole series of deductions for future use, and the use of it would be that we need no longer make the deductions one by one, but can express simultaneously the result of the whole series. If this be so, then the prodigious development of arithmetical studies, with their multitudinous applications, will suffice to put an end to the widespread contempt for analytic judgements, and to the legend of the sterility of pure logic' (ibid., p. 24).

But the fact that truths of arithmetic can be applied to particular matters of fact does not imply anything about their logical nature. The meaning and truth of an arithmetical proposition is quite distinct from its applicability. 'Mill always confuses the applications . . . which often are physical and do presuppose observed facts, with the pure mathematical proposition itself' (ibid., p. 13). Applicability, although as we saw it is this characteristic which distinguishes mathematics as a science from a formalist game with numeral signs, is not the whole of mathematics. 'It is a mistake to see in such applications the real sense of the propositions; in any application, a large part of their generality is always lost, and a particular element enters in, which in other applications is replaced by another particular element' (ibid., p. 23). It is because arithmetic like logic is more general than the particular natural sciences that its truths have their peculiarly general character. '(The sense of arithmetical formulae) will then be so general, that with the aid of geometrical axioms and physical and astronomical observations and hypotheses, manifold applications can be made to these sciences' (*Grundgesetze*, ii, 92; and see *Grundlagen*, pp. 23-4).

(iii)

Frege insisted upon the importance of a correct theory of definition. Without definitions, proofs could not be given which would satisfy his rigorous criteria; so that if the nature of definition itself were misunderstood, the nature and very content of a proof would be misunderstood. He took for his main objects of attack two theories of definition, namely the psychologistic theory and the formalistic theory. I shall not expound these theories at length; much of the interest of Frege's attacks is now historical, since new forms of the theories have arisen which are not vulnerable to his weapons. Briefly, according to the psychologistic theory a definition is a description of how we arrive at our possession of the concepts we possess, or how we come to know the objects we do know. According to the formalistic theory, it is the arbitrary assignment of certain rules of operation to the given signs of a theory, regardless of any significance possessed already by those signs. Frege insists that definitions are neither psychological descriptions of ideas nor arbitrary rulings about signs. He thought these theories suffered from a common fault, namely in being mistaken about the nature of concepts; psychologism confused concepts with ideas, formalism confused them with objects (*Grundgesetze*, i, Preface, esp. pp. XIII-XXV). And fundamentally each view denied Frege's distinction between the objective and the actual.

Frege states eight conditions in the *Grundgesetze* (i, 33) which definition must fulfil if it is to satisfy the needs of science and logic. Only four of these are of general importance, and I shall describe them rather than use Frege's own words. (i) Every introduced name must be determined to have a definite reference, and it must be laid down in the definition that it has the same reference as some other already defined or known name. (ii) The name so defined and introduced must always be replaceable in future contexts by the original defining name. (iii) No name shall be defined more than once. (iv) Only simple names shall be defined. Now it must be understood that the term 'name' here has its widest sense, i.e. that it covers not only proper names but function-names. For both objects and concepts can, according to Frege, be defined; the introduction and use in science of both proper names and concept expressions must therefore conform to these general conditions of definition.

Instead of looking at definition from the side of the defined sign, we can look at it from the side of the defined entity. Frege says that 'really all there is to definition is that something is *brought out*, precisely *limited*, and *given a name*' (*Grundgesetze*, i, Preface p. 145: my italics). And if properly understood, this explanation corresponds precisely to the conditions later mentioned.

Both objects and concepts can be defined. In the passage of the *Grundgesetze* in which he states his rules of definition Frege also gives a set of rules for the correct formation and introduction of function names, i.e. functional signs. The most important of these is the condition of completeness, that every complete proper name formed by inserting a logically valid proper name into the function name shall itself have reference. For concepts, this is the condition that every sentence formed of the concept expression together with a proper name should be definitely true or false. Now in ordinary usage many such formations do not have definite truth-values, and in such cases we are told to stipulate some value. It appears that this technique is inconsistent with Frege's view that definitions can be correct or incorrect; how can a definition be anything but arbitrary, if we are allowed to stipulate references in doubtful cases? The answer, I think, is that so long as those sentences which in ordinary usage have a definite truth-value are assigned precisely the same truth-values in the definition in question, it just does not matter what values are assigned to the rest. A definition is correct enough if it gives a correct account of the ordinary contexts of a word. For contexts which do not arise in the ordinary use of language, different criteria may be applied; here criteria of usage cannot be relevant.

The condition of completeness is also applied to proper names. A name does not strictly speaking have any definite reference unless every function-name which it completes as argument term into a complex name itself has definite reference. The truth-value of every possible sentence about the object whose name is introduced in the definition must be definitely laid down.

The fourth of the principles I cited above was that only *simple names* are to be defined. A name is *simple* if it is the name of one definite object, if it has this definite reference on its own, if it contributes to the reference of any name of which it is part, and if it can enter as part into different names. A name is *complex* if it contains as a separable component a simple name. Complex names may not be defined, but they may be *introduced*, and there are definite conditions for such introductions of complex names. In particular a complex name must be formed only out of simple names that have been introduced already themselves, i.e. correctly defined. The fulfilment of this condition guarantees a definite reference, according to Frege, for the introduced complex name.

So far we have been concerned only with the reference of defined terms. Frege adds in the same passage (*Grundgesetze*, i, 26–33) that an introduced name must be given the same sense as well as the same reference as the already known term by means of which it is introduced possesses. This can be seen more easily in the case of concepts; for here the problem of defining the sense of a sentence reduces to the problem of reproducing the conceptual content of the sentence in other words. In the *Grundlagen* this is effectively the method of definition Frege adopts. Given a sentence 'f(A)' of which we want to define either the named object or the named concept, we find some sentence '$g(B)$' equivalent in sense to '$f(A)$', such that the 'values' of '$g( )$' and 'B' are already known. Then the unknown term, for instance '$f( )$', can simply be read off as the solution to what is now an equation in one unknown. It is the condition for sameness of sense which distinguishes statements of definition from possibly informative and synthetic statements of identity. For it is essential, on Frege's account, that the two proper names that occur in the latter kind of sentence should have different senses; it is this alone which makes the sentences synthetic.

Frege specifically distinguishes definitions, i.e. statements of definition, both from assertive sentences and from axioms. 'The definition of an object does not, as such, really assert anything about the object, but only lays down the meaning (*Bedeutung*) of a symbol. After this has been done, the definition transforms itself into a judgement, which does assert about the object; but now it no longer introduces the object, it is exactly on a level with other assertions made about it' (*Grundlagen*, p. 78). And in the *Grundgesetze* too he says that a definition 'goes over' into a sentence (i, 27). We can introduce the numeral '3' as a name for the object we already know as the sum of the numbers 1 and 2. Introducing the name of an object is defining the object. But the very same sentence that introduced '3' as a name for the number 1+2 can then be read as asserting the identity of 3 and 1+2. It is because of the same distinction that Frege attacked Hilbert's view of definitions as axioms, according to which axioms can be regarded as implicitly defining the symbols they contain. The confusion is between two distinct ways of reading the same identity statements, namely either as asserting a relation between two signs, or as asserting something about the object signified by one of the signs. This may seem to clash with the sense-reference theory of statements of identity, but does not really do so; for we are in any case prevented from trying to define something as 'the such-and-such' or 'a such-and-such' by the principles already laid down.

The definition of concepts can be performed in either of two ways. We may on the one hand lay down truth-values for all possible sentences into which the concept expression in question can enter. We may on the other enumerate a set of component concepts of the concept in question, supposing that these have themselves already been defined correctly. 'All there is to definition is that something is brought out, precisely limited, and given a name' (*Grundgesetze*, i, Preface, p. 145); and 'even the mathematician cannot create things at will, any more than the geographer can; he too can only discover what is there and give it a name' (*Grundlagen*, pp. 107–8). This makes it clear that the process of determining truth-values is really not defining a concept; it is simply an essential part of the complete process of defining one. For it might well happen that the extensions of two different concepts coincided. The extensions of the concepts *Man* and *Rational animal* might happen to coincide, so that whatever object one applied to the other too applied to. It would not follow that the concepts themselves were identical. This shows that by defining, i.e. limiting, the extension of a concept, we do not put ourselves in a position to say which concept we have defined. By this method alone we should not be able to distinguish the concept *Man* from the concept *Rational animal*. The essential first step is to specify what properties an object must possess if it is to fall under the concept in question, that is, to specify the marks of the concept.

Another objection can be raised to this notion; it applies equally well against the idea discussed above that axioms may be regarded as implicit definitions of the concepts and objects contained in them. It is an objection which derives from Frege's rejection of the principle that the reference, or sense, of some component of an expression is itself a component of the reference, or sense, of the complete expression. For it follows from this that the concepts and objects contained in an axiom or a set of axioms are 'under-determined' by these axioms, i.e. by their contexts; the sense, or reference, of a complete axiom together with the sense, or reference, of some component does not sufficiently determine the sense, or reference, of the remainder. This objection can also, in fact, be raised against the method of definition adopted by Frege himself in the *Grundlagen* (pp. 74 ff.).

Concepts can, according to this method, be defined in a way different from either of the two mentioned above, namely by analysing a given expression. 'The most fruitful type of definition is a matter of drawing boundary-lines that were not previously given at all. What we shall be able to infer from it, cannot be inspected in advance; here, we are not simply taking out of the box again what we have just put into it. The conclusions we draw from it extend our knowledge . . . and yet they can be proved by purely logical means, and are thus analytic . . . They are contained in the definitions, but as plants are contained in their seeds, not as beams are contained in a house' (*Grundlagen*, pp. 100–1). This explains why Frege often says that definitions can be and should be useful; that they 'show their worth by proving fruitful'. For the whole purpose of defining concepts and objects is to ensure the rigour of proof and to limit the validity of propositions. Definitions, like the primitive laws of logic, are among the basic propositions to which everything must be reduced if we are to achieve clarity and certainty about derivative truths.

'The aim of proof is in fact not merely to place the truth of a proposition beyond all doubt, but also to afford us insight into the dependence of truths upon one another' (*Grundlagen*, p. 2). And 'the further we pursue these enquiries, the fewer become the primitive truths to which we reduce everything'. Knowledge of these primitive truths will enable us not only to fulfil the demand made by the nature of mathematics itself, as a science, for rigour of proof and inference but to answer the questions raised by philosophy about the nature of mathematics, or whichever science is in question.

(iv)

Frege believed that what was 'logically simple' could not be defined ('On Concept and Object', pp. 42–3; 'Function and Concept', p. 32; *Grundgesetze*, i, Introduction, p. 151). He gives at different places in his writings examples of notions which are too simple to be defined. The notions of object, concept, function, thought, judgement and incompleteness are all said to be indefinable for this reason. The reason is not merely that these notions are *simple*, but that their simplicity makes logical *analysis* impossible. There is nothing more simple out of which such concepts are compounded, or more basic to them in logic. Frege calls such notions *logically simple* notions. What is logically simple can, he says, be reached only by analysis or 'scientific work'; and when reached it can only be pointed to or indicated. It cannot be defined or described. This idea is the same as Moore's idea of the connection between analysis, simplicity and definition, e.g. as expounded in *Principia Ethica* (Chapter I, sections 6 to 8).

Since definition is out of place here, we must resort to a different method. Frege describes this as 'hinting', 'elucidating' or 'explaining' (*Erklaerung*). The hearer or reader must be got by any possible means to understand the meaning of the term in question, i.e. to apprehend the logically simple notion it is meant to indicate. We should therefore take it that everything said by Frege himself about such logically simple notions as I mentioned above is only elucidation. It is not proper definition, and Frege did not think it was or intend it to be such. For the writer must often resort to figures of speech, metaphorical expressions and other devices of ordinary language in order to get his readers to appreciate his meaning. Explanation of this sort cannot be direct. 'We cannot come to an understanding with one another apart from language, and so in the end we must always rely on other people's understanding words, inflexions and sentence-construction in essentially the same way as ourselves' ('On Concept and Object,' p. 45). Of his own work he says in the same essay that he has not been 'trying to give a definition (of the notion of a concept), but only hints; and to this end I appealed to the general feeling for the German language'.

There is a second distinct group of indefinable notions. These are indefinable not just because they are logically simple and primitive, even if they are, nor because of the impossibility of an infinite regress in definition, but because an understanding of them is presupposed in the understanding of all definitions, i.e. in the notion of definition itself. Such notions are identity, truth and definition itself; presumably we should add at least the notion of reference and perhaps others. Any definition, by Frege's account, must be a potential statement of identity, and therefore must itself contain the relation of identity of reference. Any definition must be a potential truth; and of course it is necessarily already a definition. We could not learn from definition what definition was; for if we did not understand what definition was, how could we understand the definition which defined the notion? Frege does give us indirectly to understand what identity and truth are, in ways similar to those recommended for notions of the first group. The Leibnizian axiom that identicals may be substituted for one another without affecting the reference of the whole is said to 'bring out the nature' of identity, although without being a strict definition ('Review of Husserl', pp. 80–1). And the meaning of the word 'true' is said in 'The Thought' to be 'contained in the laws of truth'; to show someone the laws of Excluded Middle and Contradiction together with the rules for using the truth-tables of propositional logic is not to define, but to illustrate or elucidate or point to, the notion of truth.

One of the mistakes made by psychologistic logicians was to confuse the notions of definition and elucidation, *Erklaerung*. 'When the author feels himself obliged to give a definition, yet cannot, then he tends to give at least a description of the way we arrive at the object or concept concerned . . . Such explanations are never referred to again in the course of the subsequent exposition. For teaching purposes, introductory devices are certainly legitimate; only they should always be clearly distinguished from definitions' (*Grundlagen*, Introduction, p. VIII). As applied to Frege's own work, this confusion would amount to thinking that his remarks about functions, concepts, incompleteness and so forth need only be taken as remarks about expressions, language and facts of grammar. But he only mentions such facts in order to get us to understand his real meaning, and this is something concerning logic or reality, not simply language. It would be a bad mistake to rest content with applying his theories to words, sentences and symbolic notations, or to see them as misleadingly phrased expressions of the requirements of a logically adequate language. They are certainly this, but Frege believed they were more.

He believed that they pointed to the facts about logic which underlay and generated such requirements of language.

(v)

For Frege, a science consisted of a body of propositions known to be true, some of which constituted the axioms and others the theorems, together with a body of propositions which constituted the necessary definitions, the specified modes of inference used in that science, and any general logical laws used as premisses. The connection between the notions of science and knowledge is essential in this view. It means that the criteria for modes of inference and procedures within the science are determined by the criteria for knowledge; and these are the laws of logic, or the laws of truth. Theorems in a science are sentences which express true propositions in a set notation. Therefore symbols of the chosen notation must conform to the requirements of sense and reference. And this shows that every science can be construed as a body of propositions concerning objects which are peculiar to that science, namely the objects named by the defined simple names of the symbolism.

Frege took pure mathematics and logic as examples of science. This entails several consequences. The axioms and theorems of arithmetic and logic are truths; and it is peculiar to logic that self-evidence is a criterion for their acceptability as true. Since in Frege's view arithmetic is simply a branch of logic, the same holds there too. Propositions in each of these sciences are meaningful, i.e. have definite senses that can be apprehended, expressed and communicated. In a different way the sciences themselves are *meaningful* and not merely formal (*Grundgesetze*, ii, 88 ff. '*inhaltlich*'). They are indeed not in-formal; it is possible to interpret the presentation of logic or mathematics in the form of axioms and theorems as a purely formal system. But Frege thought this would be pointless (*Grundgesetze*, ii, 101), since it would remove the possibility of explaining why the laws of logic and arithmetic are what they are, i.e. not arbitrary, and the possibility of explaining their applicability to real phenomena. It also follows that the names in logic and arithmetic refer to peculiar objects of these sciences, and the function-names to correspondingly peculiar concepts. In arithmetic the objects presented to us by the notation are the natural numbers; Frege sometimes calls it the science of number. On the other hand there are no such logical objects, since the propositions of logic are completely general and contain no designating signs, but instead only letters which indefinitely indicate. It is because of this complete absence of particularity that the propositions of logic can be applied to any object whatever. There are of course certain concepts peculiar to logic, namely the two second level concepts known as the universal and the existential quantifier. Besides these, there are also the so-called logical constants, i.e. the notions 'and', 'or' and others of the same kind. Frege does not discuss these much (though see *Begriffsschrift*, sections 5 to 7).

Frege speaks in the *Grundlagen* of objects of reason. There is an obvious ambiguity in the expression, and the passage should be quoted. 'The proper object of reason, *Vernunft*, is reason. In arithmetic we are not concerned with objects which we come to know as something alien from without through the medium of the senses, but with objects given directly to our reason, and as its nearest kin (*ihr Eigenstes*), utterly transparent to it (*welche sie. . . vollig durchschauen kann*)'. This passage should be compared with the earlier passage in the same book in which he defines what is objective as what is independent of sensation, intuition and imagination, but dependent on reason, 'for what are things independent of reason?'. In the same section he says that 'objectivity cannot of course be based on any sense-impression . . . but only, so far as I can see, on the reason' (*'Der Grund der Objectivitaet kann . . . liegen . . . nur in der Vernunft'*) (*Grundlagen*, p. 36). The general flavour of these remarks will, I think, be familiar to someone who has read Kant's *Critique of Pure Reason*, and particularly the *Transcendental Aesthetic*; in the *Grundlagen* Frege was deliberately covering much of the ground of that section of the *Critique* in a spirit not unsympathetic to Kant. (See pp. 99–102).

What is it about reason that makes it the ground of objectivity, when sensation and intuition are rather grounds of subjectivity? If we remember that the problem of objectivity can be reduced to the problem of the objective truth or falsehood of propositions about concepts and objects, the answer is near. The laws of logic, which are laws of objective truth, can also misleadingly be called laws of thought. We could also call them 'laws of reason'; Frege later described logic as the study of *mind*, as opposed to psychology, the study of *minds*. To say that reason is the ground of objectivity is therefore in part to say that the mental operations subsumed under this heading, when correctly performed, guarantee the objectivity of the sense and reference of the thoughts that result, whereas other mental operations do not. It is easy to specify some of the operations of reason; namely apprehension of truths, understanding, inference, calculation. Perhaps Frege's term 'conceptual thinking' is an expression which covers all of these. We must not, of course, assume that just any thinking or inferring guarantees the objectivity and conformity to the required logical laws of its object propositions. But if these operations are performed correctly, the conditions for objective sense and truth-value will be fulfilled. For example only objectively true conclusions can be deduced in accordance with logically valid modes of inference from premisses correctly recognised to be true.

One such operation is that called by Frege 'recognition', and it plays a central role in his discussion of the derivation of arithmetic from logic. Given a logical object, there must be given too some criterion of identity for the object; we must have some means of recognising it as the same again under different guises. This is a special case of the general requirement that 'for every object there is one type of proposition which must have a sense, namely the recognition-statement, which in the case of numbers is called an identity' (*Grundlagen*, p. 116; and see p. 73). At the end of his appendix to the *Grundgesetze* Frege writes: 'The prime problem of arithmetic may be taken to be the problem; How do we apprehend logical objects, in particular numbers? What justifies us in recognising numbers as objects?' We must, for example, have some general method of deciding which objects are identical with the number 4 and which are not. And Frege demands that we should have some general method for deciding in face of any object whatever whether it is a number or not, even before we identify it with a particular number. So we shall not have to compare the given object with every number in order to decide whether it is a number or not; we simply use the general method. As we shall see in the next chapter, Frege's general method involves defining numbers as the extensions of concepts of a certain type. So we can say in advance, by comparing a given object with this general notion of the extension of a concept of the known type, whether the object is a number or not.

It is here that the *fundamental law of logic* comes in, i.e. the law that permits us to transform the general equality of values of two functions into the particular equality of their two value-ranges. For Frege says it is this law that gives us the general means of apprehending or recognising numbers. And it was because Russell's paradox forced him to abandon the fundamental law, and hence his only available means of recognising numbers in general, that he saw this paradox not merely as a threat to his logical system of mathematics, but as a threat to his whole conception of mathematics as a science.

SOURCES FOR CHAPTER ELEVEN

Grundgesetze, ii, 56–67; 139–47; Appendix; 'On Concept and Object'; *Grundlagen*, passim; especially Introduction; sections 1–4, 14–16, 22, 26–7, 46–8, 52–3, 56–7, 62–7, 87–91, 105; *Begriffsschrift*, sections 1, 4, 11; 'The Thought'.

CHAPTER TWELVE

THE NATURE OF NUMBERS

IN this final chapter I discuss Frege's definition of the concept of a natural number. I shall use Sections 55 to 73 of the *Grundlagen* as the basis of my discussion, rather than the corresponding sections of the later *Grundgesetze*, because the former is more accessible than the latter and also exhibits more fully certain general philosophical difficulties. Nearly every theory so far examined will be seen to play a part in the definition, and I presuppose no more than a certain understanding of these theories. My purpose is twofold; first, in returning to the theory of functions to show how all Frege's theories are interrelated; second, to show how his philosophical doctrines grew from and served his logical inquiries into the foundations of mathematics, and how on the other hand his theory of mathematics itself derived from a general philosophical outlook of which these specific philosophical doctrines are also expressions.

Frege identifies the *extension* of a concept with the *value-range* of a function. Extensions are a special class of value-ranges, namely the value-ranges of those functions that are concepts, i.e. whose values are always either The True or The False. Frege introduces the notion of a value-range in a particular context, and extensions must be considered in a similar context if needless confusion is to be avoided. When two functions always have the same value for a given argument, we may transform this general statement of equality into a statement of the identity of two particular objects, namely the value-ranges of the two functions. This transformation of one statement of equality into another, i.e. their identification, is called by Frege the recognition of something common to the two functions. The general identity and the particular identity statement thus seem to express different senses but possess identical references. Now value-ranges, and hence extensions also, should at first be treated simply as the entities introduced in the way described, i.e. as determined by their role in the 'fundamental law' and by nothing else. Therefore at first all that we may say about extensions is this: when two concepts have the same truth-value for every particular argument, i.e. object, then we may take them to have something in common. And this common element is their *extensions*.

There are two questions raised at once by this limitation of the idea of an extension. First, can the idea be so generalised as to become independent of the context in which it is introduced? Can we come to speak of the extensions of concepts in contexts different from those in which we are comparing the truth-values of concepts for a given argument? Is there a general definition of extensions which will allow us to recognise whether any given object is or is not the extension of some concept? Second, are extensions on this account to be identified with a kind of class or aggregate of objects? For we can move from saying that two concepts F and G have the same truth-value for every argument to saying that whatever falls under F also falls under G and vice versa; and we can, it seems, also make the converse move. And in the latter version we certainly seem to be talking about classes of objects. Moreover, Frege often speaks unmistakably as if the extension of a concept consisted of the objects which fell under it.

There is nevertheless some distinction to be drawn, though it is not clear between what and what. 'The extension of a concept is constituted in being, not by the individuals, but by the concept itself; i.e. by what is asserted of an object when it is brought under a concept' ('Review of Schroeder', p. 102). And 'the concept is logically prior to its extension; and I regard as futile the attempt to take the extension of a concept as a class, and make it rest, not on the concept, but on single things . . . The extension of a concept does not consist of objects falling under the concept, in the way, e.g. that a wood consists of trees; it attaches to the concept and to this alone. The concept thus takes logical precedence of its extension' (ibid., p. 106). The point, I think, is not so much that extensions are not merely sets of objects, but that even classes are not. Frege's remarks apply equally to the notion of a *class*. For we can think of classes either as mere aggregates of unrelated objects, or as 'determined by the properties that individuals in them are to have' (ibid., p. 104). And classes thus determined are extensions of concepts. What Frege attacked was not the identification of extensions with classes, but the identification of classes with mere aggregates of individuals. This is why he brings in the notion of a concept. It is a concept which serves to constitute some set of objects as a class.

The difference between these two notions of class goes with the difference between what Frege calls 'domain-calculus' or class-calculus and what he calls *logic*. The main difference is that in the class-calculus there is no distinction drawn between objects and classes; every individual object can be taken as a class having just one member. It follows from this assimilation that the relations of class-membership and class-inclusion, i.e. the relation of an object to a class it belongs to and the relation of a class to another class it is part of, cannot be distinguished. Both are assimilated in the single notion of the relation of part to whole. And the most obvious difficulty here concerns the notion of the empty class. For if classes are identified with the objects they contain, it seems that there cannot be an empty class, i.e. a class containing no members; nor can there be any infinite classes either.

Frege thought it was not only an inconvenience but actually an error to assimilate these two relations. He distinguishes them as the *sub* relation and the *subter* relation. 'If we want to make clear to ourselves the distinction between the two relations, we must regard classes as extensions of concepts . . .' ('Review of Schroeder', pp. 93–4). We can then distinguish them as (a) the relation of an object to the extension of a concept which it falls under and (b) the relation of the extension of one concept to the extension of another when the first concept is contained in the second, i.e. when whatever falls under the first falls under the second.

It does not, I think, follow that class-membership and falling under a concept are identical relations, i.e. that extensions must be identified in this way with classes. For when an object *A* falls under the concept *F* it has the relation of class-membership to the extension of the concept *F*; but the concept *F*, to which it has the relation of falling under, is not its own extension. Similarly, class-inclusion and falling within are not identical. Frege seems, however, to identify the relation of *A* to the extension of *F* with the class-membership relation, and the relation of two extensions described above as class inclusion, although it looks possible to distinguish the relation of an object to the extension of a concept under which it falls from the class-membership relation. Frege's assimilation of extensions to classes, if correctly construed, is in line with his theory of classes. He says himself that 'in many respects my position may be closer to the author . . . than to those who could in contrast to him be termed intensionalist logicians' (ibid., p. 106).

Frege says that extensions are value-ranges ('On Sense and Reference', p. 31). But in introducing the notion of a value-range he was certainly talking not about the arguments of functions but about their values. It should follow that extensions too are intrinsically related not to the possible arguments of concepts but to their possible values;

but we have just seen that Frege identifies extensions with sets of arguments, i.e. objects falling under a concept. Is there a real contradiction here? I do not think so. To say that two functions have the same value-range is simply to say that for any argument they yield the same value. Therefore to say that two concepts have the same value-range is simply to say that for any argument, i.e. object, they yield the same value; which is to say that for any argument their truth-values are identical, i.e. that one is true if and only if the other is, and false if and only if the other is. And this is to say that the two concepts are true of the same objects and false of the same objects as one another, i.e. that whatever falls under one falls under both.

The possibility of confusion arises from the existence of five equivalent propositions. These are (i) A is F; (ii) A falls under the concept F; (iii) 'A is F' is true; (iv) A belongs to the extension of the concept F; (v) A is a member of the class of objects which are F. All these propositions may be taken to have the same complete sense, but to be analysed into different components having different particular senses. Just as in the case of (i) and (ii) Frege allows us to talk about an object called 'the concept F' instead of the concept F itself, so a similar method can be applied to the other forms. Therefore we may talk about the extension of the concept F instead of about the concept F itself; or about the class of objects which are F instead of the extension of the concept F. And in general we can move from one idiom to another, since the sense as a whole of our remarks will remain the same.

(ii)

Frege's definition of the concept of a number (*Grundlagen*, pp. 67–96) falls into three parts. First, he discusses and rejects a fairly simple attempt based on Leibniz' definitions to define 0, 1 and the notion of following after. Next, he introduces a new kind of definition, using as an example to illustrate it the case of parallelism of lines and equivalence of direction. Third, he gives his own definition of number in terms of the notion of extension. In this section I shall discuss the two rejected methods.

Earlier in the *Grundlagen* Frege has shown that the content of a number-statement, i.e. a sentence which assigns a definite number to a set of objects, is an assertion about a concept rather than an object. What the number is really assigned to is a concept. In Section 55 he proposes the following three definitions as a basis for arithmetic. (i

The number o belongs to a concept, if the proposition that *A* does not fall under that concept is true universally, whatever *A* may be; (ii) the number 1 belongs to a concept *F*, if the proposition that *A* does not fall under *F* is not true universally, whatever *A* may be, and if from the propositions '*A* falls under *F*' and '*B* falls under *F*' it follows universally that *A* and *B* are the same; (iii) The number *N*+1 belongs to a concept *F*, if there is an object *A* Falling under *F*, and such that the number *N* belongs to the concept *Falling under F, but not A*. There are two related objections, however, which show up the incompleteness of these definitions. 'We can never . . . decide by means of our definitions whether any concept has the number JULIUS CAESAR belonging to it, or whether that same familiar conqueror of Gaul is a number or not'; we are told that o and 1 are numbers, but are not given any means of deciding what other objects are numbers. Second, these definitions are not sufficient to prove that if the numbers *A* and *B* both belong to one concept, then necessarily *A*=*B*. Therefore we are not justified in using the expression 'the number of the concept . . .', and cannot in general prove numerical identities. What is still lacking is this; 'we have only defined the sense of the phrases 'the number o belongs to' and 'the number 1 belongs to;' but we have no authority to pick out the o and 1 here as self-subsistent objects that can be recognised as the same again'. The first method of definition fails to conform to the requirements for defining *objects*; it serves only to define certain predicates in which apparent proper names, i.e. 'o' and '1' occur, but not to define these proper names in isolation from their predicative contexts of occurrence. It does not tell us how to deal, for example, with the context of identity-statements, i.e. '. . .=the number 1'.

Frege adds here two more theses to his original views. Numbers are objects of some kind, and therefore expressions for numbers, i.e. numerals and number-words, are essentially only parts of predicative expressions. Number-statements are in logical form statements of identity between numbers. His reasons for construing numbers as objects seem, in this work, to be that the expressions for referring to numbers conform to the conditions for a proper name, and that we say things about numbers that are only strictly appropriate to objects, i.e. that they are identical with or different from each other. It follows from this that number-referring expressions cannot occur as the grammatical predicates of sentences in which they occur. Therefore all such 'number-statements' must be construed as statements of identity of the form 'The number of so-and-so's is Such-and-such'.

At this point he prepares for the second attempt to define the concept of number. 'For every object there is one type of proposition which must have a sense, namely the recognition-statement, which in the case of numbers is called an identity'. The problem therefore becomes to define the sense of propositions of the form 'The number which belongs to the concept F (i.e. the number of F's) is the same as (=) the number which belongs to the concept G'. And this is the problem of reproducing the content of this proposition in other terms without using the expressions 'the number which belongs to the concept F' and 'the number which belongs to the concept G'. This will provide us with a general criterion for the identity of numbers.

For his second attempt, Frege uses the concept of a line's *direction* as an analogy to the concept of a concept's *number*. It is important to be clear just what is being defined and just what is being taken as known for the purposes of the definition. The doubt here is whether the concept of number is taken as known for the purposes of defining the concept of numerical identity or whether it is the other way round. We might expect that we are to deduce the concept of numerical identity from a knowledge of the concept of identity and of the concept of number. This is not the way Frege adopts. In his method it is the concept of numerical identity which must be taken as known, since it is the concept of number which is to be defined. Analogously, by Frege's method we take as known the general concept of identity and the particular concept of identity of direction, i.e. parallelism, and from these two we are to deduce the concept of a line's direction.

The method is as follows. We take a sentence of the form 'Line A is parallel to Line B', and construe it as a kind of statement of identity. We then give as an equivalent the sentence 'The direction of the line A is identical with the direction of the line B'. In this latter sentence we could rewrite 'is identical with' as ' = ', since here we are dealing with the general concept of identity. The method comes to this; by means of the equivalence of these two sentences we have now defined the concept of a *direction* as 'that with respect to whose *identity lines* are *parallel*'. And here the terms *identity*, *line* and *parallel* are all taken to denote known notions.

For the case of the number of a concept the method would work as follows. We take a sentence of the form 'concept F is one-one correlatable with concept G', and construe it as an identity-statement. We can then give as an equivalent the sentence 'The number of the concept F is identical with the number of the concept G'. Thus we have defined the notion of the number of a concept as 'that with respect to whose *identity concepts* are *one-one correlatable*', where the italicised terms denote known notions. Frege does not doubt that one-one correlation, i.e. the possibility of 'correlating' objects from two classes one to one, is the criterion for numerical identity (ibid., pp. 73–4).

But against the use of this second method of definition Frege raises three objections. He answers the first, and the second, but the third forces him to reject this method and move on to his final attempt. This third objection is substantially the same as one of the objections to the first attempt at defining number, namely that it does not give us a sufficiently general criterion for number-hood or direction-hood. It provides us with a criterion for identity of directions, or numbers, and therefore for direction-hood, or number-hood, only in contexts of the form 'The direction (number) of the line (concept) $F=$the direction (number) of the line (concept) G'. It 'says nothing as to whether the proposition, 'The direction of a is identical with q' should be affirmed or denied, except for the one case where q is given in the form of 'the direction of b' '. We still lack a general concept of direction or number.

(iii)

In expounding his final definition of number Frege again uses the analogy between the number of a concept and one-one correlation, and the direction of a line and parallelism. I shall therefore describe this method by setting down two sets of propositions, one relating to the notion of direction and to other to that of number.

A

1. Line A is parallel to Line $B=$The extension of the concept 'Parallel to line A' is identical with the extension of the concept 'Parallel to line B'.

2. Line A is parallel to line $B=$The direction of line A is identical with the direction of line B.

3. The direction of line A is identical with the direction of line $B=$ The extension of the concept 'Parallel to line A' is identical with the extension of the concept 'Parallel to line B'.

4. The direction of line $A=$The extension of the concept 'Parallel to line A'.

5. The direction of line $A=$The concept 'Parallel to line A'.

B

1. Concept F is equal to concept $G=$The extension of the concept 'Equal to concept F' is identical with the extension of the concept 'Equal to concept G'.

2. Concept F is equal to concept $G=$The number of concept F is identical with the number of concept G.

3. The number of concept F is identical with the number of concept $G=$The extension of the concept 'Equal to concept F' is identical with the extension of the concept 'Equal to concept G'.

4. The number of concept $F=$The extension of the concept 'Equal to concept F'.

5. The number of concept $F=$The concept 'Equal to concept F'.

Not all of these propositions occur explicitly in Frege, and the two numbered (5) appear acceptable only if one rejects Frege's own version (4). They will be discussed in Section (v) below, however, since there is some authority in Frege's text for upholding them, and since they are in themselves relevant to Frege's own position. Proposition A (1) is stated in Section 68 of the *Grundlagen*; A (2) in Section 65; and A (4) in Section 68 as a definition. The corresponding B (4) is also stated as a definition in Section 68; B (3) is stated as if obviously true in Section 69; and B (1) and B (2) are proved in Section 73. B (5), the alternative definition of number which I have said he does not adopt, is implicitly described in a footnote to Section 68, immediately following B (4). I shall now try to trace the movement of thought through these two parallel structures of propositions.

It looks at first sight as if the final definitions of 'direction' and 'number', i.e. the propositions numbered (4), are derivable from the earlier propositions in each list. Consider list A, dealing with direction. It seems that (1) and (2) together entail (3). Now (3) is of the general form: '$(f_1=f_2)=(g_1=g_2)$', and it seems natural enough to move from this to '$f_1=g_1$ and $f_2=g_2$'. And proposition (4) seems to exemplify part of this general form. What is wrong with this inference is that it plays upon an ambiguity in the symbol '$=$'. This symbol, when it occurs between two propositions as in the propositions (1) to (3), can be read either as 'is true if and only if' or as 'has the same sense as', and on Frege's account of meaning and truth the second reading is stronger than the first and is not entailed by the first, although it entails the first. This ambiguity affects the apparent inference from (1) and (2) to

(3) and from (3) to (4) and its possible companion. In proposition (1) the symbol '=' must be read as the weak 'is true if and only if', but in proposition (2) as the strong 'has the same sense as'. It follows that in proposition (3) the sign '=' must be read as the *weak* 'is true if and only if'. But (3) would only entail (4) if the sign were to be read as the *strong* 'has the same sense as'.

If we consider the structures of propositions (1)–(4) as inferences, then the derivation of (4) is logically unjustified. For the moves from (3) to (4) in each list are moves of the same form as the move from '$(x=y)=(2x=2y)$' to '$x=2x$ and $y=2y$', which is obviously unjustified. And it is easy to show that the general form of inference exemplified in the list of propositions is not universally applicable. Consider the propositions numbered (1) in each list. They are of the general form:

The $f(A)$ has such-and-such a relation to the $f(B)$=The extension of the concept 'has such-and-such a relation to the $f(A)$' is identical with the extension of the concept 'has such-and-such a relation to the $f(B)$'.

And we may write this for the sake of perspicuity in the short form:

$$a \ R \ b=(x) \ x \ R \ a=x \ R \ b$$

Now quite clearly this is in general false. It is true only of those relations which are symmetrical, i.e. such that if $a \ R \ b$ then $b \ R \ a$, and such that a term may have this relation to itself, i.e. such that $a \ R \ a$. These two conditions apply to Frege's cases, namely the relations of being one-one correlatable with and of being parallel with. It also applies to relations such as being the same height as, liking the same food as and knowing the same poems as. This shows why Frege describes part of his method of definition as replacing by 'the more generic symbol =, *das allgemeinere* =' some particular symbol. The method is only applicable to cases where the relation involved is a 'species' of the general relation of identity.

However the order in which the propositions of list B occur, and the ways in which Frege introduces them, show that indeed he did not proceed in the kind of manner described. He did not try to *infer* the definition of number contained in B (4) from the other propositions in list B. Instead, he begins by laying down the definition and then draws the consequences; first, to see whether they agree with our standing conceptions, and second, to show that these consequences are fruitful for mathematics. He begins by supporting the general identification of numbers with the extensions of concepts. To this end he produces proposition B (3) as if obviously true, calling it a 'basic assertion we make', i.e. a common and non-philosophical non-mathematical assumption. This merely shows the definition to be possible; it does not yet show it to be fruitful.

In order to show its fruitfulness Frege defines the notion of one-one correlation, which has so far been used informally (pp. 81–5). Correlation in general is defined as follows. 'If every object which falls under the concept *F* stands in the relation φ to an object falling under the concept *G*, and if to every object which falls under *G* there stands in the relation φ an object falling under *F*, then the objects falling under *F* and under *G* are correlated with each other by the relation φ'. In order to make the correlation one-one, two further conditions are introduced. '1. If *d* stands in the relation φ to *a*, and if *d* stands in the relation φ to *e*, then generally, whatever *d*, *a* and *e* may be, *a* is the same as *e*. 2. If *d* stands in the relation φ to *a*, and if *b* stands in the relation φ to *a*, then generally, whatever *d*, *b* and *a* may be, *d* is the same as *b*'.

Then 'the concept *F* is equal to the concept *G*' may be accurately defined, where it was previously taken as true but undefined, as meaning the same as the following. 'There exists a relation which correlates one to one the objects falling under the concept *F* with the objects falling under the concept *G*'. And with this definition in hand, Frege finally defines the expression '*N* is a number' to mean the same as 'There exists a concept such that *N* is the number which belongs to it'. Since 'the number which belongs to the concept . . .' has already been defined, this general definition of the notion of number does not contain a circle.

It is now necessary to show that if the numbers of two concepts are equal then the concepts themselves are 'equal' in the sense defined. This is proposition B (2). Since we already know from the definition, i.e. B (4), that the number of a concept is the extension of the concept 'equal to the concept . . .', the problem of proving (2) is the same as the problem of proving (1). And both are easily shown to be true. It is simply a matter of showing that if two concepts are equal then any concept equal to either is equal to both. It is easy to produce a one-one relation which ensures this. For by hypothesis there is a one-one relation between the equal concepts, and another one-one relation between the third concept and one of the two equal ones.

(iv)

Just before publication of the second volume of the *Grundgesetze*, which contains Frege's formalisation of the theory of real numbers, and his critical comments on several theories of irrational numbers, e.g. those of Cantor, Dedekind, Weierstrass and the Formalists, Russell communicated his discovery of a contradiction latent in Frege's set of axioms. We can gauge the seriousness of this discovery to Frege's work by turning to his Preface. He had there written as follows: 'The whole of the second part is really a test of my logical convictions. It is improbable that such an edifice could be erected on an unsound base . . . As a proof of the contrary, I can only admit the production by someone of an actual demonstration that upon other fundamental convictions a better and more durable edifice can be erected, or the demonstration by someone that my premisses lead to manifestly false conclusions. But nobody will be able to do that. May my book then . . . contribute to a revival of logic' (p. 147). It was his view that the prevailing logic of his time, as represented particularly by B. Erdmann, was 'infected by psychology' (ibid., p. 146). A large part of the Preface is concerned with psychologistic logic, since Frege regarded this as more dangerous than formalism.

He had seen himself that the weak link in his foundations was the 'fundamental law of logic', namely the law that if two functions have the same values for the same arguments, then they may be said to have identical value-ranges, and vice-versa. In the same Preface he allows that a 'dispute can arise' about the status of this law. However at this stage he clearly regarded the law both as true and as containing a notion of the highest importance in his whole theory of mathematics. This had not always been the case. In the *Grundlagen* he had remarked in his concluding words 'I attach no decisive importance even to bringing in the extensions of concepts at all' (p. 117). But by 1903 his position had become more definite, and he was now convinced of the need for his notion of a concept's extension. 'I do not see how arithmetic can be *scientifically established*; how numbers can be *apprehended* as *logical objects*, and brought under *review*, unless we are permitted—at least conditionally—to pass from a concept to its extension . . . What is in question is not just my particular way of establishing arithmetic, but *whether arithmetic can possibly be given a logical foundation at all*' (ibid., Appendix, p. 234; my italics). It was because Russell's paradox sprang directly from the Fregean notion of an extension that it appeared to threaten not just Frege's particular axiomatisation of arithmetic but his whole conception of arithmetic as a science. This is shown by the phrases I have italicised in the quotation just given. The status of arithmetic stood or fell, in Frege's view, with the object-hood of numbers. This in turn depended upon the intuitive notion of a concept's extension, and this notion was expressed in the two implications which make up the fundamental law of logic. The Appendix to the *Grundgesetze*'s second volume is therefore devoted to an examination of the fundamental law, in which Frege searches for a modification of it which will escape Russell's paradox, and tries to see how this modification will affect the scientific status of arithmetic.

The paradox is very well known and I shall state it only briefly. An object is said to belong to a certain class if it falls under the concept whose extension the class is. To belong to a class, to fall under a concept and to be part of a concept's extension are taken as identical. If we now consider the concept *Class that does not belong to itself* we see that its extension consists of those classes that do not belong to themselves, i.e. that are not members of themselves. This is itself a class, namely a class of classes. Now does it belong to itself or not? If it does, then it must fall under the concept *Class not belonging to itself*, i.e. it does not belong to itself; and here is one contradiction. If it does not, then it must fall under the concept *Class belonging to itself*, i.e. it does belong to itself; and here is another. And these alternatives are taken as inescapable; there is no third possibility.

Frege describes several different attitudes we might adopt in the face of this paradoxical situation. First, we might restrict the law of Excluded Middle. We might say that it held for all objects except classes or extensions. Then we could say that the class of classes which are not members of themselves neither is nor is not a member of itself, so that neither form of the paradox would arise for us. But Frege believed that such denial of the law of Excluded Middle amounted to denial that classes were objects. Against this drastic move he brought considerations of grammar of the kind discussed in Chapter 3. 'What we usually consider as the name of a class . . . has rather the nature of a proper name; it cannot occur predicatively, but can occur as the grammatical subject of a singular proposition' (Appendix, p. 235). Therefore it might be less drastic and more plausible to regard classes as 'improper objects'. We could thus allow classes to be the possible arguments of only some functions or concepts. We could stipulate that their logical impropriety consisted precisely in their not being possible arguments to the kind of concept involved in the Russell paradox. This would be to deny the applicability of the law of Excluded Middle to just those cases in which it generates contradiction.

Frege however objects to this second attempt that it involves setting up 'a complete system of rules for deciding which objects are allowable arguments of which functions' (ibid., p. 236), i.e. an explicit theory of types such as Russell later adopted. Frege regarded any such move as necessarily inadequate, but in any case he doubted whether this notion of an 'improper object' was a justifiable one.

There is still a third possible attitude. This would be to regard classes and extensions as 'apparent objects', i.e. to regard class-names as 'sham proper names' (ibid., p. 236). If class-names were only apparent proper names, but were in fact inseparable components of more complex expressions, then they could no longer be construed as referring components of complex names. Then numbers could no longer be taken as objects, since numerals could now occur only as parts of referring expressions, and would not be separable. It would therefore be impossible to define numbers and numerals in Frege's way; we could define only the complex expressions containing numerals. This would mean in turn that we could no longer justifiably replace numerals by variable letters; we could still have an arithmetic and an algebra, but there would not be any connection between arithmetical and algebraic expressions.

Frege concludes that it is not possible to deny full object-hood to classes and extensions; and that therefore we must continue to hold that the law of Excluded Middle applies to them. Instead, 'the interpretation we have so far put on the words 'extension of a concept' needs to be corrected' (ibid., p. 237). This is his own attitude in the face of the Russell paradox; and he reconstructs his notion of a concept's extension by means of a partial rejection of his 'fundamental law of logic', i.e. the previously noticed weak link in his foundations.

The fundamental law can be formulated as two implications; (i) if whatever falls under either of two concepts falls under both, then they are equal in extension, and (ii) if two concepts are equal in extension, then whatever falls under either falls under both. Frege locates the only possible root of the paradox in (ii) and therefore rejects it. He then provides a general proof of the falsehood of (ii), concluding that 'if in general, for any first-level concept, we may speak of its extension, then the case arises of concepts having the same extension, although not all objects that fall under one fall under the other as well' (ibid., p. 241). But to abandon (ii) is to abandon the notion of a concept's extension, since this notion is implicitly defined in the two components of the fundamental law. Frege therefore tries to make clear the implications of this by providing an alternative to (ii) which avoids the paradox, and by stating a new criterion for equality in extension. 'The extension of one concept coincides with that of another, when every object that falls under the first concept, except the extension of the first concept, falls under the second concept likewise, and when every object that falls under the second concept, except the extension of the second concept, falls under the first concept likewise' (ibid., p. 243). And the new version of (ii) may be stated as follows: 'if two concepts are equal in extension, then any object, which is not the extension of one of them, falls under one if and only if it falls under the other'. The reconstructed version of the complete fundamental law may now be read as follows: 'Two concepts have equal extensions if and only if any object, which is not the extension of one of them, falls under one if and only if it falls under both'.

Frege's reconstruction thus preserves two principles that he held very strongly; first that logic could notice only the broadest categories of entity, i.e. those of concept and object, and that it could make no special cases within, e.g., the category of object; and second that the law of Excluded Middle could not be abandoned by logic, since it provided a means for deciding the admissibility of expressions to which the alternatives were impracticable and perhaps also unthinkable. Moreover it allows him to keep the notion of a value-range, which he regarded by now as 'indispensable for laying the foundation of arithmetic' (ibid., p. 239). There is, however, still another possible way of escape from Russell's paradox, which Frege mentions two or three times. This is to abandon the notion that every concept necessarily has an extension. That he saw this as a genuine possibility is clear from the fact that, as he remarks himself, all his discussion presupposes that 'the extension of the concept . . .' is a logically correct function-name. But at the time of writing this Appendix he thought this too radical, and he nowhere discusses it seriously in the *Grundgesetze*, or indeed elsewhere.

(v)

I mentioned in Section (iii) a possible definition of number, alternative to Frege's own in the *Grundlagen*, namely the definition of the number of the concept F as the *concept* 'Equal to the concept F'. In the footnote on p. 80 Frege says that we could simply write 'concept' for 'extension of the concept', and this is the suggestion I have made explicit. He then mentions two possible objections to his rewriting, but says that 'both these objections can be met'.

The first we are not immediately concerned with here, except that it is relevant to the possibility of defining number as a second-level concept rather than as an object. It is the objection that the new definition would appear to contradict Frege's assertion that numbers are objects. Frege's point is, I think, a familiar one. The expression 'the concept 'Equal to the concept *F*' ' which takes concepts of the first level as its arguments, will be the expression for a second level concept. But if we take a particular first level concept, e.g. the concept *Man*, as its argument, we shall get the expression 'The concept 'Equal to the concept *Man*' '; and this must be taken as a proper name. It stands for a definite object, namely some large integer or other.

The second objection is the one we are principally concerned with. It is the objection 'that concepts can be of the same extension without coinciding, *ohne zusammenfallen*'. This might simply be a denial of the proposition numbered (1) in my list B above, namely a denial of Frege's belief that two concepts are equal if and only if their extensions are equal. But it might also be related to Frege's own denial of part (ii) of the fundamental law of logic in the Appendix to the second volume of the *Grundgesetze*. It might be the objection that two concepts can be equal in extension although not everything that falls under one falls under both. This would amount to a denial of the proposition which Frege accepts as cardinal, namely the proposition that the numbers of two concepts are equal if and only if the extensions of the concepts 'Equal to concept *F*' and 'Equal to concept *G*' are identical. For it seems that rejecting this proposition, my B (3), entails rejecting also B (1), in which case the whole structure of the Fregean definition seems to collapse. Moreover, the rejection of these two propositions entails a reinterpretation of the notion of an extension. Crudely, it will no longer be possible simply to define a concept's extension as the class of objects which fall under that concept.

It seems that here we have one ground for doubting the efficacy of a definition of number as extension. There is another; in order for the definition to do what Frege requires the notion of an extension has to be taken as self-evident. It was a defect in the first method of definition that Frege rejected that it did not provide any such means of deciding in the face of objects whether or not they were numbers. Frege remarks in the same footnote (*Grundlagen*, p. 80) that 'I assume that it is known what the extension of a concept is'. It is now presupposed that we can recognise extensions, e.g. that we can tell that Julius Caesar is not the extension of any concept. Without this possibility, Frege's method does not have the advantage claimed for it over the rejected method.

But he says himself in the *Grundgesetze* that there is no general way of recognising extensions (vol. i, 10). It is only when an object is given to us in the particular form of the value range expression '$\grave{\varepsilon}f(\varepsilon)$' that we can recognise it as a value-range or extension. If it is not so given, we can neither tell in general whether the object in question is an extension or not, nor of what function or concept it is the value-range or extension. We might think that any object can be taken as an extension, namely as the extension of that concept under which it alone falls; and that there always is such a concept for any object x, namely the concept *Identical with x*. But if the object is already given to us in the form of an extension, this simple trick will not work. For suppose it is given to us as 'the extension of the concept F'. Then on the method proposed we should say that the extension of the concept F was to be identified with the extension of the concept 'Identical with the extension of the concept F'. This would be to say that whatever fell under the concept F was identical with the extension of the concept F. But clearly this applies only to some very special cases, and is of no use in general. There is still no general method for recognising objects as extensions.

(vi)

Frege's attitude towards these difficulties in his conception of number seems to have altered over the years. It is only in the *Grundgesetze* that the notion of an extension is taken as fundamental both to this system and to the whole idea of mathematics as a science. In the *Grundlagen* he says that the notion is not essential, and envisages alternative solutions (p. 117). What is throughout essential is that some means of identifying certain objects as numbers should be provided. This suggests that the ultimate sources of his difficulties and indeed his whole theory should be thought of as general and philosophical, rather than merely technical. It was because he held these general philosophical views that he could not abandon his belief that numbers are objects of some kind. Holding this belief necessitated guaranteeing the possibility of their identification, and the method of extensions came to seem to Frege the only guarantee.

A glance at the headings of certain sections of the *Grundlagen* will show some essential points in this philosophical position. Frege believed that arithmetical formulae are provable, and are objective truths. They

are statements about numbers, which can be defined as objective entities, namely as objects. Mathematics is a science, and therefore its
propositions and expressions, i.e. arithmetical formulae and numerals,
are meaningful; the science is itself meaningful, in that it deals with
general facts about reality. Mathematical formulae are significant and
must therefore be true or false. It follows from this that they contain
referential signs, i.e. numerals, and this amounts to saying that numbers
are definite objects.

It is clear even in this brief formulation of an early position how the
various elements of Frege's general outlook contribute to the whole.
What seems to be crucial in generating and upholding difficulties of
the kind discussed in this chapter is that part of his outlook which concerns the notions of meaning, truth, and knowledge. This, especially
the kind of topic I dealt with in Chapter 11, is certainly the least
original part of Frege's philosophy, though not necessarily the most
objectionable. It is sometimes said that Frege was a Platonist, or that
his theory of mathematics and logic is a Platonistic theory. As it stands,
this can be seriously misleading; for instance it suggests quite falsely
that he attributed some kind of real existence to concepts, and that he
construed concepts as objects of some peculiar kind. Frege spent much
of his time destroying these two views, which are undoubtedly
Platonistic.

But there are two characteristics of Frege's thought which explain
the epithet. The first is his emphasis on the notion of *objectivity* together
with its use in his rejection of psychologism. Even if he distinguished
objectivity from existence, the fact that he described concepts, thoughts
and senses as objective entities is enough to class him as a philosophical
realist. The second is his notion of 'objects'. The fact that he calls
numbers, for instance, objects is not by itself what counts, since we do
not know just from this what use he makes of the term 'object'. It is
this use that is significant. I argued earlier that this use can be explained
by pointing to Frege's view that truth and falsity are themselves
'logical objects' and are objective entities. This means for Frege first
that propositions are not dependent for their truth-values on any
psychological event, in particular on their being discovered to be true
or believed to be true; second that this independence of truth from
everything psychological amounts to the actual subsistence of true
propositions before they come into relation to any mind.

Surely Frege drew a sharp distinction between objectivity and existence; what then justifies my using the term 'subsistence' in place of his

'objectivity'? He seems to have held two positions, at first a fairly undefined one but in the end a fairly rigid one. In the *Grundlagen* the notion of objectivity is deployed as an alternative to the notions of subjectivity and actuality; numbers are objective since number-statements are neither about psychological facts nor physical facts, and their truth-values are dependent on reason and not on sensation or intuition. In the late essays, particularly 'The Thought', these earlier negative notions are interpreted in a positive way. Now the fact that objectivity is an alternative to subjectivity and actuality is condensed in the metaphor of the three realms. Thus objectivity is put on a level with the other two, and comes to seem just a different kind of existence, e.g. subsistence or 'being'. This is largely the fault of Frege's language, which is Platonic in the extreme. Frege's position in the Preface of the *Grundgesetze*, intermediate in time between these two, is also intermediate in doctrine. Objectivity is upheld against subjectivity and actuality, as in the *Grundlagen*, but upheld in terms of the independence of truth-values from the occurrence of thoughts.

Frege's application of this theory of the objectivity of truth to the propositions of logic and mathematics reinforces the description of him as a realist. It was his view that in doing logic and mathematics we are investigating the most general facts about the structure of reality; though in the *Grundlagen* he perhaps thought that these facts were rather facts about the structure of our thought about reality. The *Grundlagen* is very strongly influenced by Kant, and it seems possible to give a Kantian interpretation of its foundations. However in either case it is Frege's assimilation of logic and mathematics to the positive sciences that counts. It is his view that the notions of truth and falsity apply to logical and mathematical propositions as well as to others. I have tried to demonstrate in the structure of this book how these notions underlay and helped to shape many of Frege's particular philosophical doctrines.

SOURCES FOR CHAPTER TWELVE

Grundlagen, sections 55 ff.; 'Review of Schroeder's *Algebra der Logik*'; *Grundgesetze*, ii, 146–7 and Appendix.

I have made no attempt at a comprehensive list of works dealing with Frege. More titles can be found in *Funktion, Begriff, Bedeutung: Fuenf logische Studien* (Vandenhoek and Ruprecht, Gottingen, 1962), which is a reprint of five of Frege's most important articles, namely 'Function and Concept', 'On Concept and Object', 'On Sense and Reference', 'What is a Function?' and the article 'Ueber die wissenschaftliche Berechtigung einer Begriffsschrift' of 1882. The list I give includes only the works that I have found most helpful in dealing with Frege. Excellent bibliographies for general study can be found in such works as *The Development of Logic* by Professor and Mrs. Kneale, *Mathematical Logic* by Professor Quine, *Formal Logic* by Professor Prior, and *Logical Positivism*, edited by Professor Ayer.

1. *Books*
> Geach, P. T. and Anscombe, G. E. M., *Three Philosophers: Aristotle, Aquinas, Frege* (Blackwell 1961)
> Kneale, W. and M. A., *The Development of Logic* (O.U.P. 1962)
> Koerner, S., *The Philosophy of Mathematics* (Hutchinson 1960)
> Anscombe, G. E. M., *Introduction to Wittgenstein's Tractatus* (Hutchinson 1959)
> Church, A., *Introduction to Mathematical Logic*, vol. 1 (Princeton University Press 1956)
> Nidditch, P. H., *The Development of Mathematical Logic* (Routledge & Kegan Paul 1962)
> Strawson, P. F., *Individuals* (Methuen 1959)
> Russell, Bertrand, *The Principles of Mathematics*, *Appendix A* (Allen & Unwin, 2nd edn. 1937)

2. *Articles*
> Kneale, W. C., 'Gottlob Frege and Mathematical Logic', in *The Revolution in Philosophy* (Macmillan 1960)
> Black, Max, 'Frege on Functions', in *Problems of Analysis* (Routledge & Kegan Paul 1954); 'Presupposition and Implication', in *Models and Metaphors* (Cornell University Press 1962)
> Church, A., 'A Formulation of the Logic of Sense and Denotation', in *Structure, Method and Meaning: Essays in Honor of Henry M. Sheffer* (New York 1951)
> Wells, R. S., 'Frege's Ontology', *Review of Metaphysics* 1950
> Wienpahl, P. D., 'Frege's *Sinn und Bedeutung*', *Mind* 1950,
> Marshall, W., 'Frege's Theory of Functions and Objects' *Philosophical Review* 1953; 'Sense and Reference: A Reply', ibid. 1956

Dummett, M., 'Frege on Functions: A Reply', *Philosophical Review* 1955;
    'Note: Frege on Functions', ibid. 1956
Quine, W. V., 'On Frege's Way Out', *Mind* 1955
Geach, P. T., 'Class and Concept', *Philosophical Review* 1955
Bergmann, G., 'Frege's Hidden Nominalism', *Philosophical Review* 1958
Klemke, E. D., 'Professor Bergmann and Frege's "Hidden Nominalism"',
    Philosophical Review 1959
Jackson, H., 'Frege's Ontology', *Philosophical Review* 1960
Grossmann, R., 'Frege's Ontology', *Philosophical Review* 1961